A HISTORY OF THE
PAPACY

✝

A HISTORY OF THE
PAPACY

ALAN HALL

THUNDER BAY
P·R·E·S·S

This edition published in 1998 by
Thunder Bay Press
5880 Oberlin Drive, Suite 400
San Diego, California 92121
1-800-284-3580

http://www.advmkt.com

Produced by
PRC Publishing Ltd,
Kiln House, 210 New Kings Road, London SW6 4NZ

ISBN 1 57145 155 2

1 2 3 4 5 98 99 00 01 02

Printed and bound in China

Page 2:
St. Silvester's shroud; a Russian seventeenth century embroidery.
Hermitage, St. Petersburg, Russia/
Bridgeman Art Library, London

CONTENTS

✝

INTRODUCTION

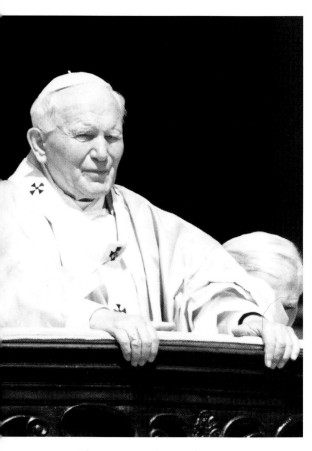

Above: Pope John Paul II is destined to be remembered as one of the most popular—and populist—popes. As the millennium approaches, he presides over a flock of almost a billion souls and is given credit for helping to tear down the Iron Curtain across Europe.

IT IS A MOVEMENT MIGHTIER THAN COMMUNISM and more enduring than capitalism. It brooks little in the way of change and dissenters are ruthlessly dismissed. Millions of devotees gather at mass meetings and in solitude in the tiniest of chapels and churches scattered around the globe.

"It" is Catholicism, and as the world rushes headlong into the new millennium, it is more popular than ever before. Ruling supreme and effectively unchallenged over the faithful is the Papacy, the supreme authority of the Holy See, invested in the pope and his headquarters, the Vatican City in Rome. Few can doubt the goodness and sincerity that emanates from the reigning Holy Father, the Polish Karol Wojtyla, better known to his flock as Pope John Paul II: but this pontiff is the successor to many not-so-holy men. In fact, a history of the papacy is a bloody trip through time exposing some of the worst excesses of the human spirit.

Financial corruption, sexual excesses, venality, greed, and even murder—many of the popes who preceded John Paul II displayed all these dubious qualities in their long and inglorious reigns. Of course, there were good men too, shining beacons of devotion and faith in bleak times. Angelo Giuseppe Roncalli, better known to the world as John XXIII, was one of the best loved and most revered religious leaders of all, as was Eugene I, one of the earliest popes who was known as a lover of peace. But good or bad, their lives and times, their reigns, their decrees, and their interpretations of the teaching of Christ have had a profound effect on western civilization, because they literally shaped the world we know. Entire countries were often placed under papal rule, giving the church enormous sway over society—and leading to the corrupting influence of power that so many popes found irresistible. Their story is a fascinating and complex one, that makes the fleeting rules of monarchs, ministers and tyrants seem tame in comparison.

The papacy is, first and foremost, the authority of the office of the pope and the recognition of the supreme pontiff as a legitimate spiritual force in history. By being appointed Bishop of Rome, the pope automatically, in Catholic faith, is successor to its first bishop, St. Peter. The pope, therefore, claims to be the shepherd of all Christians and representative—the Vicar or Viceregent—of Christ. The church further holds that God will not permit the pope to make an error in solemn official declarations concerning matters of faith—this is the infamous Papal "Infallibility," which is rejected by non-Catholic Christians.

Above: Christopher Columbus: navigator, explorer, adventurer, but even he had to seek papal permission to go on his epic voyages.

While the pope is all-important, the Catholic church in general, and the papacy in particular, are enormous multinational businesses supported by layers of bureaucracy that have their nerve center in Rome. Day-to-day the papacy exercises power in several ways, perhaps the greatest being its absolute authority over the Catholic faith everywhere in the world. It has papal courts, which can excommunicate and discipline those who fail to toe the line (as divined by the pope and his aides); it has the authority to interpret divine laws; it has the responsibility for spreading the faith, and the right to bestow or to withold privileges and grants; it has a well-oiled publicity machine that seeks to exert ever-mounting pressure on governments that it believes are at odds with Catholic teachings—controversial subjects like abortion and contraception fall within this department's mandate.

The Holy See—also known as the Apostolic See—has the pope as

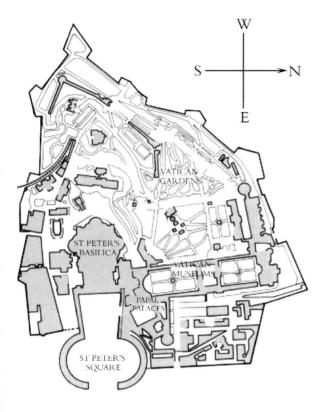

Above and Top: The Vatican City and its location in Italy.

Above Right: View over St. Peter's Square, whose colonnades were designed by Bernini.

Right: Today the papacy is not involved in the sort of armed politics that was usual in the twelfth century. Here Alexander III blesses Doge Ziani after his victory over the Imperial fleet in 1271.
Palazzo Ducale, Venice,
Italy/Bridgeman Art Library, London

its supreme ruler, but he is far too busy to oversee the vast machine of the Vatican; instead the Roman curia wields the daily power. The curia is, in essence, the central government of the Catholic church with thousands of salaried workers, assisted by priests and clerics from around the world who come to Rome to serve their pontiff. *Curia*—Latin for court—derives its name from the ancient practice of delegates to Rome receiving from the pope or his court any duties he wished to delegate.

The curia is now an extensive bureaucracy, governed by the regulations laid down in the *Regolamento Generale della Curia Romana*, (General Rules of the Roman Curia), which was issued in March 1968 under Pope Paul. This official "handbook" of the papacy instructs its members as to the working week—33 hours—holidays, suggested attire, and the protocol to be used when dealing with cardinals and such-like. The most important post within the curia is that of secretary of state, always a cardinal and always hand-picked by the Holy Father himself to be his right-hand man.

There was a time when the curia—founded in 1588—had far more administration on its hands than now. The Vatican once held sway over territorial possessions far greater than the tiny enclave of the Vatican City itself. The Papal States, *Lo Stato della Chiesa*, were the physical symbol of the great spiritual and temporal power wielded by the papacy; substantial tracts of land that the popes ruled from the eighth

Above: Today little is left of the "Patrimony of Peter" or the Papal States—but this has not reduced the importance or influence of the papacy: indeed, it enters the twenty-first century after the birth of Christ at the head one of the two most significant religions of the world.

century until 1870 when the last territory slid from the Vatican's grasp. At one time the Papal States encompassed 16,000 square miles of Italy, including the present regions of the Marche, Emilia-Romagna, Umbria, and Latium. At various times popes also claimed suzerainty over Naples, Sicily, and Sardinia, and it is hardly surprising the tenacity with which some pontiffs clung to these territories. Much of this land had come the way of the church following the collapse of the Roman Empire; it was then supplemented by large donations of territory by pious noblemen. But the actual Papal States came about due to the turmoil raging in Italy in the sixth and seventh centuries. Bequeathed a massive chunk of the country in 756AD by King Pepin the Short, the papacy in the form of Pope Stephen II found itself with considerable territory and considerable influence. However, while the Papal States were fine resources for food and raw materials for the papacy, they were poorly run and unrest among a discontented population was not uncommon. These states became the battleground for feuding warlords and much blood was spilled in the name of Christ.

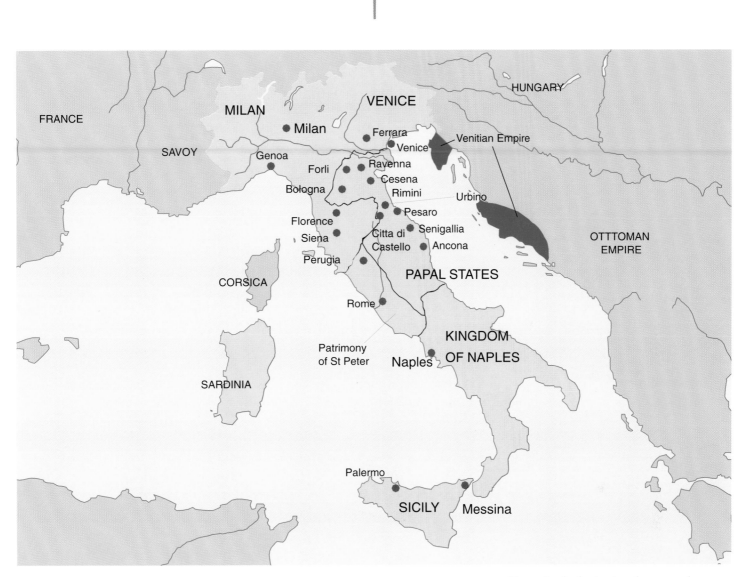

Above: In the beginning there was the "Patrimony of Peter," which Pepin, king of the Franks, expanded and defended against the Lombards. Popes such as Innocent III added to this until the Papal States included Latium, Umbria, Ancona, Ravenna, and Bologna. They would be held until the reunification of Italy—the "Risorgimento," which culminated in the taking of Rome by King Victor Emmanuel's troops in September 1870. This is a map of the Papal States in the late 15th century.

Seized by Napoleon during his wars of conquest, many democratically minded statesmen were saddened when the Papal States were restored to the papacy after the Corsican's defeat at Waterloo. The Vatican continued to run them in an inefficient and arbitrary fashion and it was little wonder that these states fell with ease in 1860 to King Victor Emmanuel as he sought to bring about the unification of Italy as a single state. In 1870, Rome itself fell to his armies, bringing an end to all the church's temporal power. It was not until 1929 that the Lateran Treaty brought about the establishment of the church's sole remaining territorial foothold—the Vatican City. It was a treaty forged between the Holy See and the Kingdom of Italy that gave the pope absolute autocracy over the *Stato della Citta del Vaticano* (the State of the Vatican City). The treaty was a compromise to "free" the pope from self-proclaimed imprisonment inside the Vatican walls. When Rome fell to Victor Emmanuel, Pope Pius IX was incensed at the seizure of papal real estate. He was the longest reigning pope in history and, when the monarchy came about, declared both himself and the Vatican "inviolable."

Above: Although the Swiss Guards' finery suggests a certain "chocolate soldier" appearance, in fact they are highly trained professionals with an array of sophisticated weaponry at their command.

Right: Another view of the Swiss guard in its ceremonial uniforms.

"I am a prisoner of the Vatican," he said, and for the next 59 years every pope followed his example. It led to a perpetual state of tension between the church and the Italian state until Mussolini resolved it with the Lateran Treaty. As a consequence, the Vatican is the world's smallest sovereign nation—but some would argue it's also the most powerful. What other country has so many souls doing its bidding around the world with such devotion, ready to obey a papal edict in a heartbeat?

But while the Vatican City is the nerve center of papal power, few of its "citizens" ever get to see within its walls. Like the Kremlin in Moscow, the Vatican can be a secretive place where cardinals, bishops, and a multitude of clerical rank-and-filers wield absolute power over the faithful spread all around the world. The Vatican has its own laws, its own radio station, its own currency, stamps, and even its own armed forces, the Swiss Guards, the "Cohors Helvetica," the world-famous bodyguard of the popes, established by Pope Julius II in 1505.

Born out of the interminable warring that plagued Rome and the Papal States, Pope Julius II turned to Switzerland to raise a cadre of men to protect him and his palaces because he could find no suitable candidates within his own country. With their ornate helmets and body armor, these 100 guardians of the papacy—drawn from the purely Catholic cantons of Switzerland—are one of the most potent symbols of both the papal past and future, outdated and enduring at the same time. But anyone tempted to regard them as "chocolate soldiers" had better think again—all are masters of judo or karate, and have access to high-velocity weapons if their fearsome lances are not enough of a deterrent to any would-be assassins.

Within the walls they guard, another power exists—one that is smaller and with greater clout and reach than that wielded by the servants of the curia. It is the Pontifical Commission of the State of the Vatican City, comprising cardinals assisted by both clerical and lay officials. These cardinals are roughly the equivalent of civil servants—appointed to serve as the chief assistants to the pontiff. Matthew Bunson, compiler of *The Pope Encyclopedia*, calls the College of Cardinals "one of the most select bodies in the entire world, and its members are considered the most capable, gifted, and important leaders in the entire Church. They fulfill some of the crucial leadership positions in the administration of the Church."

The college dates from 1150 when Pope Eugene III formed it to recognize those clerics used by the pontiff as his chief advisers. There are now cardinals spread all over the world, but it is in Rome that the real power lies with the Pontifical Commission. These eminent clerics form a shield around the pontiff, advising him on policy, overseas visits, papal decrees, and a plethora of other church-related duties. In turn the cardinals live a gilded existence in the city state, benefiting from the patronage bestowed on them by the pontiff—fine apartments, servants,

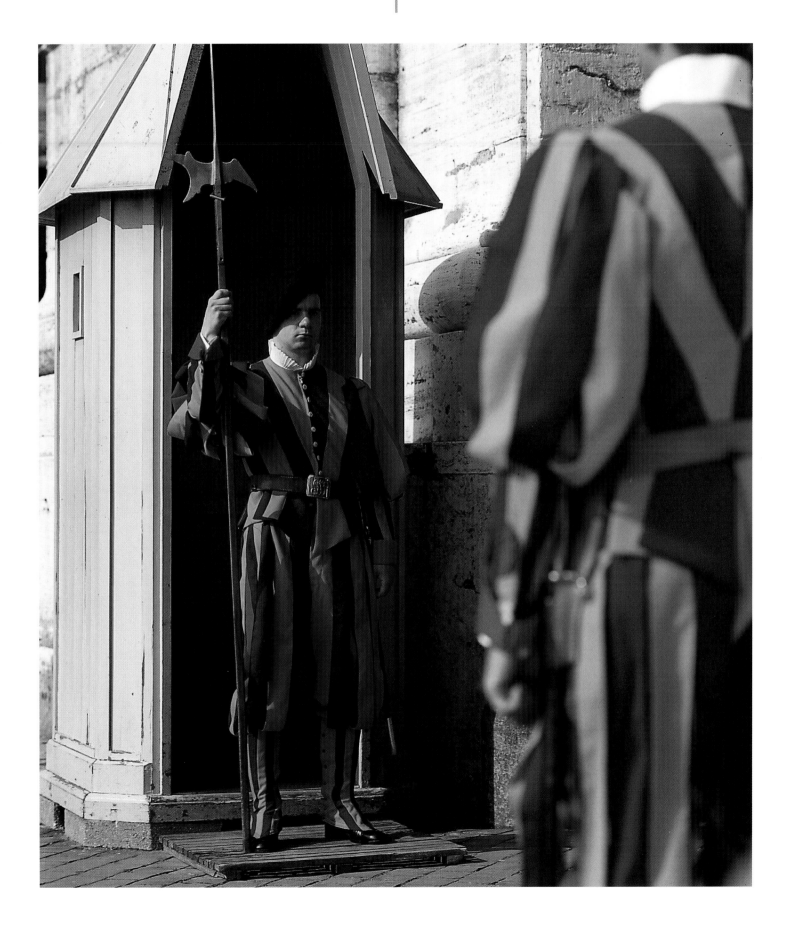

Above: A member of the Swiss Guard in his fine outfit.

assistants, cooks, and secretaries. But perhaps this is all to be expected—they are, after all, the individuals who put the pope into power in the first place. Cardinals are ordained priests who literally rise up through the ranks to become the chief lieutenants of the Supreme Pontiff. Their "promotion," as it were, is entirely at the personal discretion of the pope, who chooses them at special meetings attended by other cardinals. When he has decided to appoint someone he asks the other members present: "*Quid Vobis Videtur?*"—How does this sit with you?" There are no records of dissent.

If the pope has supreme power, it comes only after a democratic process among the cardinals who hands it to him. They can use one of three methods for choosing a new Supreme Pontiff—a secret ballot, a unanimous declaration of support referred to as the "*acclamatio,*" or they can slug it out like jurors in a sealed room, arguing sometimes for days—or, in one extreme case in history, for years—until a majority verdict, rather than a unanimous one, is reached. Whatever guides the cardinals in their quest, they must at all times be mindful of their declared belief that they are being assisted in their choice by the Holy Spirit.

This ancient method of choosing a new pope has its origins in the founding of the papacy by St. Peter in 62AD when bishops and other members of the clerical hierarchy began to develop as the dominant influences upon the lives of ordinary members of society. They started to be elected at meetings composed of other churchmen and lay members, and the practice seemed a good one—until human greed stepped in. Soon there were disagreements about this churchman or that churchman not representing the interests of minority groups. In 366AD factions for Pope St. Damasus clashed bloodily with those siding for the antipope Ursinus, leaving scores dead and much of Rome in a state of chaos.

It was becoming apparent to all concerned that a better way would have to be found, but it would not come about for hundreds of years. Succeeding popes found themselves lobbying for their position with various foreign powers that held sway over lands bordering Rome—Germans, Franks, and the Byzantine Empire, whose rulers in Constantinople demanded the right of veto over any and all pontiffs. This erratic state of affairs wasn't brought to an end until 1059 when Pope Nicholas II brought in the legislation that gave the cardinals sole power to elect the Holy Father. Further tweaking of the rules down the years gave the cardinals the framework within which they now work—including the mandatory two-thirds majority before a new pope can take up his office. Not that the cardinals have always found such profound decision-making easy—they once remained undecided for three years after the death of Clement IV in 1268, leading to a conference in the town of Viterbo that resulted in angry locals putting them on starvation rations because they were so disgusted with their tardiness!

When cardinals meet to choose a pontiff, the gathering is called a "conclave"—from the Latin "*con*," meaning with, and "*clavis*," meaning key, as they are sealed in a locked room, forbidden to come out until they have chosen the successor of the last pope. The conclave is held in the Sistine Chapel of the Vatican, but down the ages popes have been chosen in places as far apart as Avignon, Lyons, Siena, Venice, and Pisa.

The whole affair, which has captivated the entire world since the advent of television, takes place beneath the majestic fresco of the *Last Judgment* by Michaelangelo. "Not surprising," said noted American Catholic commentator George Wells, "when you think that upwards of a fifth of this planet counts themselves as Catholic. No wonder there is a huge amount of interest in who will be their spiritual leader in the months and years to come."

The election comes immediately after the death of a pope—and it is almost always a death, as retirement from being Supreme Pontiff is usually not an option. It is almost always a job for life, and only six popes have ever resigned from office. Cardinals from around the world are summoned and, once in place, are shown to spartan living quarters far different from the luxury usually associated with the Vatican. They have a simple cot bed, a chair, a wash basin, and a pitcher of cold water to wash with—all designed to make them want to make up their minds sooner rather than later!

Below: View from the southeast over St. Peter's Square to St. Peter's Basilica.

Below and Below Right: Aerial and internal views of St. Peter's Basilica. Started in 324AD by the Emperor Constantine, who built a sanctuary over the tomb of St. Peter, construction of the existing basilica was started in 1506 during the pontificate of Julius II, who wanted to be buried at the heart of it in a tomb designed by Michaelangelo. Designed by Bramante, building of the basilica was finally finished by Bernini 120 years later.

Following a mass at St. Peter's Basilica, the cardinals are escorted into the Sistine Chapel where the doors are sealed behind them and the important task at hand is tackled. Voting goes on until a two-thirds majority is reached, with no cardinal being allowed to vote for himself. Overseers in the form of "Cardinal Scrutineers"—the present pontiff was one during the election of John Paul I in 1978—count the ballots and generally make sure that decorum reigns. If no clear consensus has been reached after three days, there is a 24-hour break for prayers and meditation.

Secret ballot papers are routinely burned during this haggling process, bound up with damp straw that makes dark smoke. When there

is a decision, it is time to burn the ballot papers again, only this time with dry straw which produces the "*sfumata*," or famous white smoke that signals to the crowd outside, and indeed the entire waiting world, that a new pontiff has been chosen. The cry "*Habemus Papam*" (we have a pope) also goes out and the duty of the cardinals is over. The new pope must agree and is well within his rights to turn the decision down, as has happened several times in history. He takes up his position by saying "*Accepto*"—I accept. He then chooses a name for himself, but never Peter. It is a tradition among the highest echelons of the clergy that no man will call himself Pope Peter.

Once he has accepted the title of Bishop of Rome—and therefore

Above: With all the administration and officialdom packed into the Vatican it is easy to forget the religious events and services that are held regularly. This is one of the big events: the coronation of John Paul II.

the mantle of spiritual leader of a huge part of the globe—the new pope enters a diverse world of both grandeur and humility. His duties begin with an official coronation, the magnificence of which has been scaled back in modern times from the pageantry of the Middle Ages. The two symbols of the coronation were traditionally the tiara and the pallium, a circular band of white wool worn over the chasuble. The new pope was borne into St. Peter's on the "*Sedia Gestatoria,*" the portable throne, while aides burned bundles of rope before him, chanting the words: "*Sancte Pater sic transit gloria mundi*" (Holy Father, so passes the glory of the world). Flanked by the cardinals who elected him, the pope's tiara, or crown, was then placed upon his head with the words:

"Receive this tiara adorned with three crowns; know that thou art the father of princes and kings, victor of the whole world under the earth, the vicar of our Lord, Jesus Christ, to whom be the glory and honor without end."

The last traditional ceremony of this type came in 1963 at the coronation of John Paul VI. John Paul I and II both opted for far humbler ceremonies.

Right: Pope Alexander III presents a ring to Doge Sebastiano Ziani in this fourteenth century Venetian image. Rings were important symbols of power in the medieval period, none more so than the "Ring of the Fishermen" used by the pope as a signet ring and decorated with a picture of St. Peter in a boat.
Museo Correr, Venice/Bridgeman Art Library, London

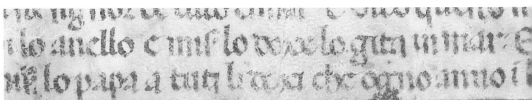

After the coronation the new pope is presented with the "Ring of the Fishermen," the *piscatorio*, used by the pope as a signet and decorated with an image of St. Peter in a boat—the allusion by Christ to St. Peter that he was a fisher of men. The ring is embossed with the name of the reigning pontiff and is used throughout his reign to seal all papal documents and edicts. When the pontificate is over, the ring's home becomes the Papal Palace of the Vatican, a veritable treasure chest of art and riches, containing some of the most important artistic artifacts anywhere in the world.

The Papal Palace, or Apostolic Palace, is a mish-mash of styles and buildings, added on by the whims and commands of various pontiffs over the years. During the years of the Avignon papacy the palace was largely abandoned, but since the accession of Gregory XI in 1370 all popes have made it their official residence. Little of the Apostolic Palace is ever seen by members of the public, but the Holy Father is expected

Above: The papacy has had a considerable influence in South and Central American politics—exemplified by John Paul II's 1997 visit to Cuba and his condemnation of the continued U.S. trade embargo, which was put in place by President John F. Kennedy. Here, Fidel Castro—rarely in a suit rather than fatigues—is seen at the Vatican to discuss the details of the visit.

to maintain the humility of the most impoverished parish priest, spending many hours alone in his own private chapel in meditation and prayer. This chapel is beautifully decorated with a stained-glass roof and a modern altar. When not praying alone the pope attends mass with the nuns who serve as his secretaries and cooks.

The day-to-day living routine is not daunting to most cardinals elected to be pope, but the clothes sometimes are! The grand papal vestments are undoubtedly the biggest shock to the system—this priestly uniform, when everything is worn for liturgical celebrations and important masses, weighs upward of 60 pounds, akin to the full pack of an infantryman on maneuvers. Perhaps sartorial discomfort, however, is a small price to pay when the "perks" of the papal job are considered.

An executive, for instance, who worked the hours or had the responsibility of the Holy Father, would appreciate things like the splendid summer retreat called Castel Gandolfo situated 13 miles from Rome on the Appian Way in Romagna, overlooking a beautiful lake. The Papal Palace is surrounded by stunning villas, the most notable of which are the Villa Barberini and the Villa Cybo. The retreat was granted in perpetuity to the Vatican in the Lateran Treaty of 1929 but has been used by popes going back 500 years. Pope John Paul II loves being there and caused something of a stir among the keepers of the papal purse strings when he requested a swimming pool. The pontiff heard mutterings from clerics about the cost of such a venture, but his Holiness is reported to have shrugged his shoulders and merely said: "Well, it is cheaper than getting a new pope!" He got it and enjoys regular swims every time he helicopters there from the Vatican for the start of long weekends or even longer vacations.

Of course, all this has to be paid for, and financial scandals are not just part of the dark and dubious past of the papacy. The Vatican banking scandal of the 1970s—discussed in a later chapter—shook the Vatican to its foundations. That it survived to bankroll the church today was due to the skill of hard-headed financial men who saw the church spiraling toward bankruptcy unless drastic measures were implemented. They were, and the Vatican Bank is now on a sound financial footing.

Officially known as the IOR, or Institute for Works of Religion, the Vatican Bank administers to the banking needs of the citizens of the Vatican State as well as working in tandem with other secular organizations that draw up the balance sheets for the running of the papacy. These are the Prefecture for the Economic Affairs of the Holy See, the Administration of the Patrimony of the Apostolic See, and the Council of Cardinals for the Study of Organizational and Economic Problems of the Holy See. Together, they plot the investment strategies for the Vatican to keep the papacy on the right side of the profit-and-loss books.

But this nonspiritual side of the pope's life belies what was, and remains, his main function—Christ's representative on earth, the symbol

for close to a billion souls on all continents who revere him. Though the popes gave the world the brutal terrors of the Inquisition, the corruption and vice of the Borgias, the chaotically ruled papal states, and have been ambivalent on issues ranging from the Holocaust to how South American despots rule their Catholic flocks, the institution of the papacy survives and thrives because, in the final analysis, in a world of spiritual hollowness, the need to believe in faith is greater than ever.

Below: His Holy Father Pope John Paul II. The ceremonial papal vestments weigh many pounds, and more than one Supreme Pontiff has been rendered weary on a hot Roman day beneath the layers of garments. It is, therefore, unsurprising that they are only worn on big occasions.

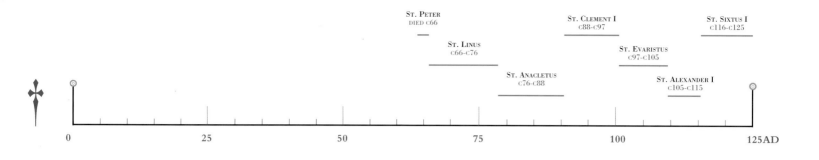

ST. PETER
DIED c66

ST. LINUS
c66–c76

ST. ANACLETUS
c76–c88

ST. CLEMENT I
c88–c97

ST. EVARISTUS
c97–c105

ST. ALEXANDER I
c105–c115

ST. SIXTUS I
c116–c125

0   25   50   75   100   125AD

THE UNDERGROUND CHURCH

Thou art Peter and on this rock I will build my Church. And the gates of Hell will not stand against it. I will give you the Keys of the Kingdom of Heaven; whatever you bind on earth will be bound in heaven; whatever you loose on earth will be loosed in heaven.

Matthew 16:18–19

THE PAPACY BEGAN WITH ST. PETER, the Prince of the Apostles and founder of the See of Rome. The disciple of Jesus chosen to serve as Vicar of Christ, his name is commemorated on the most important Catholic church in the world—St. Peter's in Rome. He is a figure of such importance in establishing the papacy that it is sometimes easy to forget that he lived as a simple fisherman for much of his life in Galilee. It was there that, according to St. Luke's Gospel, he was called by Christ to be a disciple after he caught a miraculous number of fish. Originally named Simon, Christ called him *Cephas*, meaning "rock," which was later translated in Greek as *Petros*, leading to the name for which the world knows him.

St. Peter was indelibly bound up with Christ during the years of his ministry, becoming a formidable miracle worker in his own right, able to heal the sick by his shadow alone. After the Resurrection he became the foremost of all the apostles, the unquestioned head of the fledgling Christian church that was to grow into such a world force. As a preacher, he moved across to a Europe still dominated by the pagan Roman Empire, whose citizens worshiped numerous deities and performed human sacrifices; it was, say scholars, inevitable that St. Peter would wind up at the center of the empire—Rome itself.

The evidence of his life in Rome is fragmentary and circumstantial, but no serious Biblical scholar disputes he was there. The church at that time was a secret organization, an underground religion that was not tolerated by the autocratic Roman rulers. It was in the year 49AD that Emperor Claudius expelled Jews from the capital when news of the Messiah filtered through from what we now know as the Holy Land: Then it was called Judea. The Roman Church met in the homes of gentile Christians. Paul sends greetings to these house-churches and to 29 named individuals in the final chapter of his letter to the Romans, but there was no mention of Peter in them. He does, however, receive a mention in the New Testament in 1. Peter 5:13, which sends greetings from Babylon—a euphemism in those times for the imperial capital. Peter is understood to have been the author of this letter.

Father Michael Miller, an American priest who authored a book about the papacy called *The Shepherd and the Rock*, said:

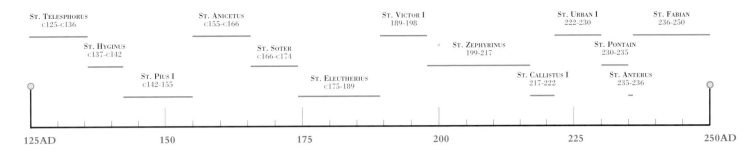

ST. TELESPHORUS c125-c136		ST. ANICETUS c155-c166		ST. VICTOR I 189-198		ST. URBAN I 222-230	ST. FABIAN 236-250
ST. HYGINUS c137-c142		ST. SOTER c166-c174		ST. ZEPHYRINUS 199-217		ST. PONTAIN 230-235	
ST. PIUS I c142-155		ST. ELEUTHERIUS c175-189		ST. CALLISTUS I 217-222	ST. ANTERUS 235-236	

| 125AD | 150 | 175 | 200 | 225 | 250AD |

St. Peter was indelibly bound up with Christ during the years of his ministry, becoming a formidable miracle-worker in his own right, who was able to heal the sick by his shadow alone.

"Even though Peter had preached at Antioch and Jerusalem, playing an important role in both places, no tradition grew up there which held that its bishop succeeded to Peter's ministry. At Rome, however, the story is different. From the oldest evidence available, this church alone claimed that its bishop succeeded to Peter's office in the church, a prerogative recognized by the other churches. Peter himself left no record of why he went to Rome to preach. What we can piece together are the reasons which make that choice remarkably fitting. In the ancient world 'all roads led to Rome.' Peter probably went there because it was fertile ground for missionary activity."

Above: St. Peter, the fisherman who came to Rome as a simple servant of God and who ended up dying a martyr's death at the hands of the bloodthirsty Emperor Nero. His passing, however, did not see a diminution in the faith of his followers and Christian beliefs continued to grow throughout the Roman Empire.

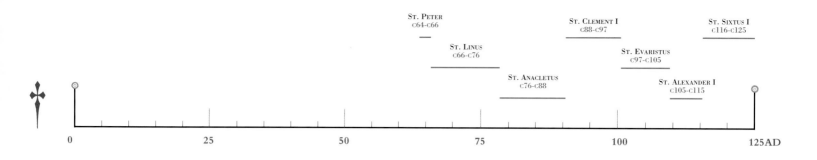

St. Peter c64-c66		St. Clement I c88-c97	St. Sixtus I c116-c125	
St. Linus c66-c76		St. Evaristus c97-c105		
St. Anacletus c76-c88		St. Alexander I c105-c115		

0   25   50   75   100   125AD

As someone spreading a seditious religion, it was also inevitable that St. Peter came under the scrutiny of the authorities and, ultimately, the emperor, who earned himself an infamous place in history as the first persecutor of Christians—Nero. Having murdered a boy he was guardian of, then his mother, followed by his wife, Nero managed to burn down half of Rome, supposedly "to see what Troy would have looked like when it was in flames." While the flames consumed Rome's imperial splendor, he chanced upon an easy scapegoat for the catastrophe—the fledgling Christians with their peculiar religion.

Nero instituted a pitch of terror that the Nazis in a later age would have envied; people burned alive, disemboweled, fed to lions, crucified, and tortured to reveal the identity of others in the church. The Roman historian Tacitus chronicled Nero's insane quest for revenge in a series of articles. Although he sided with his emperor over the spreading of "deadly superstition" by the Christians, he, too, was repelled by the sadism displayed in dealing with them. Christians were sewn in animal skins to be torn apart by half-starved dogs; others were coated with pitch and burned like torches to illuminate the splendor of Nero's gardens. All the while the emperor himself rode through Rome in a chariot disguised as a humble Roman legionary to witness his handiwork. The massacre began on October 13, 64AD, and it is almost certain Peter was there then, although some dispute this. The earliest literary evidence for his martyrdom in the city is from Clement's first letter. This was written in about 96AD, by the Roman bishop to the church of Corinth, and lists Peter among those who suffered death "as a result of jealousy."

Pope Eusebius, often referred to as the "Father of Church History," wrote before his death in 340AD that Peter preached and died in Rome. He said a letter from the Bishop of Corinth told him:

"In this way by your impressive admonition you have bound together all that has has grown from the seed which Peter and Paul sowed in Romans and Corinthians alike. For both of them sowed in our Corinth and taught us jointly; in Italy, too, they taught jointly in the same city and were martyred at the same time."

Before St. Peter's martyrdom, his work was recognized in Rome as establishing a religious primacy, with the Petrine (meaning from Peter) See enjoying a position above all others. Peter's successors, therefore, as Bishops of Rome, would hold the same authority as Peter himself, the chosen ones claiming primacy over the entire church. But the exact date of his death is not known, although Catholic historian John Jay Hughes places it between 65AD and Nero's death in 68AD. "Literary and archaeological evidence indicates that Roman Christians knew the site

Above: Nero has had bad press historically—and much of the opprobrium is merited. Remembered for having fiddled while Rome burned, he was also responsible for persecution of Christians, burning them at the stake and feeding them to lions. He can hardly have suspected that the fisherman he martyred was proselytizing a faith that would last longer than the Roman Empire.

Right: St. Peter's tomb was discovered in 1939 under the High Altar in St. Peter's Basilica, long after he was put to death on Nero's orders.

ST. TELESPHORUS
c125-c136

ST. ANICETUS
c155-c166

ST. VICTOR I
189-198

ST. URBAN I
222-230

ST. FABIAN
236-250

ST. HYGINUS
c137-c142

ST. SOTER
c166-c174

ST. ZEPHYRINUS
199-217

ST. PONTAIN
230-235

ST. PIUS I
c142-155

ST. ELEUTHERIUS
c175-189

ST. CALLISTUS I
217-222

ST. ANTERUS
235-236

125AD   150   175   200   225   250AD

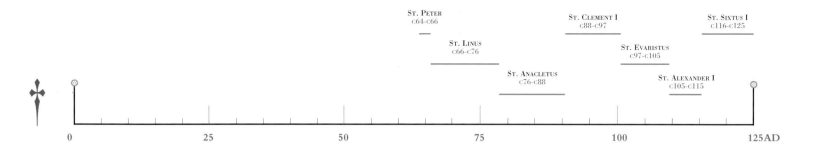

| St. Peter c64-c66 | St. Linus c66-c76 | St. Anacletus c76-c88 | St. Clement I c88-c97 | St. Evaristus c97-c105 | St. Alexander I c105-c115 | St. Sixtus I c116-c125 |

0   25   50   75   100   125AD

of Peter's tomb on Vatican Hill before the middle of the second century. This supports the view that he was executed alone, under conditions that permitted reverent burial," he said.

It is probable, although not confirmable, that St. Peter died by crucifixion upside down, because he allegedly told Nero that he did not want to be crucified in the same way as Jesus. As he refused to recognize the deities and gods of the Romans, he was charged by Nero's officials with both anarchy and "hatred of civilized society." In the Roman theory of government, the state was central, religion being a branch of the civil service. "He had to die," said papal expert John Williams. "But in his death the Romans merely laid down the foundations of the strongest religion ever. It was the exact opposite of what they hoped for in his demise."

It was not until 1939 that the Vatican made the stunning discovery of the tomb of St. Peter beneath the high altar of St. Peter's Basilica itself. In 1950, after two decades of excavations, Pope Pius XII announced to the world that his resting placed had indeed been found. "Has the tomb of St. Peter really been discovered?" he asked. "To that question the answer is beyond all doubt 'yes.' A second question, subordinate to the first, refers to the relics of St. Peter. Have they been found? At the site of the tomb remains of human bones have been discovered. However, it is impossible to prove with certainty that they belong to the body of the apostle." In fact it was Pope Paul VI during his reign in the 1960s and 1970s who announced that St. Peter's bones had been discovered in the site. It is a matter of faith, not certainty, whether or not one believes that they are the mortal remains of Peter. What is certain is that, in his death, the Romans created a force that would outlive their, and other, empires.

The successor to Peter as Bishop of Rome was St. Linus who reigned from 67AD to 76AD. Very little is known about his time but he was the first Italian appointed pope and during his tenure the Romans burned Jerusalem in 70AD. St. Anacletus was the third successor to Peter. He established the organization of the Holy See in Rome into 25 parishes before he, too, fell foul of Roman barbarism and was put to death. It wasn't until the appointment of St. Clement I in 88AD that the papacy began to take on a distinctive power structure, a portent of the supremely authoritative body that the church was to become.

Clement was born a slave in the household of Titus Flavius Clemens, a cousin of the Emperor Domitian, and he obtained his

Domitian, (Above), ruled the Roman Empire 81-96AD; Pope Clement I was born a slave in the house of a cousin of the emperor.

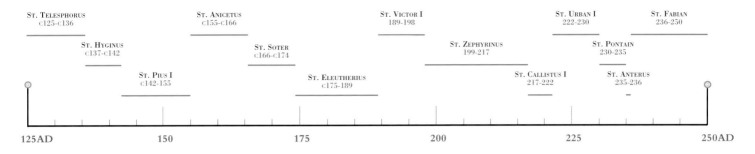

freedom as a young man. It is thought that he probably knew both St. Peter and St. Paul, falling under the spell of the new religion after hearing Peter preach one day in Rome. His reign saw the first example of the Petrine See exercising its authority over that of other churches. "The First Letter to the Corinthians" came about due to a revolt of the church in Corinth, where some duly elected officials had been deposed. The letter sent from Clement urged the Corinthians to restore "peace and fervor" to the church and called for the reinstatement of the deposed ministers. Michael Miller in his book *The Shepherd and the Rock*, says:

"All commentators draw attention to the highly unusual nature of this Roman intervention in another church's affairs. For at least four reasons this step was atypical. First, the early churches did not routinely write to one another using the imperious tone evident in the letter. Second, the church at Rome did not like riding on the shirt-tails of civil authority as a pretext to interfere. Thirdly, Corinth was the older church and should therefore have dictated to Rome, if there was any dictating to do. Fourthly, when the letter was written the apostle John was probably still alive and lived closer to Corinth. If the Corinthians needed fraternal support why did they not ask him, or any other apostolic church in the area to help them resolve their internal strife?"

Historians see the letter as the first authoritarian act of the Church of Rome, stamping itself early on as the supreme arbiter in church affairs worldwide. The tone of the language in Clement's epistle itself speaks pure authority, "If any disobey the words of Him through us, let them know they will involve themselves in transgression and no small danger." Miller adds:

"The epistle betrays a tone that is more than merely admonitory. It expects the church at Corinth to obey its directives. For Church historians, the letter is no less than the single most important church document of the first century after the New Testament."

Because historical records of the age are so few and far between—and those that do exist are so often unreliable in their accuracy—it is impossible to verify what became of Clement. Legend has it that he was banished to the Crimea by authorities who then murdered him when he began preaching to the heathen masses. He is reputed to have died from drowning, tossed into the sea weighed down with a huge anchor chain around his neck. But modern Biblical scholars are loath to believe this account. Clement was a cultured man who wrote many homilies and letters other than his historical missive to the Corinthians and modern-day thinkers believe he may well have died in Rome. Either

"The epistle betrays a tone that is more than merely admonitory. It expects the church at Corinth to obey its directives. For Church historians, the letter is no less than the single most important church document of the first century after the New Testament."

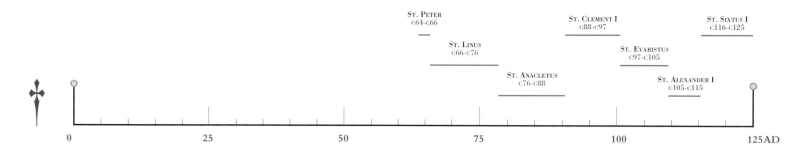

ST. PETER
c64–c66

ST. LINUS
c66–c76

ST. ANACLETUS
c76–c88

ST. CLEMENT I
c88–c97

ST. EVARISTUS
c97–c105

ST. ALEXANDER I
c105–c115

ST. SIXTUS I
c116–c125

0   25   50   75   100   125AD

Above: Pope Clement I, third successor to Peter and one of the most significant of the early pontiffs. During his pontificate the papacy began to exercise jurisdiction over other churches—as evinced by his letter to the Corinthians.

way, the likelihood is that he was killed by the authorities as they resorted to ever more desperate measures in an attempt to destroy the Christians' expanding power.

His successor was St. Evaristus, pope from 97 to 105AD. Again, little reliable information is known about him, but he is mentioned in some Roman documents as being a Jew from Bethlehem. He is also reported to have been martyred, but no grave has been discovered. St. Alexander I followed, reigning over the underground church 105–115AD. He is credited with being the founder of the tradition that mixed water with salt for the blessing of homes. Legend has it that he, too, was martyred, beheaded beside the Via Nomentana in Rome, but scholars now think this unlikely. Following him came St. Sixtus, who brought in a number of liturgical regulations governing mass. He ordered that only the minister could touch the sacred vessel during a mass, a move that established the priest as a distinctly separate entity within the church. He also established the moveable date for Easter and proclaimed, like St. Clement, that Rome was the authority to which all others must bend.

There followed eight more popes, all of whom were devoted in their own ways, but who did little to spread the power of the papacy. Not that the ninth one did much, but he was such a colorful character that there is a special place for him in the hearts of Catholics and students of the papacy. This was Pope Callistus I, later St. Callistus, whose antics were preserved for posterity by his great rival, St. Hippolytus, who set himself up as history's first antipope long before the Great Schism.

Pope Callistus I reigned from 217AD to 222AD, a time of more toleration in the Roman Empire, but not without peril for Christians. St. Hippolytus, envious that a man he considered little more than a rogue should be elevated to such a position, chronicled his early life. Hippolytus, a profound theologian who studied at Lyons before going to Rome, rose through the ranks of the church to become one of the leading figures in its intellectual community. He was a prolific writer—as is evinced upon the plinth of a statue of him, erected in Rome during his lifetime and rediscovered again in 1551. Here are listed the

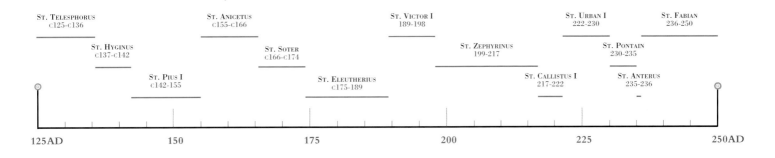

| ST. TELESPHORUS c125-c136 | | ST. ANICETUS c155-c166 | | ST. VICTOR I 189-198 | | ST. URBAN I 222-230 | ST. FABIAN 236-250 |

ST. HYGINUS c137-c142 · ST. SOTER c166-c174 · ST. ZEPHYRINUS 199-217 · ST. PONTAIN 230-235

ST. PIUS I c142-155 · ST. ELEUTHERIUS c175-189 · ST. CALLISTUS I 217-222 · ST. ANTERUS 235-236

125AD · 150 · 175 · 200 · 225 · 250AD

numerous books he wrote, including his masterwork *Refutation of all the Heresies.* He was a zealot: pious and strong-willed, he was utterly contemptuous of his rival Callistus whom he regarded as something of a dangerous buffoon.

Hippolytus tells how Callistus was a slave in the house of a freeman—a freed slave—called Carpophorus, who was taken in by the easy manner and glib charm of his new servant. He let the young man have more and more responsibility, finally entrusting him with the day-to-day running of a bank he owned. But Callistus and money did not go together very well. Hippolytus records how he made unwise investments with the money of widows and other Christians, finally losing a small fortune—which led to an angry mob besieging his master's home! Callistus packed a bag and tried to flee from Rome, but was caught by the outraged citizens who dragged him back. He was sentenced by the authorities to penance on a treadmill, but the investors bought his freedom, believing he could lead them to the loot. Unfortunately for them, Callistus was not a swindler, but a genuine failure; there really was no money left.

The next record Hippolytus presents of him is his brawling; it seems that there was an altercation between Callistus and some local Jews, ending in a fight in a Roman synagogue. The sacred Torah scrolls were hurled, artifacts were smashed, and legend has it that the future Supreme Pontiff had to be subdued by six men before he could be brought under control. It was inevitable that he would face stern punishment for his latest outrage, and he was sentenced to one of the most feared penal colonies of the old world—the silver mines of Sardinia.

These mines were notorious deathtraps, and all Christian slaves who toiled within them had one eye burned out and a silver coin placed in the hole, a mark for all to see of their crime and punishment. Callistus escaped this fate by the narrowest of margins: luckily he was freed through the intervention of Marcia, the mistress of the Emperor Commodus. This act caused eyebrows to be raised in polite society. What was

Below: It must be remembered that the papacy before Constantine's reign was very much an underground church, and the pagan Roman Empire was at its most powerful. This is Antoninus Pius, who ruled the empire from 138AD to 161AD having been adopted by Hadrian and succeeded him. The name "Pius" was probably earned by his insistence that Hadrian was deified—something completely impossible within Christian beliefs.

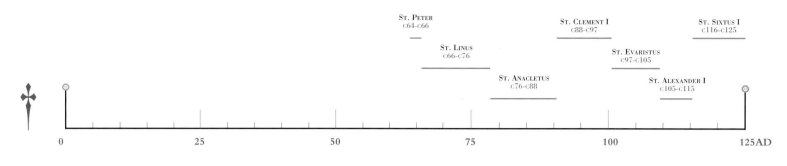

ST. PETER c64-c66		ST. CLEMENT I c88-c97		ST. SIXTUS I c116-c125
ST. LINUS c66-c76			ST. EVARISTUS c97-c105	
	ST. ANACLETUS c76-c88		ST. ALEXANDER I c105-c115	

| 0 | 25 | 50 | 75 | 100 | 125AD |

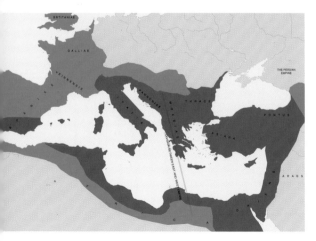

an emperor's mistress doing speaking out for a Christian slave? Hints of further impropriety between the two have been made down the years, but Hippolytus makes no mention of it—and if he could have done so, most think he would.

The headstrong young man apparently saw the error of his ways before it was too late and entered the church before his teens were out, finally becoming a deacon in 216. He was given a pension by Pope Victor I and became his chief counselor. By now his charm and energy had been channeled into more creative tasks and he proved himself a worthy administrator. Having won the confidence of Rome's Christians, he was appointed pope in 217AD. As pontiff he is best remembered for bringing to the church the doctrine of forgiveness and repentance. As pope he admitted back into the church adulterers and fornicators, and granted absolution to hitherto "untouchables"—murderers and the like—but only after they had displayed supreme contrition for their acts. This became an important concept of the church's "salvation through repentance" ethos which has lasted to this day. At the time it served to make him an even greater enemy of Hippolytus, who became the first, but by no means the last, antipope to be a thorn in the side of the papal establishment.

Hippolytus wrote much that incurred the wrath of Callistus and his criticisms continued until Urban I became supreme pontiff. Hippolytus was exiled to Sardinia by the Christian-hating Emperor Maximus Thrax, where he died, but he was reconciled with the church before the end because his body was brought back to Rome and solemnly interred. As for Callistus, his end is unclear; some legends have it that he died as a martyr, but there are insufficient facts to prove or disprove this. Certainly Alexander Severus, emperor at the time, was not known for any major pogroms against Christians, although it is likely that individual persecutions did take place. All that is known is that Callistus was buried in Trastevere, on the Via Aurelia, and not in the cemetery that was named after him, the Cemetery of San Callisto. Having showed such a vagabond spirit in his youth, he went on to become a man of great faith and piety, one who exemplified the tradition of forgiveness which lies at the very heart of the Catholic faith. But forgiveness was not a maxim learned by the Roman rulers of the time. Even though emperors came and went, with varying degrees of tolerance and persecution of Christians as their trademarks, the church was still very much an institution balanced on a knife-edge of acceptability.

Nothing illustrates the capriciousness of Roman rule better than the case of St. Fabian, who reigned 236-250AD. He was one of the most promising of all supreme pontiffs, tireless in his work as an organizer and responsible for dividing Rome into seven districts, each one supervised by a deacon and sub-deacons. This organization became the foundation stone for the later College of Cardinals, which would in turn become

30

| St. Telesphorus c125-c136 | St. Anicetus c155-c166 | St. Victor I 189-198 | St. Urban I 222-230 | St. Fabian 236-250 |

St. Hyginus c137-c142   St. Soter c166-c174   St. Zephyrinus 199-217   St. Pontain 230-235

St. Pius I c142-155   St. Eleutherius c175-189   St. Callistus I 217-222   St. Anterus 235-236

125AD   150   175   200   225   250AD

the supreme authority invested with the power to appoint popes. St. Fabian also ordered extensive works on the catacombs, the myriad caves outside Rome that were the traditional burial place of Christians. But his promising work was cut short by the brutal excesses of Emperor Trajanus Decius, who stated, "I would rather face a usurper supported by five legions of men than hear another pope had been elected."

The emperor took his venom out on Christians, starting with Fabian, whom his men murdered in the street. It was to be a long time before the threat of Roman terror and retribution was lifted from the church. Then, the papacy would become victim of the Dark Ages soon to settle across Europe.

Above: Another view of the interior of St. Peter's, Rome.

Above left: Over 300 popes and antipopes have succeeded St. Peter (seen here holding the key to the Kingdom of Heaven) as head of the Roman Catholic Church. Some have been worldy, some warlike, and some holy: the history of the papacy has been anything but dull!

Below left: The Roman Empire in the third century A.D.

31

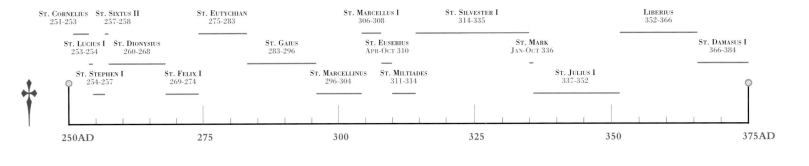

ST. CORNELIUS 251-253   ST. SIXTUS II 257-258   ST. EUTYCHIAN 275-283   ST. MARCELLUS I 306-308   ST. SILVESTER I 314-335   LIBERIUS 352-366

ST. LUCIUS I 253-254   ST. DIONYSIUS 260-268   ST. GAIUS 283-296   ST. EUSEBIUS APR-OCT 310   ST. MARK JAN-OCT 336   ST. DAMASUS I 366-384

ST. STEPHEN I 254-257   ST. FELIX I 269-274   ST. MARCELLINUS 296-304   ST. MILTIADES 311-314   ST. JULIUS I 337-352

250AD   275   300   325   350   375AD

THE DARK AGES

THE DISINTEGRATION OF THE ROMAN EMPIRE left a void that the church was not immediately able to fill. For all its sacrifices, its pagan worship, its unquenchable thirst for domination and conquest, the Roman Empire had promoted the arts, learning, and letters, and had established a rule of law which kept barbarism in check. Upon Rome's collapse the forces of darkness were masters of a divided and fearful continent. Christianity would rise from the ashes of the collapse of Rome to fill this gap in knowledge, in faith, in learning—but not before it, too, became a victim of the great shadow that was cast all the way from the Urals to the coast of the English Channel.

Before Rome finally fell, there emerged Romans who proved themselves ready to embrace a religion that they had been unable to stamp out. Constantine the Great is credited with founding the Christian Empire. Though ultimately a despotic ruler who moved his capital from Rome to Byzantium (which was rebuilt as Constantinople), he was the first of the Roman emperors to tolerate both paganism and Christianity. Initially a warrior, Constantine I saw off rivals for his title in a series of battles across Europe.

By 312AD the pagan-worshiping emperor was already sympathetic to the Christian doctrine and claimed to have seen a vision of a flaming cross in the sky with the words "In this sign thou shall conquer" inscribed upon it. Constantine took up the cross as his emblem and was victorious in the final fight against his rival Maxentius along the banks of the Tiber just outside Rome. It is this battle that is considered to be the turning point for Christianity.

Along with his fellow emperor Licinius, Constantine issued the so-called Edict of Milan in 313AD, confirming Emperor Galerius's ruling of 309AD that Christianity would be tolerated. Constantine's backing effectively made Christianity a legal religion across the empire. In the uneasy peace that followed—until Constantine killed off Licinius in 324AD and became the sole ruler of the empire—he set about strengthening Christianity.

The Bishop of Rome at that time was Silvester, an unassuming cleric who was very much in the shadow of the towering Constantine. Silvester, believed to be himself a Roman, benefited from Constantine's tolerance and generosity, and his lasting legacy was the construction of

Above: Constantine adopted the cross as his symbol, encouraged Christianity throughout the empire, and is recognized as the Roman emperor who changed history by tolerating Christianity—but he himself was not baptized until he was close to death in 337AD.

Above: Christianity spread through the Roman Empire by sea around the Mediterranean coastline, first to Asia Minor and Greece, then to Italy and further afield.

the first major churches including St. Peter's, St. Paul's, and the Basilica Constantiniana. The emperor also gave him the Lateran Palace, which became home to popes until the end of the 14th century.

The mediocre Silvester, pope during the periods of great change between 314AD and 335AD, seems to have been content to take a back seat while Constantine made the changes. His claim to fame came centuries later when the Donation of Constantine—now considered to be one of history's most famous forgeries—was exposed. The donation, or to give it its Latin name *Constitutum Constantini*, was said to have been given by Constantine to Silvester, granting the popes spiritual control across Christendom. Throughout the Middle Ages popes used it to wield wide-ranging powers, and it was not until the 15th century that scholars began to question its authenticity.

According to the story in the document, Constantine was avidly persecuting the Christians (as his forefathers had done before him)

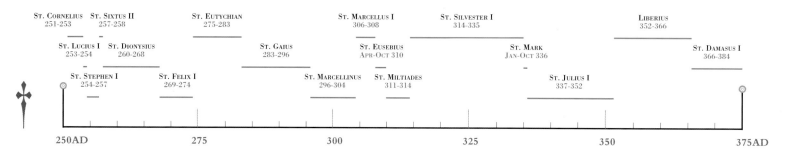

| ST. CORNELIUS 251-253 | ST. SIXTUS II 257-258 | | ST. EUTYCHIAN 275-283 | | ST. MARCELLUS I 306-308 | | ST. SILVESTER I 314-335 | | LIBERIUS 352-366 |

ST. LUCIUS I 253-254 | ST. DIONYSIUS 260-268 | ST. GAIUS 283-296 | ST. EUSEBIUS APR-OCT 310 | ST. MARK JAN-OCT 336 | ST. DAMASUS I 366-384

ST. STEPHEN I 254-257 | ST. FELIX I 269-274 | ST. MARCELLINUS 296-304 | ST. MILTIADES 311-314 | ST. JULIUS I 337-352

250AD   275   300   325   350   375AD

Constantine described himself as the conqueror of the Huns—some 50 years before they even arrived in Europe!

when he was afflicted by leprosy. St. Peter and St. Paul appeared to him in a vision stating that only Silvester could cure him. The elderly pope duly cured him and in gratitude Constantine ordered that Christianity should be worshiped across the Roman Empire. In fairness, the Donation of Constantine sticks fairly close to the truth about how the Lateran Palace became the Pope's residence with Constantine himself supervising the building of the basilicas. A humble clerk named Christophorus is generally believed to be the forger. No one for sure knows whether he intended the document to deceive or whether he was merely writing a whimsical story to amuse himself. The result, however, nicely suited the future popes who could claim their power was granted by Constantine. They got away with this until the fifteenth century when scholars looked closely at the donation and spotted the glaring historical errors. For instance, Constantine described himself as the conqueror of the Huns—some 50 years before they even arrived in

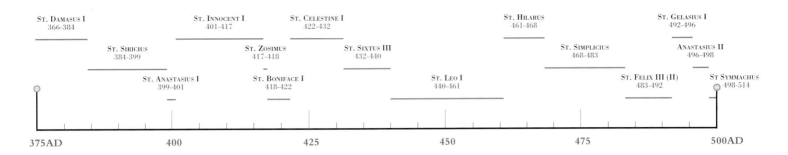

| ST. DAMASUS I 366-384 | ST. INNOCENT I 401-417 | ST. CELESTINE I 422-432 | ST. HILARUS 461-468 | ST. GELASIUS I 492-496 |

ST. SIRICIUS 384-399 · ST. ZOSIMUS 417-418 · ST. SIXTUS III 432-440 · ST. SIMPLICIUS 468-483 · ANASTASIUS II 496-498

ST. ANASTASIUS I 399-401 · ST. BONIFACE I 418-422 · ST. LEO I 440-461 · ST. FELIX III (II) 483-492 · ST SYMMACHUS 498-514

375AD — 400 — 425 — 450 — 475 — 500AD

Believing himself the founder of a second and religious empire, his legal reforms were considered humane and in keeping with Christian beliefs. Yet the early historians differ greatly on Constantine's beliefs.

Left: Constantine the Great is credited as being the emperor who converted the Roman Empire to Christianity. Proclaimed emperor in Britain in 306AD, his main rival was Maxentius, whom he defeated at the battle of Ponte Milvio, near Rome in 312AD. It was before this battle that Constantine saw a vision of a flaming cross inscribed with the words "In this sign thou shall conquer."

Europe! Additionally, the Bishop of Rome was not called "Pope" at that time: it would be another 200 years before this name was officially linked to the office. But one legacy of the forger did stick; according to the donation, Constantine gave the Bishop of Rome a crown, "the purple mantle also and the scarlet tunic and all the imperial trappings."

The reality, as history has shown, was that Constantine was initially a pagan ruler with Christian sympathies. He was eventually converted to Christianity on his deathbed after restoring properties confiscated during the Diocletian persecutions, and rebuilding many of the

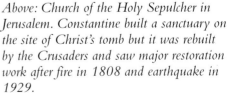

Above: Church of the Holy Sepulcher in Jerusalem. Constantine built a sanctuary on the site of Christ's tomb but it was rebuilt by the Crusaders and saw major restoration work after fire in 1808 and earthquake in 1929.

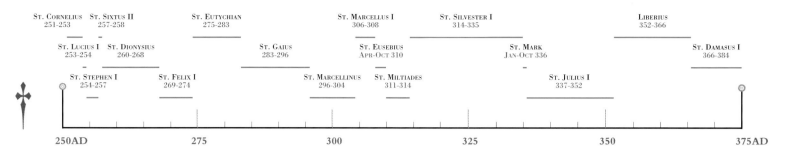

| ST. CORNELIUS | ST. SIXTUS II | ST. EUTYCHIAN | ST. MARCELLUS I | ST. SILVESTER I | LIBERIUS |
| 251-253 | 257-258 | 275-283 | 306-308 | 314-335 | 352-366 |

ST. LUCIUS I 253-254 · ST. DIONYSIUS 260-268 · ST. GAIUS 283-296 · ST. EUSEBIUS APR-OCT 310 · ST. MARK JAN-OCT 336 · ST. DAMASUS I 366-384

ST. STEPHEN I 254-257 · ST. FELIX I 269-274 · ST. MARCELLINUS 296-304 · ST. MILTIADES 311-314 · ST. JULIUS I 337-352

250AD · 275 · 300 · 325 · 350 · 375AD

Above: St. Augustine of Hippo, who lived 354-430AD, was a Tunisian who converted to Christianity at Cathage; he wrote Confessions and City of God. One of the great fathers of the church, his rules for clerical living would be used as the basis for the monastic Rule of St. Augustine. He also promoted the belief in divinely authorized violence which would influence the crusaders of the eleventh century.

churches. He also helped his mother Helena (later canonized) build the Church of the Nativity in Bethlehem and the Church of the Holy Sepulcher in Jerusalem. The clergy also flourished under Constantine, particularly as he excused them from military duties and made church property exempt from taxation.

When he moved his empire to Constantinople in 330AD, he chose a city that was already predominantly Christian and dedicated to the Virgin Mary. Believing himself the founder of a second and religious empire, his legal reforms were considered humane and in keeping with Christian beliefs. Yet the early historians differ greatly on Constantine's beliefs. He is often described as a devout convert, yet in 320AD he executed his son Crispus for adultery, and his first wife; others see him as a political genius cleverly using Christianity to unite his empire. His true motives and beliefs have been lost in the mists of time but for Silvester and the early Christians, he paved the way to changing the religion of the Roman world.

Constantine's legacy was cemented by the First Council of Constantinople in 381AD when it was decreed that "The Bishop of Constantinople shall have the primacy of honor after the Bishop of Rome because Constantinople is new Rome."

Later edicts were to order equal rights between the two cities and their bishops and it took Pope Leo I to remove the competition from Constantinople in 452AD, arguing that St. Peter was chief of the apostles and the man on whom the church was founded. As political power shifted away from Rome with the rise of Constantinople and the erosion of the empire by the barbarian invasions, the Bishop of Rome became more powerful in his own capital, taking on civil functions as well as religious.

Leo, who ruled 440-461AD, advanced the cause of the Bishops of Rome greatly. Interfering with the affairs of Gaul, Spain, and Illyricum (now pre-civil war Yugoslavia), he pushed for more and more power. He is also credited with saving Rome from Attila the Hun and from the Gaiseric the Vandal, through his statesmanship. Leo, a Roman who rose rapidly through the clergy to become deacon after serving under St. Celestine I and Sixtus III, persuaded Emperor Valentinian to grant him ecclesiastical powers over the West. In his book *Tome of Leo* he emphasized the church's orthodox teachings, persuading many Christians in the more rigid Eastern empire that Christ was both human and divine. But his major claim to fame was coming to the aid of the Empire—by standing up to Attila the Hun and then the Vandals.

In 452AD Leo rode to confront Attila at Mantua and persuaded him to leave. Three years later he approached King Gaiseric at the gates of Rome pleading with him not to sack the city. The Vandals wrecked Rome but kept their promise to him not to murder the inhabitants. For this Leo is one of only two pontiffs granted the title "the Great" after his

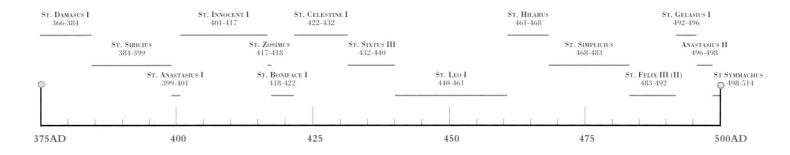

| St. Damasus I | | St. Innocent I | | St. Celestine I | | | St. Hilarus | | St. Gelasius I |
| 366-384 | | 401-417 | | 422-432 | | | 461-468 | | 492-496 |

| | St. Siricius | | St. Zosimus | | St. Sixtus III | | | St. Simplicius | | Anastasius II |
| | 384-399 | | 417-418 | | 432-440 | | | 468-483 | | 496-498 |

| | St. Anastasius I | | St. Boniface I | | | St. Leo I | | | St. Felix III (II) | St Symmachus |
| | 399-401 | | 418-422 | | | 440-461 | | | 483-492 | 498-514 |

| 375AD | 400 | 425 | 450 | 475 | 500AD |

name. The other is St. Gregory, ironically an aristocratic monk who had no wish to become pope.

When elected he implored Emperor Maurice to refuse consent—and when his letter to the Emperor was intercepted Gregory tried to flee from Rome. In the early months after his ordination in 590AD, Gregory's surviving letters show his sadness at giving up the rigid monastic life. But by January 591AD he had more or less accepted his role, writing to Archbishop Natalis of Salona: "I undertook the burden of this dignity with a sick heart. But seeing that I could not resist the divine decrees, I have recovered a more cheerful frame of mind."

Gregory was born around 540AD into an aristocratic Roman family with strong papal ties. His great-great-grandfather was Pope Felix III, a married man when he was ordained as a deacon. (Although Gregory and earlier pontiffs tried to insist on celibacy among the clergy, at that stage in the shaping of the church it was not an edict that affected those coming late into the priesthood.) Felix was widowed by the time he became pope in 483AD, but another married ancestor, Agapitis,

Above: Church of the Nativity, Bethlehem. In 323AD Constantine ordered the building of the original basilica over the cave where Christ is said to have been born at the behest of his mother, Saint Helen, who came to the Holy Land to supervise the work in 326AD. Little of the original building survives today.

37

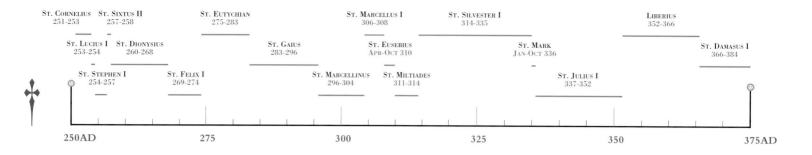

| ST. CORNELIUS | ST. SIXTUS II | ST. EUTYCHIAN | | ST. MARCELLUS I | ST. SILVESTER I | | LIBERIUS |
| 251-253 | 257-258 | 275-283 | | 306-308 | 314-335 | | 352-366 |

ST. LUCIUS I 253-254   ST. DIONYSIUS 260-268   ST. GAIUS 283-296   ST. EUSEBIUS APR-OCT 310   ST. MARK JAN-OCT 336   ST. DAMASUS I 366-384

ST. STEPHEN I 254-257   ST. FELIX I 269-274   ST. MARCELLINUS 296-304   ST. MILTIADES 311-314   ST. JULIUS I 337-352

250AD   275   300   325   350   375AD

served as pope 535-536AD. Gregory, in common with other aristocratic families of the day, had seen his family's wealth and power diminish through wars with the Lombards and the shift of government to the Eastern Empire. Gregory's father Gordianus was a Roman senator and cleric; his mother, Sylvia, was a devout Christian who went into religious seclusion after her husband's death. Three of Gregory's aunts were nuns, although one (Gordiana) scandalized the family by running off to marry the caretaker of her estates.

As a young man Gregory administered the family estates, which included a palatial home in Rome, neighboring farms, and extensive holdings in Sicily. He followed his father's lead by holding high office in Rome's civil government. But on his father's death he too decided to join the holy orders. He turned the family home into the monastery of St. Andrew and founded another six monasteries on his Sicilian estates. Looking back on his life, Gregory maintained this was when he was at his happiest. In a telling letter while pope, he wrote:

"When I was in the monastery I could curb my idle talk and usually be absorbed in my prayers. Since taking on the burden of pastoral care, I have been unable to keep steadily recollected because my mind is distracted by many responsibilities."

He complained he was forced to listen to "aimless chatter" and found himself enjoying the gossip. He reflected: "So I end by wallowing where I had first dreaded to fall."

Gregory's monastic life lasted just four short years. In 579AD, with the Lombards baying at the gates of Rome, Pope Pelagius II ignored his protests and ordained him deacon. To Gregory's horror he was then sent to Constantinople as the Emperor's papal envoy. His job was to plead for aid against the invading Lombards. Although his seven-year stint as envoy proved fruitless in that he failed to gain much military aid against the Lombards, Gregory made friends with the Emperor and other noblemen, which held him in good stead in the years that followed.

Called back to Rome by Pelagius in 586AD, Gregory tried to resume his simple monastic lifestyle, but the pope had other ideas. He gave Gregory complicated diplomatic missions. Then in 589AD floods

Above: Pope Leo I, pontiff from 440 to 461AD, was one of only two popes granted the title "The Great." (The other was Gregory I, pope from 590 to 604AD.) He earned his title by persuading Attila the Hun to leave Italy and stopping the Vandal Gaiseric from burning Rome in 455AD.

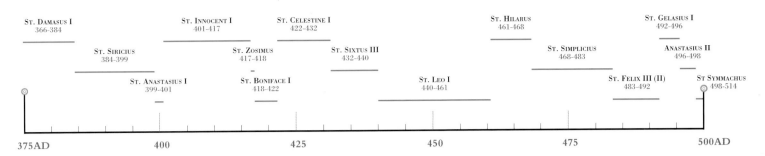

St. Damasus I 366-384		St. Innocent I 401-417	St. Celestine I 422-432		St. Hilarus 461-468		St. Gelasius I 492-496
St. Siricius 384-399		St. Zosimus 417-418	St. Sixtus III 432-440		St. Simplicius 468-483		Anastasius II 496-498
St. Anastasius I 399-401	St. Boniface I 418-422			St. Leo I 440-461		St. Felix III (II) 483-492	St Symmachus 498-514

| 375AD | 400 | 425 | 450 | 475 | 500AD |

"When I was in the monastery I could curb my idle talk and usually be absorbed in my prayers. Since taking on the burden of pastoral care, I have been unable to keep steadily recollected because my mind is distracted by many responsibilities."

devastated northern Italy and Rome. The overflowing River Tiber destroyed several ancient churches and the papal granaries that fed most of the city. Plague followed and one of the first to succumb was Pope Pelagius. Although considered young at 50, Gregory's contemporaries decided he was the only candidate as the 64th pope. Gregory was horrified—knowing that holding office would finally end his hopes of returning to his beloved monastery—and he did everything in his power to halt the inevitable.

At that stage the Emperor still had to give his consent and it was to him that Gregory wrote imploring him to refuse. However, Gregory's brother, Palatinus, read the letter first and substituted his own, saying Gregory had been elected pope unanimously. When the Emperor's consent reached Rome six months later, Gregory attempted to flee. Again his plans were intercepted and on September 3, 590AD, he was

Above: Attila was the King of the Huns who attacked both Eastern and Western Roman Empires. Here he is seen watching storks leave the northern Italian city of Aquilia—a sign of impending victory which saw the fall of the city in 452AD. Intervention by Leo the Great saved Rome and Attila left Italy.

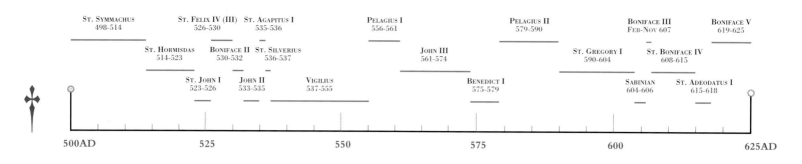

St. Symmachus 498-514	St. Felix IV (III) 526-530	St. Agapitus I 535-536	Pelagius I 556-561	Pelagius II 579-590	Boniface III Feb-Nov 607	Boniface V 619-625
	St. Hormisdas 514-523	Boniface II 530-532 St. Silverius 536-537	John III 561-574	St. Gregory I 590-604	St. Boniface IV 608-615	
	St. John I 523-526 John II 533-535	Vigilius 537-555	Benedict I 575-579	Sabinian 604-606	St. Adeodatus I 615-618	

500AD   525   550   575   600   625AD

Above: Gregory the Great was a monk, became pope in 590AD, and sent St. Augustine to convert the English. Known as a brilliant administrator, Gregory suppressed slavery and promoted monasticism.

Gregory's 14-year rule as pope was marked by his ill health brought on as a result of gout and excessive fasting as a monk.

ordained. Gregory's 14-year rule as pope was marked by his ill health brought on as a result of gout and excessive fasting as a monk. He wrote many letters—which have survived and provide one of the most illuminating pictures of papal life in the early years of Rome—complaining of his woes in graphic detail. He was bed-ridden for the final six years of his life and in one letter he admitted that he expected his death daily. He showed a keen interest in medicine and even pacified a Lombard warrior by sending him a milk diet for his own stomach ailments.

Gregory's other overriding conviction was that the end of the world was near. He saw symbols everywhere, from the plagues that regularly swept through the country, the floods, Lombard invasions, and the decay of Rome, which he described as "once mistress of the world." Even when bedridden, Gregory's fears led him to a flurry of activity to appease God. At that stage, the papacy was the biggest landowner in Italy, with estates dotted over much of the western Empire. They were run by rectors, and intended to provide money for the clergy, the poor, and the upkeep of churches, monasteries, and other religious foundations. This once vast income had become a trickle over the years due to incompetent rectors, invaders, and bad administration. One of Gregory's first jobs was to revamp the financial system, ordering regular audits and extracting oaths made over the sacred tomb of St. Peter from rectors to administer their roles honestly.

Gregory's papal purse often provided food for the poor and military aid for Rome's sparse garrison when money failed to appear from the Emperor. He also paid huge sums to the ever-marauding Lombards in the hope that they would leave. For this he received a number of rebukes from the Emperor, who felt he was exceeding his authority. Historians later argued that Gregory was trying to negotiate with the Lombards out of necessity when no help was forthcoming from Constantinople.

Gregory was also keen to convert the pagan peasants of Britain, Gaul, Sicily, Corsica, and Sardinia to Christianity before his feared end of the world. He was not averse to playing on the twin fears of plague and invasion to promote Christianity, and suggested his missionaries use those fears. One of his most successful missions was that of St. Augustine (not to be confused with St. Augustine of Hippo) to Britain. Augustine received a friendly welcome from King Aethelbert, who was baptized on Christmas Day 597AD along with 10,000 of his loyal subjects. Gregory and Augustine's legacy was to launch the church in England, and thus starting the process of preaching Christianty beyond the Mediterranean. Until Henry VIII's split with Rome in 1533 over Pope Clement VII's refusal to grant him a divorce from Catherine of Aragon, the church in England was the most loyal of all to Rome.

Although Gregory has also been credited with major liturgical reforms, today's historians believe that the Gregorian Sacramentary and

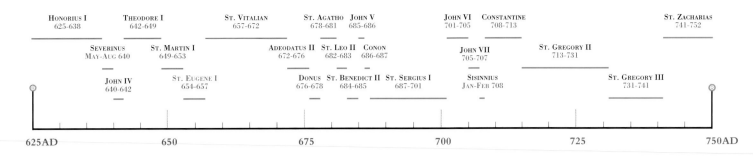

HONORIUS I 625-638	THEODORE I 642-649		ST. VITALIAN 657-672		ST. AGATHO 678-681	JOHN V 685-686		JOHN VI 701-705	CONSTANTINE 708-713			ST. ZACHARIAS 741-752

SEVERINUS MAY-AUG 640   ST. MARTIN I 649-653   ADEODATUS II 672-676   ST. LEO II 682-683   CONON 686-687   JOHN VII 705-707   ST. GREGORY II 713-731

JOHN IV 640-642   ST. EUGENE I 654-657   DONUS 676-678   ST. BENEDICT II 684-685   ST. SERGIUS I 687-701   SISINNIUS JAN-FEB 708   ST. GREGORY III 731-741

625AD   650   675   700   725   750AD

Gregory's other overriding conviction was that the end of the world was near. He saw symbols everywhere, from the plagues that regularly swept through the country, the floods, Lombard invasions, and the decay of Rome, which he described as "once mistress of the world." Even when bedridden, Gregory's fears led him to a flurry of activity to appease God.

Above: Gregory the Great dictates the Book of Job to his scribe Peter; a twelfth century illustration to sixth century text. Bibliotheque Municipale, Laon/ Bridgeman Art Library, London

the Gregorian chant should be ascribed to Gregory II, who was pope 713-731AD. However, as John Jay Hughes points out in his book *Popes Who Shaped History*, Gregory the Great was a prolific writer and the most widely read author of the Middle Ages. He also composed 82 of the 927 prayers in the *Sacramentary*.

Gregory died in March 604AD and was succeeded by his trusted deacon Sabinian. The Tuscan native's career under Gregory was marred by his failure as papal envoy to Constantinople to stop that city's bishop using the fawning title "Ecumenical Patriarch." Recalled to Rome by Gregory in 595AD, he recovered his standing sufficiently to succeed his mentor. His two-year tenure as pontiff is noted more for his wheeler-dealing ways and the mob riot at his funeral than for his work.

Sabinian ended Gregory's policy of giving grain away to the poor

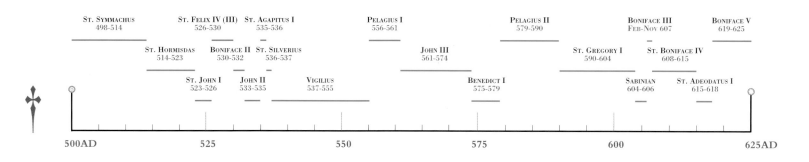

ST. SYMMACHUS
498-514

ST. FELIX IV (III)
526-530

ST. AGAPITUS I
535-536

PELAGIUS I
556-561

PELAGIUS II
579-590

BONIFACE III
FEB-NOV 607

BONIFACE V
619-625

ST. HORMISDAS
514-523

BONIFACE II
530-532

ST. SILVERIUS
536-537

JOHN III
561-574

ST. GREGORY I
590-604

ST. BONIFACE IV
608-615

ST. JOHN I
523-526

JOHN II
533-535

VIGILIUS
537-555

BENEDICT I
575-579

SABINIAN
604-606

ST. ADEODATUS I
615-618

500AD   525   550   575   600   625AD

According to legend, Constantine had granted the territories to St. Peter via Silvester and they rightfully belonged to the pope. Incredibly, both Pepin and the ailing Byzantines accepted the story as fact. It took the Romans a full 10 years to realize the implications of the new Papal States.

Right: Charlemagne, king of the Franks, was the most powerful European monarch of the period, ruling an empire that stretched from Saxony to Lombardy. In return for his protection the papacy conferred on him the mantle of the Western Roman Empire and thus started a relationship—often stormy—between emperors and popes that would last for hundreds of years.

and needy by selling it instead. With famine still gripping the entire area he infuriated the starving Romans, who got their own back by going on the rampage after his death in February 606AD. A baying crowd blocked his funeral procession and his body had to be carried around the city walls to reach its final resting place at St. Peter's Basilica.

Life was no less easy for the succeeding popes. Lombard invasions, barbarian uprisings, and the tussle for power between the church and the empire all took their toll well into the next century.

As Italy's Byzantine power ebbed, the Lombards became the conquering strength. It took Pope Stephen III—also known as Stephen II because his namesake predecessor died of a stroke just three days after his election—to turn to another potential ally, the Franks, for support. Stephen met with the Frankish leader Pepin in 754AD, pleading with him to save the papacy from the Lombards. In exchange, Stephen gave him the title "Patrician of the Romans," a title he had no right to bestow but which proved tempting to Pepin. The Franks then marched on Rome and defeated the Lombards. Two years later Pepin's army also snatched Ravenna and other extensive territories, all of which he handed to Stephen in a gift known as the Donation of Pepin. These areas became known as the Papal States.

It was around this time that the fraudulent Donation of Constantine moved from whimsical fiction into fact. According to legend, Constantine had granted the territories to St. Peter via Silvester and they rightfully belonged to the pope. Incredibly, both Pepin and the ailing Byzantines accepted the story as fact. It took the Romans a full 10 years to realize the implications of the new Papal States. In effect, the Pope was now an incredibly wealthy feudal lord and as such the pontiff's crown became a much sought-after trophy for the rich and powerful families of Rome.

The first papal riots resulting from Pepin's legacy broke out in 767AD, when on the death of the reigning pope, one aristocrat rode into Rome to propose his own brother, a layman, as successor. "The fact that the brother was disqualified because he was a layman was easily overcome, for he was ordained cleric, sub-deacon, deacon, and priest—and then consecrated as bishop and pope on the same day," wrote E.R. Chamberlin in his book *The Bad Popes.*

Not to be outdone, two more would-be popes appeared. The first had his eyes gouged out and was left for dead; the second was murdered by a mob. Ironically Christophorus, believed to be the author of the Donation of Constantine, was also killed in one of the riots. The third papal candidate survived only because he appealed to the Lombards for protection.

The links established between the Franks as natural protectors of the pope became even more apparent 50 years later when Pepin's son, Charlemagne, helped Leo III to retain his position as pope in the face of

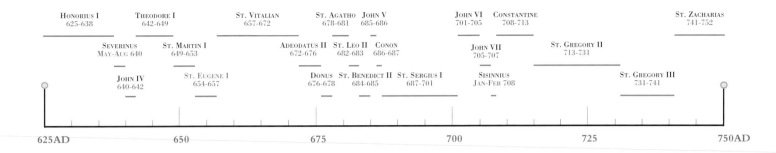

| HONORIUS I | THEODORE I | | ST. VITALIAN | | ST. AGATHO | JOHN V | | JOHN VI | CONSTANTINE | | | ST. ZACHARIAS |
| 625-638 | 642-649 | | 657-672 | | 678-681 | 685-686 | | 701-705 | 708-713 | | | 741-752 |

SEVERINUS   ST. MARTIN I   ADEODATUS II   ST. LEO II   CONON   JOHN VII   ST. GREGORY II
MAY-AUG 640   649-653   672-676   682-683   686-687   705-707   713-731

JOHN IV   ST. EUGENE I   DONUS   ST. BENEDICT II   ST. SERGIUS I   SISINNIUS   ST. GREGORY III
640-642   654-657   676-678   684-685   687-701   JAN-FEB 708   731-741

625AD   650   675   700   725   750AD

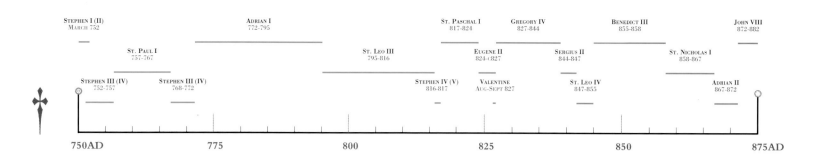

| STEPHEN I (II) MARCH 752 | ADRIAN I 772-795 | | ST. PASCHAL I 817-824 | GREGORY IV 827-844 | BENEDICT III 855-858 | JOHN VIII 872-882 |

ST. PAUL I 757-767   ST. LEO III 795-816   EUGENE II 824-c.827   SERGIUS II 844-847   ST. NICHOLAS I 858-867

STEPHEN III (IV) 752-757   STEPHEN III (IV) 768-772   STEPHEN IV (V) 816-817   VALENTINE AUG-SEPT 827   ST. LEO IV 847-855   ADRIAN II 867-872

750AD   775   800   825   850   875AD

considerable opposition. As successor to Adrian I, Leo's election on December 26, 795AD, had been unanimous, but was soon marred by supporters of the previous pontiff and other Romans who hated his governmental style.

Leo, a Roman by birth, successfully quelled his detractors and kept the problems at bay for just over three years until the simmering anger erupted into full scale rioting on April 25, 799AD. A baying mob attacked Leo and almost succeeded in cutting out his tongue and gouging out his eyes. He was locked up in a monastery, accused, among other things, of perjury and adultery (charges that certainly seemed well-founded), but managed to escape, fleeing to the court of Charlemagne.

This is where the papal friendship with the Franks paid off. Supported by Charlemagne and his powerful Frankish army, Leo returned to Rome and was dramatically cleared of all the charges. Keen to repair his tarnished image, Leo repaid Charlemagne by crowning him Emperor of the West on Christmas Day 800AD, as the warrior leader knelt in prayer at St. Peter's Basilica—a move Leo had no right to make as the reigning emperor was already in situ in Constantinople. Among other things, this set a precedent that all future Holy Roman Emperors should receive their crowns from the pope, thus ending the reliance of the Byzantines for favor and protection.

Until Leo's death in 816AD there followed a harmonious pact between the church and the empire. The illiterate Charlemagne had a burning desire to educate himself under Leo. He set up universities, inspired architecture and great sculptures, and his genuine feel for farming is said to have led to the three-tier system of agriculture still used to this day of rotating crops while leaving one field fallow. Stone castles sprang up across Italy and the peasants lived nearby for protection. Monasteries followed as a natural course, creating towns and cities that still remain.

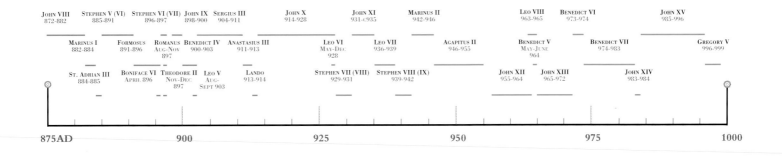

| JOHN VIII 872-882 | STEPHEN V (VI) 885-891 | STEPHEN VI (VII) 896-897 | JOHN IX 898-900 | SERGIUS III 904-911 | | JOHN X 914-928 | | JOHN XI 931-c935 | | MARINUS II 942-946 | | | LEO VIII 963-965 | BENEDICT VI 973-974 | | JOHN XV 985-996 |

| MARINUS I 882-884 | FORMOSUS 891-896 | ROMANUS AUG-NOV 897 | BENEDICT IV 900-903 | ANASTASIUS III 911-913 | | LEO VI MAY-DEC 928 | LEO VII 936-939 | | AGAPITUS II 946-955 | | BENEDICT V MAY-JUNE 964 | | BENEDICT VII 974-983 | | GREGORY V 996-999 |

| ST. ADRIAN III 884-885 | BONIFACE VI APRIL 896 | THEODORE II NOV-DEC 897 | LEO V AUG-SEPT 903 | LANDO 913-914 | | STEPHEN VII (VIII) 929-931 | STEPHEN VIII (IX) 939-942 | | | JOHN XII 955-964 | JOHN XIII 965-972 | | JOHN XIV 983-984 |

| 875AD | 900 | 925 | 950 | 975 | 1000 |

Exactly 30 years later violence again erupted in Rome when 10,000 warring Saracens landed at the mouth of the River Tiber, ransacking the stricken city, taking away ancient relics, and pillaging St. Peter's of its treasures. The embattled Romans blamed the then pope, Sergius II, and his over-bearing all-powerful brother, Bishop Benedict of Albano.

Sergius, a Roman nobleman, was already elderly and in a bad health when he was elected pontiff in 844AD. He had served with distinction under several popes including Pope Gregory IV, and was elected by his contemporaries to counterbalance the people's choice of the antipope John. The noblemen's troops put an end to the opposition by crushing the rising rebellion and installing Sergius as pontiff. His enemy, John, was allowed to live only after Sergius intervened.

Sergius immediately found himself at the center of a synod investigation because he had been elected without the permission of Emperor Lothair I. But once cleared, Sergius repaid the Frankish ruler by building great churches across the empire. Unfortunately, Sergius and his brother funded their ambitious construction projects by auctioning off honors and offices to raise money. When the Saracens attacked it was seen by the Romans to be divine punishment for their power-hungry actions.

The ill-fated Sergius died in January 847AD, five months after the bloody sack of Rome, leaving his successor, Leo IV, with the unenviable task of defending Rome from the marauding Saracens. His pontificate—which lasted until his death in 855AD—was important because he built new walls along the Tiber, ringing St. Peter's, and organized the military alliance between the Holy See, Naples, and Amalfi that ultimately defeated the Saracens in 849AD. The tough pope also ordered the execution of several imperial officials accused of murder, in the process straining relations with the Frankish Emperor Louis II.

Another ninth century pope who combined the church with military leadership was John VIII, who eventually paid with his life and holds the dubious honor of being the first pope to be assassinated.

John, a trusted Roman cleric who served under Nicholas I and Adrian II before his own election in 872AD, used his political ambitions to interfere with the affairs of the empire, using his energy to take on the still warring Saracens. Further strengthening Rome by building walls around St. Paul's Basilica and organizing a papal fleet, he unsuccessfully tried to forge an alliance with the Muslims. But eventually John VIII was forced to buy them off by crowning Charles the Bald emperor in exchange for new territories and political favors. When Charles died six years later in 881AD, John then gave his blessing to Charles the Fat, crowning him emperor. But this proved to be a disaster; the new emperor failed to support John VIII against the Saracens and was eventually deposed by his own sons.

Left: Another view of the coronation of Charlemagne by Pope Leo III—St. Leo—at St. Peter's, Rome in 800AD. The dealings between popes and Holy Roman emperors were crucial to the politics of the medieval papacy.
Giraudon/Bridgeman Art Library, London

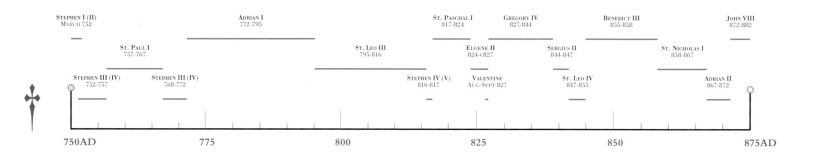

STEPHEN I (II)
MARCH 752

ADRIAN I
772-795

ST. PASCHAL I
817-824

GREGORY IV
827-844

BENEDICT III
855-858

JOHN VIII
872-882

ST. PAUL I
757-767

ST. LEO III
795-816

EUGENE II
824-c.827

SERGIUS II
844-847

ST. NICHOLAS I
858-867

STEPHEN III (IV)
752-757

STEPHEN III (IV)
768-772

STEPHEN IV (V)
816-817

VALENTINE
AUG-SEPT 827

ST. LEO IV
847-855

ADRIAN II
867-872

750AD   775   800   825   850   875AD

"The corpse was provided with a council, which kept wisely quiet, while Pope Stephen raved and screamed his insults at it."

Aside from his disappointment in Charles the Fat, John VIII was also infuriated by the Roman nobility. Vexed by their ambition and furious that they did not support his coronation of Charles, he excommunicated several, including Formosus, the Bishop of Porto who later became pope. The final years of his 10-year reign were filled with trouble. While he succeeded in securing an uneasy peace between Constantinople and Rome, he failed to quell the warring factions in his own court. Records are sketchy but, according to the *Annales Fuldenses*—the Annals of Fulda—the unfortunate John was murdered by his supposedly trusted lieutenants, who poisoned him and then beat him to death in December 882AD. Marinus I was quickly installed as pope and he immediately pardoned the excommunicated noblemen, including the future pontiff Formosus.

The unfortunate Formosus owes his place in history solely to what happened after his death when, in possibly the most grotesque papal act, his rotting corpse was dug up and ordered to stand trial. He was probably a Roman by birth and was elected pope in 891AD after two stints as Bishop of Porto. As pontiff, Formosus's main acts appear to have been crowning a succession of warring emperors and failing to heal the rift between the East and West. He died on April 4, 897AD, and was immediately succeeded by Boniface VI, who, having been elected at the height of a riot, promptly died 15 days later.

Stephen VI and the grotesque Cadaver Synod, or Synod Horrenda, followed. In his book *The Bad Popes*, E.R. Chamberlin described the social disintegration of the church in Rome thus:

"In March 896, the ghastly Synod Horrenda, which sat in judgment upon a corpse, marked the moment when the city plunged finally into anarchy and delivered, as inescapable result, the Chair of Peter to whosoever was bold enough to ascend it."

Stephen, who had been appointed a bishop against his will by Formosus, was a supporter of Lambert of Spoleto, now virtual ruler of Italy. Lambert had sworn revenge on Formosus for crowning the Frankish leader Arnulf emperor instead of his father. His planned revenge was cut short by the deaths of both Arnulf and Formosus, but he ordered Stephen to convene a synod to try the dead pontiff on charges of perjury and canonical violations.

Formosus's corpse was dug up and the rotting remains of the eight-month dead pope were once again dressed in papal robes and propped up on the throne to stand trial. As E.R. Chamberlin writes, "The corpse was provided with a council, which wisely kept quiet, while Pope Stephen raved and screamed his insults at it."

Formosus's sin, according to the synod, had been to accept the role of pontiff while still bishop of another diocese—the reality was that he

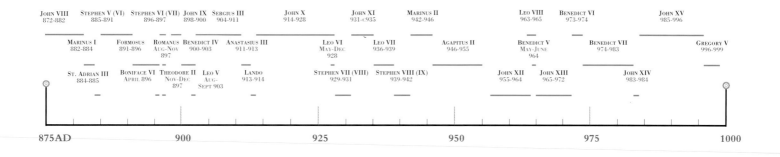

JOHN VIII 872-882	STEPHEN V (VI) 885-891	STEPHEN VI (VII) 896-897	JOHN IX 898-900	SERGIUS III 904-911	JOHN X 914-928	JOHN XI 931-c935	MARINUS II 942-946	LEO VIII 963-965	BENEDICT VI 973-974	JOHN XV 985-996
MARINUS I 882-884	FORMOSUS 891-896	ROMANUS Aug-Nov 897	BENEDICT IV 900-903	ANASTASIUS III 911-913	LEO VI May-Dec 928	LEO VII 936-939	AGAPITUS II 946-955	BENEDICT V May-June 964	BENEDICT VII 974-983	GREGORY V 996-999
ST. ADRIAN III 884-885	BONIFACE VI April 896	THEODORE II Nov-Dec 897	LEO V Aug-Sept 903	LANDO 913-914	STEPHEN VII (VIII) 929-931	STEPHEN VIII (IX) 939-942	JOHN XII 955-964	JOHN XIII 965-972	JOHN XIV 983-984

875AD   900   925   950   975   1000

had crowned the wrong emperors. Not surprisingly, Formosus was found guilty. But Lambert and Stephen were not content to simply record the fact in the annals of history.

The corpse was stripped and the three fingers of his right hand—traditionally used to bless lesser mortals—were hacked off. Formosus's remains were then dragged into the street and thrown to a baying mob. The crowd in turn threw the body into the Tiber, where it was rescued by a group of fishermen. Legend has it that a hermit later gave the unfortunate Formosus a second burial in a common grave. Immediately after the synod's horrendous judgment, Rome was hit by an earthquake that wrecked the Lateran Basilica. The superstitious Romans took this as a sign from God that Stephen had gone too far and, as stories circulated of an angry St. Peter seen saluting the dead Formosus, Stephen himself was seized, thrown into jail and ultimately strangled in August 897AD.

It took Pope John IX, who lasted just two years himself, from 898 to 900AD, to annul the Cadaver Synod's actions, but by then the precedent had been set for discarding unpopular popes.

After Stephen's death in jail, his followers had elected a Cardinal Sergius as pope, in direct opposition to a rival candidate. Violence erupted and Sergius was chased out of Rome. Over the next year a further four popes were elected: some lasted weeks, others days, before they were killed by rivals. In the next six years seven popes and an antipope were elected, until Cardinal Sergius returned and retook the papal crown in January 904AD.

Records from this time are sparse or nonexistent. The Dark Ages had truly befallen Rome. According to sketchy reports, Sergius ordered the deposed Pope Leo V and the antipope Christopher to be murdered and claimed his reign had begun not in 904AD but 897AD, making Popes John IX, Benedict IV, and Leo V all illegitimate and their edicts null and void. Sergius III relied on the Roman nobleman Theophylact and his ambitious wife Theodora to enforce his will. Legend has it he fathered a son—the future Pope John XI—by Theodora's 15-year-old daughter Marozia. Sergius died in 911AD, his only apparent legacy was the restoration of the Lateran Basilica.

John was elected pope 20 years later in what Matthew Bunson, author of *The Pope Encyclopedia,* describes as "a truly bleak period in papal history." By now the much feared Marozia ruled Rome and John was very much under her thumb, presiding over her unconventional marriage to her brother-in-law Hugh of Provence in 932AD. The wedding sparked another uprising in Rome led by John's half brother Alberic. After a spell in prison, John continued as pope until his death in December 935AD under the watchful eye of his sibling, now installed as Emperor Alberic II.

It would be left to new popes, in a new epoch, to try to bring light back in again after a dark age.

Over the next year a further four popes were elected: some lasted weeks, others days, before they were killed by rivals.

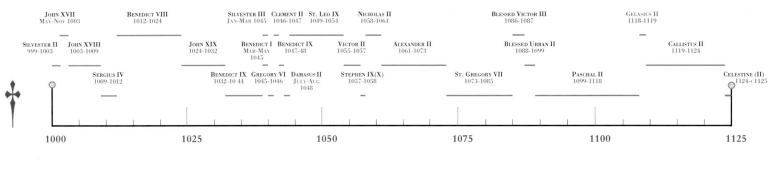

JOHN XVII
MAY-NOV 1003

BENEDICT VIII
1012-1024

SILVESTER III
JAN-MAR 1045

CLEMENT II
1046-1047

ST. LEO IX
1049-1054

NICHOLAS II
1058-1061

BLESSED VICTOR III
1086-1087

GELASIUS II
1118-1119

SILVESTER II
999-1003

JOHN XVIII
1003-1009

JOHN XIX
1024-1032

BENEDICT I
MAR-MAY
1045

BENEDICT IX
1047-48

VICTOR II
1055-1057

ALEXANDER II
1061-1073

BLESSED URBAN II
1088-1099

CALLISTUS II
1119-1124

SERGIUS IV
1009-1012

BENEDICT IX
1032-10 44

GREGORY VI
1045-1046

DAMASUS II
JULY-AUG
1048

STEPHEN IX(X)
1057-1058

ST. GREGORY VII
1073-1085

PASCHAL II
1099-1118

CELESTINE (II)
1124-c1125

1000   1025   1050   1075   1100   1125

THE MIDDLE AGES

The papacy was still reeling from the horrors of the late ninth and tenth centuries, when Leo IX, a count's son from Alsace, became Bishop of Toul in 1027.

EARLY IN 1049 A DASHING GERMAN NOBLEMAN walked through the gates of Rome dressed as a pilgrim. To rapturous cheers from the city's inhabitants, Bruno of Egisheim was crowned Pope Leo IX and thus began a period of reform that would become known in papal history by the name of Leo's successor, Gregory. The papacy was still reeling from the horrors of the late ninth and tenth centuries, when Leo IX, a count's son from Alsace, became Bishop of Toul in 1027. His patrons included the Emperor Henry III, who respected the clergyman's zealous reforms in the church and put forward his name as pope on the death of Damasus II. Leo IX, a military man at heart whose battle strategies would later lead to his downfall, was duly elected, but insisted his standing should be ratified by the people of Rome.

Dressed in the shabby garb of a pilgrim, he immediately won over the hearts of the cynical Romans and proved to be an able pontiff, making much needed church reform his priority. In this he was aided by his German contemporary Hildebrand, the future Pope Gregory VII. But Leo had good reason for his initial reluctance to become pope; two powerful Roman families had been vying for control of papacy for much of the eleventh century and their in-fighting had led to a series of unsuitable popes being overthrown.

From 1012 to 1044, the Counts of Tusculum provided three popes, including the 18-year-old Benedict IX, a spirited teenager with absolutely no clerical qualifications to hold office. The vying Crescenti family seized control in September 1044 and forced Benedict out of Rome. They replaced him with Silvester III, who lasted a matter of weeks before he, too, was overthrown. The exiled Benedict then agreed to resign in exchange for annual payments from his godfather John Gratian, who was promptly crowned Pope Gregory VI.

All went well for a year until the German King Henry III arrived in Rome to receive his own imperial crown and discovered there were three claimants to the papacy. Silvester and, surprisingly, the exiled Benedict were both disputing Gregory's claim to the title. Having heard all of the arguments, Henry decided to choose his own pope and presided over a synod meeting at Sutri on the outskirts of Rome, to decide the issue. Ultimately, all three popes were deposed and Bishop Suitger of Bamberg was duly crowned Pope Clement II on Christmas Day 1046. Clement lasted a little over six months, suddenly falling ill and dying. Rumors spread rapidly that he had been poisoned and

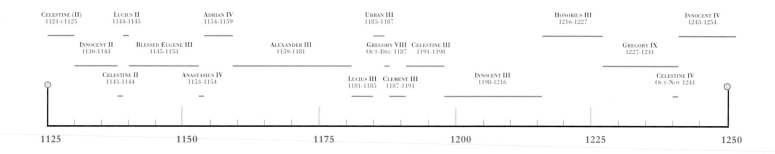

CELESTINE (II) 1124-c1125	LUCIUS II 1144-1145	ADRIAN IV 1154-1159		URBAN III 1185-1187			HONORIUS III 1216-1227		INNOCENT IV 1243-1254
INNOCENT II 1130-1143	BLESSED EUGENE III 1145-1153		ALEXANDER III 1159-1181	GREGORY VIII Oct-Dec 1187	CELESTINE III 1191-1198			GREGORY IX 1227-1241	
	CELESTINE II 1143-1144	ANASTASIUS IV 1153-1154		LUCIUS III 1181-1185	CLEMENT III 1187-1191	INNOCENT III 1198-1216			CELESTINE IV Oct-Nov 1241

| 1125 | 1150 | 1175 | 1200 | 1225 | 1250 |

seemed confirmed when Benedict made another bid to regain the papacy. Clement was buried in the cathedral at Bamberg, Germany, instead of St. Peter's Basilica. When his tomb was opened up in 1942 his bones contained a heavy concentration of lead, lending strong support to the theory that he was murdered. His successor, Damasus II, again elected by Henry III, lasted just 23 days before he too died in mysterious surroundings. Given this, it is hardly surprising that the military-minded Leo was reluctant to accept the role.

Leo's luck held out for five years and with Hildebrand at his side he set about reforming the church, establishing a committee of like-minded clergymen to sort out the twin problems of people buying their way into the priesthood and clerical marriage. Both practices were seen often in medieval times, when it was common practice for feudal lords to chose their clerics in return for payment. In return the clergy widely ignored the church's doctrine on celibacy, providing "gifts" of church property for their offspring. Such reforms were lauded across the empire, but then Leo made the first major mistake of his papacy. In 1053 he launched his own military campaign against the invading Normans in southern Italy. Leo's army was swiftly destroyed and he was taken captive. Held for nine months he was released only after granting the Normans a number of concessions, which in turn angered the Byzantines. Leo's perceived interference in military affairs led to the final break between the East and West. He died on April 19, 1054, more famous in the end for the schism than for his reforms.

Four more reforming popes, Victor II, Stephen IX, Nicholas II, and Alexander II, followed in quick succession before Hildebrand—who had become the elder statesman of church reform and had overseen all four elections—was named Pope Gregory VII on April 22, 1073. Having worked tirelessly in the preceding years to end the simony payments (selling ecclesiastical preferments) by clergy to feudal lords, marriage among the clergy, and other ecclesiastical irregularities, he vowed to make these matters the central focus of his papacy and thus gave his name to the Gregorian Reform movement.

Above: Pope Leo IX, pontiff from 1049 to 1054, won the hearts of the Romans when he entered the Eternal City dressed as a pilgrim. One of the precursors of the Gregorian reforms, his reign is best remembered for the start of the schism between eastern and western churches, and for an ill-fated military adventure against the Normans in southern Italy. It ended in his capture and imprisonment for nine months shortly after which he died.

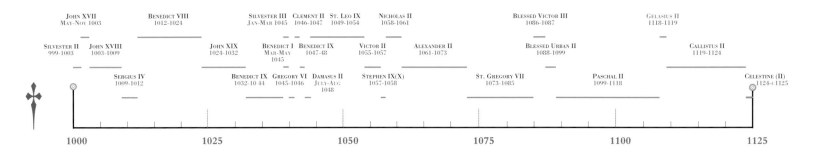

JOHN XVII MAY-NOV 1003		BENEDICT VIII 1012-1024			SILVESTER III JAN-MAR 1045	CLEMENT II 1046-1047	ST. LEO IX 1049-1054		NICHOLAS II 1058-1061			BLESSED VICTOR III 1086-1087		GELASIUS II 1118-1119
SILVESTER II 999-1003	JOHN XVIII 1003-1009		JOHN XIX 1024-1032	BENEDICT I MAR-MAY 1045	BENEDICT IX 1047-48		VICTOR II 1055-1057	ALEXANDER II 1061-1073			BLESSED URBAN II 1088-1099			CALLISTUS II 1119-1124
	SERGIUS IV 1009-1012		BENEDICT IX 1032-10 44	GREGORY VI 1045-1046	DAMASUS II JULY-AUG 1048		STEPHEN IX(X) 1057-1058		ST. GREGORY VII 1073-1085		PASCHAL II 1099-1118			CELESTINE (II) 1124-c 1125

| 1000 | 1025 | 1050 | 1075 | 1100 | 1125 |

Above: Gregory VII, pope from 1073 to 1085, was often known by his given name Hildebrand and was one of the great church reformers. St. Leo IX made Hildebrand treasurer of the Roman Church; under Nicholas II and Alexander II he was significant in shaping policy: with this background it was perhaps unsurprising that his pontificate should have initiated so much.

Unfortunately one of Gregory's well-meaning reforms, which became known as the investiture controversy, led to his downfall. For more than a century popes had been trying to stamp out the European custom of secular rulers investing abbots and bishops with the rings and staffs of their office. Rome saw the garish ceremonies as an interference and Gregory announced an edict forbidding such investitures, immediately infuriating the German boy king and future emperor Henry IV.

Initially, Gregory's relationship with Henry—who was crowned king at the age of four with his widowed mother Agnes as regent—was good. The boy promised to support the Pope's campaign against simony and clerical marriage, as well as offering to restore illegally acquired church property. He also begged pardon for associating with cardinals who had been excommunicated by Pope Alexander II for nominating an anti-papal archbishop of Milan. When the cardinals in turn lifted their excommunication on Henry himself, an easy rapport between the boy ruler and pope appeared to have begun.

However, their differences came to a head after the synod of Lent 1075 when Gregory made his ruling on lay investiture. The ceremonies were bound together with simony, making the investitures valuable properties. The feudal lords were also more interested in the personal loyalties of the clergy than their allegiance to the church. Even the rulers who agreed with the church's stand against simony and clerical marriage were aghast at the ending of the centuries old tradition. Among the most upset was the boy king Henry. Gregory hoped that the latter would understand, and wrote him a letter congratulating him on his efforts at self improvement and offering him the chance to discuss the decision. Henry responded by investing a number of his own bishops and abbots in both Germany and Italy. Gregory replied with a bitter letter attacking the king.

On January 24, 1076, Henry summoned lay rulers and his own bishops to a meeting at Worms, where they drew up a stinging reply to Gregory, accusing him of, among other things, "Filling the whole church with the stench of grave scandal by living more intimately than is necessary with a woman not of your kin." This was an unfounded reference to Gregory's friendship with the Countess Matilda of Tuscany.

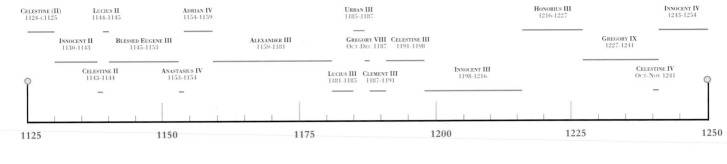

CELESTINE (II) 1124–c1125	LUCIUS II 1144–1145	ADRIAN IV 1154–1159		URBAN III 1185–1187		HONORIUS III 1216–1227	INNOCENT IV 1243–1254
INNOCENT II 1130–1143	BLESSED EUGENE III 1145–1153	ALEXANDER III 1159–1181	GREGORY VIII OCT–DEC 1187	CELESTINE III 1191–1198		GREGORY IX 1227–1241	
CELESTINE II 1143–1144	ANASTASIUS IV 1153–1154		LUCIUS III 1181–1185	CLEMENT III 1187–1191	INNOCENT III 1198–1216		CELESTINE IV OCT–NOV 1241

| 1125 | 1150 | 1175 | 1200 | 1225 | 1250 |

Above: The First Crusade was the most successful of all the crusades. It took Jerusalem in 1099 and set up the Crusader States, which included the kingdom of Jerusalem. This was held until 1187, when Saladin recaptured it. The final Crusader State was taken by the Mameluks in 1292.

Matters escalated when Henry followed that up with a stronger note denouncing the pope as "Hildebrand, no longer pope but false monk" and demanded his resignation.

Henry then sent a representative to the Lenten synod in Rome of February 14–20, to demand again Gregory's resignation. The pope's bishops reared up against Henry and only Gregory's personal intervention saved the representative from attack. The following day Gregory, in front of Henry's mother Agnes, excommunicated the bishops he believed had turned against him. He addressed Henry in the form of a prayer declaring:

"I deprive King Henry, who has rebelled against the church with unheard of audacity, of the government over the whole kingdom of Germany and Italy, and I release all Christian men from the allegiance which they have sworn or may swear to him, and I forbid anyone to serve him as king."

In later letters Gregory suggested his excommunication of Henry was provisional, in the hope the king would see the error of his ways. However, the empire responded with shock; no pope had ever excommunicated a king or tried to take away his throne, and just 30 years before the shoe had been on the other foot when Henry's father had

51

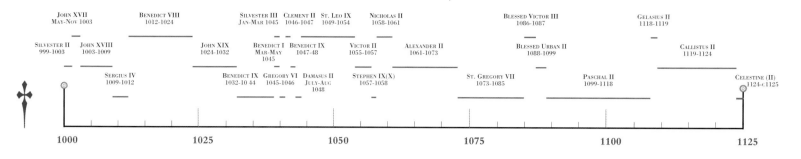

| JOHN XVII | | BENEDICT VIII | | SILVESTER III | CLEMENT II | ST. LEO IX | | NICHOLAS II | | BLESSED VICTOR III | | GELASIUS II | |
| MAY-NOV 1003 | | 1012-1024 | | JAN-MAR 1045 | 1046-1047 | 1049-1054 | | 1058-1061 | | 1086-1087 | | 1118-1119 | |

| SILVESTER II | JOHN XVIII | | JOHN XIX | BENEDICT I | BENEDICT IX | VICTOR II | ALEXANDER II | | BLESSED URBAN II | | CALLISTUS II |
| 999-1003 | 1003-1009 | | 1024-1032 | MAR-MAY 1045 | 1047-48 | 1055-1057 | 1061-1073 | | 1088-1099 | | 1119-1124 |

| SERGIUS IV | | BENEDICT IX | GREGORY VI | DAMASUS II | STEPHEN IX(X) | | ST. GREGORY VII | | PASCHAL II | | CELESTINE (II) |
| 1009-1012 | | 1032-10 44 | 1045-1046 | JULY-AUG 1048 | 1057-1058 | | 1073-1085 | | 1099-1118 | | 1124-c1125 |

| 1000 | 1025 | 1050 | 1075 | 1100 | 1125 |

Above: Urban II, pontiff from 1088 to 1099, called Christians to the First Crusade after presiding over the Council of Clermont in 1095. Justified on the grounds of defending Christians from Muslims and recovering the Holy Land, the First Crusade captured Antioch and Jerusalem and set up the Crusader States.

Right: A key moment in the history of the Third Crusade. The battling medieval monarchs of England and France, Henry II and Philip Augustus, meet at Gisors. Here the eloquence of Josias, Archbishop of Tyre, would win them over. They decided to forget their differences and to take up the cross and fight Saladin. In fact, following continued fighting and the eventual death of Henry it would be his son Richard the Lionheart who would go to the Holy Land.

deposed three popes. Henry, who now referred to Gregory as "the monk Hildebrand," seriously overestimated his own strength. Rebellious German princes sided with the recently defeated Saxons to take advantage of the split between king and church. On October 15, Henry's enemies called for an imperial Diet to choose a new ruler. In turn Gregory referred to his rival as "Henry, the so-called king" and outlined the penance required for the ruler to be restored.

A tense Henry waited on one side of the River Rhine, while his enemies on the other side discussed whether to elect a new king. Henry eventually agreed to seek forgiveness from the pope and it was agreed they would delay deciding a new ruler until February 1077, the anniversary of his excommunication. But in his letter to Gregory asking for forgiveness, Henry demanded that the pope clear his name of the immorality charges relating to the Countess Matilda. A furious Gregory then refused to receive Henry in Rome and set off to meet the king's German opponents.

Henry, who feared rebellion if the pope met with his rivals, decided to intercept Gregory. He found most of the paths blocked by his opponents but eventually made it with his wife and infant son to Mantua, 40 miles from Canossa, where Gregory had taken refuge, in January 1077. Barefoot and wearing ragged clothes, Henry waited in the snow outside the castle gates seeking forgiveness for his excommunication. Gregory feared the king would once again break his promises and that he in turn would be alienated by his German supporters. Equally he worried about being seen as a tyrant rather than a humble servant of God. Eventually Gregory capitulated and forgave the king. Incredibly, as John Jay Hughes explains in his book *Pontiffs: Popes Who Shaped History*, it was Henry who gained from Gregory's forgiveness, as it drove a wedge between the pope and his German supporters.

The Germans responded by electing a new king, Henry's brother-in-law Duke Rudolph of Swabia. For the next three years Germany was ravaged by civil war as the two kinsmen pushed their claims to the throne. A despondent Gregory initially tried to treat both men fairly but in March 1080 his patience snapped and he again excommunicated Henry, declaring Rudolph king. He also predicted at Easter Mass on April 13 that if Henry did not repent he would be dead or overthrown by the feast of Saint Peter.

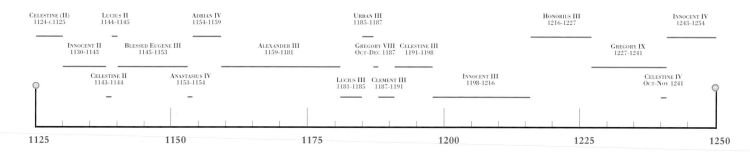

| CELESTINE (II) 1124-c1125 | LUCIUS II 1144-1145 | ADRIAN IV 1154-1159 | | URBAN III 1185-1187 | | | HONORIUS III 1216-1227 | | INNOCENT IV 1243-1254 |

INNOCENT II 1130-1143   BLESSED EUGENE III 1145-1153   ALEXANDER III 1159-1181   GREGORY VIII Oct-Dec 1187   CELESTINE III 1191-1198   GREGORY IX 1227-1241

CELESTINE II 1143-1144   ANASTASIUS IV 1153-1154   LUCIUS III 1181-1185   CLEMENT III 1187-1191   INNOCENT III 1198-1216   CELESTINE IV Oct-Nov 1241

1125   1150   1175   1200   1225   1250

The opposite happened: Henry convened two meetings of his loyal bishops to discuss the charges of immorality he had brought against Gregory at Worms four years before. He added even more outrageous charges, which included the poisoning of his four predecessors, sorcery, and heresy. Gregory was formally deposed and Archbishop Wibert of Ravenna was elected to replace him as pope. Gregory, with troops provided by the Countess Matilda, then tried to drive Wibert out, but was hopelessly defeated. At the same time Henry's rival Rudolph died of battle wounds. Henry then marched into Rome, intending to install Wibert as pope and finally receive his own imperial crown. What little support Gregory had left crumbled and when he attempted to raise money for troops he was blocked by the clergy. Ever faithful Matilda offered the only financial support when she melted down her own church plate and gave Gregory the proceeds.

Gregory sought refuge at the Castel Sant'Angelo while Henry finally entered Rome on his third attempt in 1083. Most of the rest of the year was taken up in negotiations between Henry and Gregory, but the pope refused to give Henry the imperial crown unless he first did penance. Frustrated, Henry left for southern Italy. He was then surprised in the New Year by a message from the Romans inviting him to return. Gregory's support had dwindled even more and in March 1084 Henry rode into Rome with his pope-apparent Wibert. He called a meeting of clergy and residents, inviting Gregory to give him an assurance of safe passage. They waited three days but Gregory failed to appear. At this juncture, the meeting deposed Gregory as a traitor and named Wibert as Pope Clement III. In turn Henry was crowned emperor.

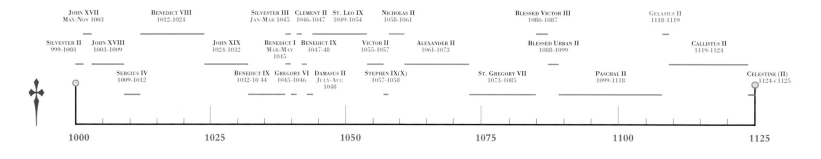

JOHN XVII MAY-NOV 1003	BENEDICT VIII 1012-1024	SILVESTER III JAN-MAR 1045	CLEMENT II 1046-1047	ST. LEO IX 1049-1054	NICHOLAS II 1058-1061	BLESSED VICTOR III 1086-1087	GELASIUS II 1118-1119

SILVESTER II 999-1003   JOHN XVIII 1003-1009   JOHN XIX 1024-1032   BENEDICT I MAR-MAY 1045   BENEDICT IX 1047-48   VICTOR II 1055-1057   ALEXANDER II 1061-1073   BLESSED URBAN II 1088-1099   CALLISTUS II 1119-1124

SERGIUS IV 1009-1012   BENEDICT IX 1032-10 44   GREGORY VI 1045-1046   DAMASUS II JULY-AUG 1048   STEPHEN IX(X) 1057-1058   ST. GREGORY VII 1073-1085   PASCHAL II 1099-1118   CELESTINE (II) 1124-c1125

1000   1025   1050   1075   1100   1125

Above: At Clermont the pope had asked his bishops to preach the crusade: in fact poorer men did a better job, particularly two Frenchmen—Peter the Hermit, an itinerant monk, and Walter the Penniless ("Sans-Avoir"), who are said to have recruited 40,000 to the cause, although the actual figure is likely to be half that.

Right: Godfrey of Boullion at the Holy Sepulcher. After the successful taking of Jerusalem, four great princes were left of those who had set out: Raymond of Toulouse, Godfrey, Robert of Flanders, and Robert of Normandy. The saintly Godfrey was chosen and refused the title of "king," becoming instead Advocatus Sancti Sepulchri—Defender of the Holy Sepulcher. He died, probably of typhoid, in 1100 and was succeeded by his brother Baldwin, who became the first king of Jerusalem.

Henry's quest for his own crown had taken a decade of savage civil war to achieve but his victory was short lived. Two months later his bitter Norman enemy, Robert Guiscard, invaded Rome and a shocked Henry withdrew without a fight. The Normans freed Gregory from the Castel Sant'Angelo and then proceeded to loot and plunder the city. The devastated Romans blamed the rout on Gregory, who left the city with his rescuers in June 1084. Gregory died a year later in May 1085 while in exile at Salerno. It took many more generations for the reforms he had presided over to be recognized. As the antipope, Clement III proved a skillful rival to the officially elected but deeply reluctant Pope Victor III, who spent most of his year as pontiff trying to resign, and then Urban II, pope from 1088 to 1099. Clement died in September 1100 having outlived and outmaneuvered both men, at times actually controlling Rome.

Urban, a Frenchman born Odo of Lagery and often known as Blessed Urban, found the papacy severely impoverished and worked slowly and patiently to try and displace Clement. For the first five years of his rule he bided his time quietly raising funds, until finally in 1093 he used some well-placed bribes to displace the antipope for a short period. He had greater success in 1095 when he appealed to the Western knights to stop fighting among themselves and help their Eastern brothers liberate Jerusalem. Thus began the First Crusade, a move that would have far-reaching consequences across the civilized world for the next 200 years. Historians differ on Urban's motives for launching the Crusades. The official record has it that Urban was responding merely to a call for help from the luckless Byzantine Emperor Alexius I, but others believe it was Urban's attempt to show force against the still troublesome western Emperor Henry IV.

Whatever the politics, the response was amazing. Urban promised total forgiveness of sins to those who marched under the banner of the cross, and while many took it to be a religious quest, others looked upon it as an adventure or as a means to earn money. Some 40,000 would-be crusaders arrived at Nicaea, in northwestern Turkey, in 1097. Of those only 5,000 were noblemen. The rest were hangers-on in the form of

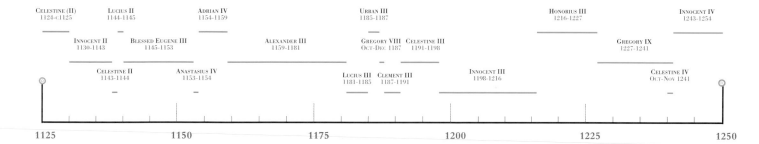

CELESTINE (II) 1124-c1125	LUCIUS II 1144-1145	ADRIAN IV 1154-1159	URBAN III 1185-1187	HONORIUS III 1216-1227		INNOCENT IV 1243-1254
INNOCENT II 1130-1143	BLESSED EUGENE III 1145-1153	ALEXANDER III 1159-1181	GREGORY VIII CELESTINE III Oct-Dec 1187 1191-1198	GREGORY IX 1227-1241		
CELESTINE II 1143-1144	ANASTASIUS IV 1153-1154	LUCIUS III CLEMENT III 1181-1185 1187-1191	INNOCENT III 1198-1216	CELESTINE IV Oct-Nov 1241		

1125   1150   1175   1200   1225   1250

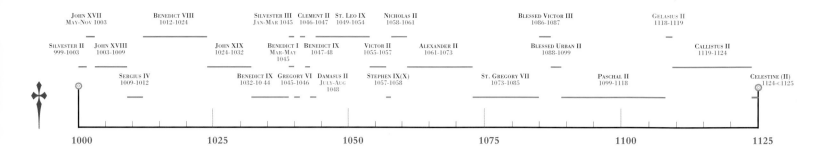

JOHN XVII MAY-NOV 1003	BENEDICT VIII 1012-1024	SILVESTER III JAN-MAR 1045	CLEMENT II 1046-1047	ST. LEO IX 1049-1054	NICHOLAS II 1058-1061	BLESSED VICTOR III 1086-1087	GELASIUS II 1118-1119

SILVESTER II 999-1003 · JOHN XVIII 1003-1009 · JOHN XIX 1024-1032 · BENEDICT I BENEDICT IX MAR-MAY 1045 1047-48 · VICTOR II 1055-1057 · ALEXANDER II 1061-1073 · BLESSED URBAN II 1088-1099 · CALLISTUS II 1119-1124

SERGIUS IV 1009-1012 · BENEDICT IX 1032-1044 · GREGORY VI 1045-1046 · DAMASUS II JULY-AUG 1048 · STEPHEN IX(X) 1057-1058 · ST. GREGORY VII 1073-1085 · PASCHAL II 1099-1118 · CELESTINE (II) 1124-c1125

1000 · 1025 · 1050 · 1075 · 1100 · 1125

Above: Peter the Hermit prays for the success of the People's Crusade.

"All who go thither and lose their lives, be it on the road or on the sea, or in the fight against the pagans, will be granted immediate forgiveness for their sins. This I grant to all who march, by virtue of the great gift which God has given me."

retainers, wives, sisters, relatives, some pilgrims, and even prostitutes, fired-up by tales of pilgrims to Jerusalem being mistreated by the Turks.

Urban II's professional aim was to recover the shrines of the Holy Land from the Muslims and bring them to Rome. For that, many a would-be warrior was prepared to go into battle, and although it may seem odd now that Christians would go to war in such a bloody way, the eleventh century followers belonged to an already violent society and thought little of murder and pillage if it was in the name of Christ. Alfred McBride, author and Norbertine priest, in his book *The Story of the Church: Peak Moments from Pentecost to the Year 2000*, summed up the differences between medieval beliefs and today's when he wrote:

"Holy wars are the most frightful of all wars. A holy war means that people think God desires it; hence they bring all the ferocity of religious conviction to the fight. War is hell enough as it is, but when religious fervor is added, it is super-hell."

Before Urban there had been an uneasy Truce of God, which forbade fighting on holy days from Wednesday night to Monday morning. Attacks on farmers, merchants, pilgrims, nuns, priests, and animals were also banned. Knights took pledges to keep the rules and then broke them. The bishops then punished the knights. Urban's Council of Clermont in 1095 sought to stop the feuding and urged all sides to take on the common cause of the crusade. Outside the eager crowd cried out *"Deus vult! Deus vult"* (God wills it). The so-called People's Crusade began the following year, fired-up by a wild-eyed bearded wanderer known as Peter the Hermit.

Breaking every rule of the Truce of God, the crusaders murdered entire Jewish communities and destroyed the farms of anyone they considered to be a heathen. In return, the victims fought back, killing crusaders as they slept by their campfires and poisoning their drinking wells. The remaining rag-tag bunch of crusaders who arrived in Constantinople terrified the Emperor Alexis, who assumed they were a

56

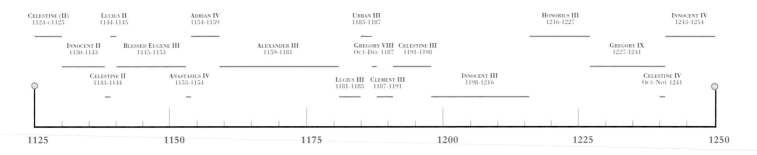

CELESTINE (II) 1124–c1125	LUCIUS II 1144–1145	ADRIAN IV 1154–1159	URBAN III 1185–1187	HONORIUS III 1216–1227	INNOCENT IV 1243–1254

INNOCENT II
1130–1143   BLESSED EUGENE III
1145–1153   ALEXANDER III
1159–1181   GREGORY VIII CELESTINE III
OCT–DEC 1187 1191–1198   GREGORY IX
1227–1241

CELESTINE II
1143–1144   ANASTASIUS IV
1153–1154   LUCIUS III CLEMENT III
1181–1185 1187–1191   INNOCENT III
1198–1216   CELESTINE IV
OCT–NOV 1241

1125   1150   1175   1200   1225   1250

threat to his kingdom. He handed them over to the Turks, who promptly massacred most of them. Yet the People's Crusade was considered to be a resounding success with the victorious Normans, still fresh from their British conquest, taking up the cudgels on behalf of Rome.

Asia Minor, Edessa, Antioch, Tripolo, and finally Jerusalem fell to the crusaders. Their hands and clothes bloodied, the holy warriors finally entered the city of Christ and knelt before his tomb.

The conquered lands were organized into four states known as *Outremer*, or the land "beyond the seas." The Knights Templar and the Knights Hospitaler were set up to defend the Outremer's fortresses along the Mediterranean coast and a further seven crusades followed to the Holy Land over the next 200 years. None matched the First Crusade and many failed to achieve anything.

Worst of all were the two Children's Crusades. A 12-year-old boy, Stephen of Cloyes, persuaded some 30,000 French children to march to Marseilles after claiming he had seen a vision from Christ. They expected the Mediterranean to open up as the Red Sea had done for Moses; instead they were captured by slave traders and sold to the Muslims. A second crusade by German children also ended in failure.

In trading terms, the crusades opened up marketing and cultural ties between the East and West, but as far as religion went, the Holy Wars merely speeded up the worsening relations between the Eastern and Western churches. Yet Urban went to his grave in July 1099 with the words of his original plea still ringing true for the crusaders:

"All who go thither and lose their lives, be it on the road or on the sea, or in the fight against the pagans, will be granted immediate forgiveness for their sins. This I grant to all who march, by virtue of the great gift which God has given me."

Urban, along with the next four popes, also sought to consolidate the papal position on lay investiture, often with dire consequences. Popes being driven into temporary exile, wars with feudal rulers and the like continued. It was in this climate that Nicholas Breakspear, the only Englishman to be elected pope, was born near St. Albans in approximately 1100.

The son of a lowly royal clerk, Nicholas entered the Augustinian monastery of St. Rufus at Avignon after studying in France. He became an abbot in 1137 and Pope Eugene III made him a cardinal in 1144, not so much as a promotion but rather to appease the monks in his charge who were unhappy at Nicholas's severe disciplinary ways. He was then appointed papal legate to Scandanavia where he proved more than adept at reorganizing the church there. For that reason he was elected pope on December 4, 1154, choosing the name Adrian IV.

His first job as pope was to defend the rights of the papacy against

Above: The storming of Antioch by the Crusaders in 1098.

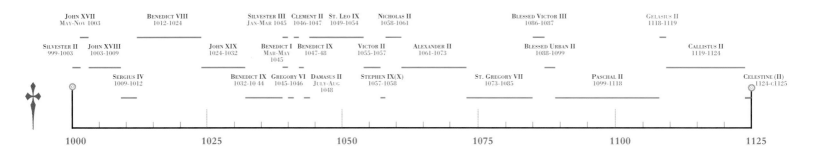

JOHN XVII MAY-NOV 1003	BENEDICT VIII 1012-1024	SILVESTER III JAN-MAR 1045	CLEMENT II 1046-1047	ST. LEO IX 1049-1054	NICHOLAS II 1058-1061	BLESSED VICTOR III 1086-1087	GELASIUS II 1118-1119

SILVESTER II 999-1003 · JOHN XVIII 1003-1009 · JOHN XIX 1024-1032 · BENEDICT I MAR-MAY 1045 · BENEDICT IX 1047-48 · VICTOR II 1055-1057 · ALEXANDER II 1061-1073 · BLESSED URBAN II 1088-1099 · CALLISTUS II 1119-1124

SERGIUS IV 1009-1012 · BENEDICT IX 1032-1044 · GREGORY VI 1045-1046 · DAMASUS II JULY-AUG 1048 · STEPHEN IX(X) 1057-1058 · ST. GREGORY VII 1073-1085 · PASCHAL II 1099-1118 · CELESTINE (II) 1124-c1125

1000   1025   1050   1075   1100   1125

the troublesome elements of Rome—namely the marauding King William I of Sicily and the radical religious reformer Arnold of Brescia. When one of his cardinals was killed in broad daylight, Adrian fled to Viterbo to plead with Emperor Frederick I Barbarossa for help. Arnold was arrested, put on trial, condemned to death, hanged, and then burned at the stake in 1155, but this did little to endear Adrian to the troublesome Rome commune. The execution also did little to secure the friendship of Emperor Frederick. The two men fell out over Adrian's insistence that the imperial crown was a gift of the pope, a disagreement that would rumble on long after both their deaths.

As an Englishman, Adrian did much to advance his own country's causes in the ongoing troubles with Ireland. He granted King Henry II of England the bull *Laudabiliter* to recognize his over-lordship of Ireland, an act that has long been studied by historians. Adrian died in 1159 and was succeeded by his closest ally, Alexander III.

Born Orlando Bandinelli in Sienna around 1100, Alexander became one of the most respected lawyers of his day. Called to Rome as a canon by Pope Eugene III, he was rapidly promoted and became one of Emperor Frederick's greatest enemies. On Adrian's death, he was elected pope by only a small majority. Hostilities broke out with the opposing candidate Cardinal Ottaviano, who was for a while elected under the name Victor IV and became an antipope. Alexander was finally crowned at Ninfa, near Velletri, on September 20, 1159, but his long papacy (until 1181) was marked by infighting with the Emperor Frederick and continued violence across Italy. In 1162 the warring factions became too much for Alexander and he fled to France, returning briefly three years later. But his negotiations with the Lombard League of Italy helped defeat Frederick in 1176.

Alexander then turned his sights on King Henry II of England, first trying to reconcile him with Thomas à Becket and then severely punishing him for Becket's murder in Canterbury Cathedral in December 1170. With England in turmoil over the martyring of Becket, Alexander tried to make amends by presiding over the Third Lateran Council, whose most noted decree was to order the election of a pope by a two-thirds majority of cardinals.

Still unpopular, Alexander was again forced out of Rome by the inhabitants in 1179 and was replaced by the antipope Innocent III. He never returned, dying

Below: Nicholas Breakspear, the only English pope, who became Adrian IV in 1154.

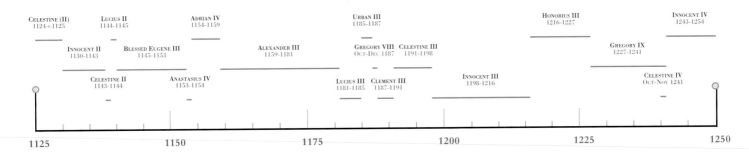

CELESTINE (II) 1124–c1125	LUCIUS II 1144–1145	ADRIAN IV 1154–1159	URBAN III 1185–1187		HONORIUS III 1216–1227	INNOCENT IV 1243–1254

INNOCENT II 1130–1143 · BLESSED EUGENE III 1145–1153 · ALEXANDER III 1159–1181 · GREGORY VIII Oct–Dec 1187 · CELESTINE III 1191–1198 · GREGORY IX 1227–1241

CELESTINE II 1143–1144 · ANASTASIUS IV 1153–1154 · LUCIUS III 1181–1185 · CLEMENT III 1187–1191 · INNOCENT III 1198–1216 · CELESTINE IV Oct–Nov 1241

1125   1150   1175   1200   1225   1250

on August 30, 1181. Innocent III had died the year before. There then followed the short reigns of four more pontiffs before Lothair of Segni—also confusingly called Innocent III—was elected pope in 1198.

Innocent was just 37 years old and considered something of a whiz-kid when he was elected. The intellectual nobleman, and nephew of Pope Celestine III, studied in Paris and Bologna before his uncle made him a cardinal. He had floundered under his immediate predecessor Celestine III due to a long-standing family feud, and spent most of that pontiff's eight-year reign writing great theological papers. He also traveled extensively and was deeply moved by the shrine of the quickly canonized St. Thomas à Becket at Canterbury. But on Celestine's death—at the then extraordinary old age of 93—the young cardinal managed to persuade the older clergy he was capable of becoming the Bishop of Rome. He was elected unanimously on the second ballot, although there were misgivings. A German writer commented: "Oh the Pope is so young! Lord, help your church."

Innocent, who was rapidly promoted from deacon to priest before he was made pope, was the first pontiff to make wide use of the phrase "Vicar of Christ." Since the beginning the popes had described themselves as Vicar of Saint Peter, after the first Bishop of Rome, but as the Roman Empire declined and the papal influence across the globe became stronger, the term became outdated. Innocent described the pope's role as "the mediator between God and man, placed below God but above men, less than God, but greater than man." Nowadays, the phrase seems shockingly arrogant but Innocent was merely describing himself as a sort of head servant, who coordinated God's other servants.

Despite his youth Innocent was a traditionalist and he refused point blank to grant King Philip II of France a marriage annulment, arguing

Above: Archbishop Thomas à Becket, who was murdered on the altar steps at Canterbury Cathedral by Henry II's knights.

59

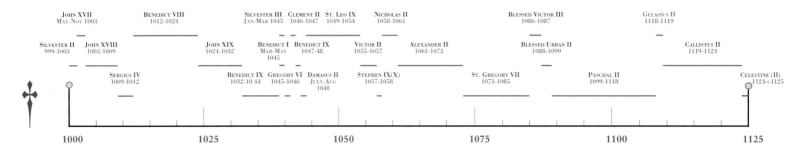

| JOHN XVII MAY-NOV 1003 | BENEDICT VIII 1012-1024 | SILVESTER III JAN-MAR 1045 | CLEMENT II 1046-1047 | ST. LEO IX 1049-1054 | NICHOLAS II 1058-1061 | BLESSED VICTOR III 1086-1087 | GELASIUS II 1118-1119 |

SILVESTER II 999-1003   JOHN XVIII 1003-1009   JOHN XIX 1024-1032   BENEDICT I MAR-MAY 1045   BENEDICT IX 1047-48   VICTOR II 1055-1057   ALEXANDER II 1061-1073   BLESSED URBAN II 1088-1099   CALLISTUS II 1119-1124

SERGIUS IV 1009-1012   BENEDICT IX 1032-10.44   GREGORY VI 1045-1046   DAMASUS II JULY-AUG 1048   STEPHEN IX(X) 1057-1058   ST. GREGORY VII 1073-1085   PASCHAL II 1099-1118   CELESTINE (II) 1124-c1125

1000   1025   1050   1075   1100   1125

Above: The struggles between church and state were typified by the relationship between Holy Roman Emperor Frederick I Barbarossa and the papacy. Crowned by English pope Adrian IV, Barbarossa supported the claims of antipopes against Alexander III during the schism that followed Adrian's death in 1159. Alexander had the last laugh following Barbarossa's defeat by the Lombards in 1176. Here Barbarossa receives a magnanamous kiss of peace from Pope Alexander in 1177.

he could be accused of heresy and forced out of his own office. In another case a man ordained as a sub-deacon after he had separated from his wife was ordered to forfeit his new role and return to his wife. Innocent argued that the wife had a divine right to her husband, while the laws ruling the clergy were human.

Innocent, who also saw himself as a mediator, often found himself drawn into political squabbles. When he became pope, the all-powerful emperor's seat was technically empty as Henry VI had died the previous year. His widow, Constance, acted as regent as their heir, Frederick, was just four years old. Constance appointed Innocent as the boy's guardian and gave him Sicily as a feudal fiefdom until the boy reached his majority at 14. Meanwhile, there were two other would-be emperors claiming the throne was rightfully theirs. The power struggle between Philip of Swabia and Guelph Otto of Brunswick rumbled on for more than 10 years until Philip was murdered.

The diplomatic Innocent then crowned Otto as emperor, having extracted a promise that he would respect the papal interests in Italy and Sicily. Otto immediately broke his promise and a furious Innocent excommunicated him, throwing his papal support once again behind his ward Frederick. Otto's enemies sided with Innocent and Frederick was finally crowned Holy Roman Emperor in 1212.

Three years later Innocent found himself negotiating for the English King John and declaring that the Magna Carta was null and void because the warring barons had extracted the king's signature using "force and fear." In return he received lands from the king.

Innocent also turned his attention to the crusades. At his urging, the Fourth Crusade was set to start by sea from Venice. But too many ships were ordered and the crusaders could not afford the charter fees. As payment, the Venetians demanded that the knights first help them

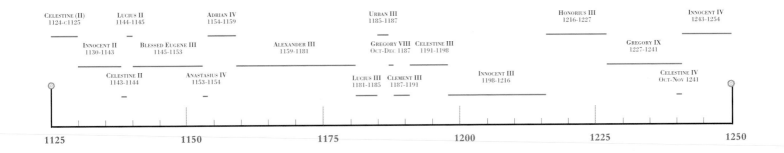

CELESTINE (II) 1124-c1125	LUCIUS II 1144-1145	ADRIAN IV 1154-1159		URBAN III 1185-1187			HONORIUS III 1216-1227		INNOCENT IV 1243-1254
	INNOCENT II 1130-1143	BLESSED EUGENE III 1145-1153	ALEXANDER III 1159-1181	GREGORY VIII OCT-DEC 1187	CELESTINE III 1191-1198			GREGORY IX 1227-1241	
	CELESTINE II 1143-1144	ANASTASIUS IV 1153-1154		LUCIUS III 1181-1185	CLEMENT III 1187-1191	INNOCENT III 1198-1216		CELESTINE IV OCT-NOV 1241	

| 1125 | 1150 | 1175 | 1200 | 1225 | 1250 |

capture Zara, then an important Adriatic port. From there the crusaders sailed to Constantinpole hoping for further support. The knights waited a year and then, in sheer frustration, overran Constantinople in April 1204.

The Byzantine Empire never recovered from the three-day-long rampage, opening up old feuds that to this day have never really been healed. The warring crusaders then made for Jerusalem but failed to get there.

A deeply disappointed Innocent—who further outraged the Byzantines by trying to reunite East and West with the appointment of a Venetian leader in Constantinople—refused to abandon crusading ideals and set about taxing the clergy to raise funds for another mission.

He promised to send the knights off himself from Messina, but on July 16, 1216, as he traveled across Italy in the hopes of reconciling old enemies to join the crusade, he died. Innocent III was 55 years old. His body was attacked by thieves on the night he died and discovered the following day naked and decomposing in the midday sun. He was hastily buried in the nearest church, St. Lawrence at Perugia. Later his remains were dug up and kept in a box at Perugia Cathedral along with the remains of two later popes, Urban IV and Martin IV. The box was reopened in 1605 but contained only a few broken bones. When Pope Leo XIII decreed in 1892 that Innocent III should have a proper burial in Rome, the bones were packed into a suitcase and taken to Rome by train.

History has shown Innocent III to be one of the most important popes of the Middle Ages; the kings of England, Poland, Sweden, and Denmark agreed with his view that he was God's servant on earth and abided by his rulings. As a political negotiator he generally proved a good mediator, although the disastrous Fourth Crusade marred his 18-year tenure.

Above: Innocent III, who reigned from 1198 to 1216, was one of the most influential medieval popes. He supported the Fourth Crusade of 1204 but was appalled when, far from crusading in the Holy Land, the crusaders attacked and sacked Constantinople.

JOHN XVII MAY-NOV 1003	BENEDICT VIII 1012-1024	SILVESTER III JAN-MAR 1045	CLEMENT II 1046-1047	ST. LEO IX 1049-1054	NICHOLAS II 1058-1061	BLESSED VICTOR III 1086-1087	GELASIUS II 1118-1119

SILVESTER II 999-1003 · JOHN XVIII 1003-1009 · JOHN XIX 1024-1032 · BENEDICT I MAR-MAY 1045 · BENEDICT IX 1047-48 · VICTOR II 1055-1057 · ALEXANDER II 1061-1073 · BLESSED URBAN II 1088-1099 · CALLISTUS II 1119-1124

SERGIUS IV 1009-1012 · BENEDICT IX 1032-10 44 · GREGORY VI 1045-1046 · DAMASUS II JULY-AUG 1048 · STEPHEN IX(X) 1057-1058 · ST. GREGORY VII 1073-1085 · PASCHAL II 1099-1118 · CELESTINE (II) 1124-c.1125

1000   1025   1050   1075   1100   1125

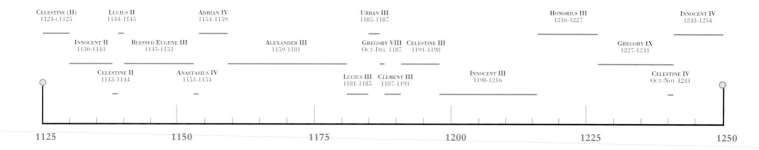

| CELESTINE (II) 1124-c1125 | LUCIUS II 1144-1145 | ADRIAN IV 1154-1159 | URBAN III 1185-1187 | HONORIUS III 1216-1227 | INNOCENT IV 1243-1254 |

| INNOCENT II 1130-1143 | BLESSED EUGENE III 1145-1153 | ALEXANDER III 1159-1181 | GREGORY VIII Oct-Dec 1187 CELESTINE III 1191-1198 | GREGORY IX 1227-1241 |

| CELESTINE II 1143-1144 | ANASTASIUS IV 1153-1154 | LUCIUS III 1181-1185 CLEMENT III 1187-1191 | INNOCENT III 1198-1216 | CELESTINE IV Oct-Nov 1241 |

1125   1150   1175   1200   1225   1250

Innocent's successor, Honorius III, was old and in poor health when he was unanimously elected. But he quickly proved to be another good administrator before falling out with the still young German king Frederick II, whom he twice crowned king and once emperor in a bid to get his support for another crusade. Frederick dithered and Honorius was on the verge of excommunicating him when he died, leaving his unfortunate successor Gregory IX to continue with the fight.

Soon after his election in March 1227, Gregory, a count's son born Ugolino of Segni, proved to have the same forceful personality as his uncle Pope Innocent III, and swiftly moved to excommunicate Frederick for failing to aid the crusades. Even when Frederick managed to brilliantly negotiate a treaty that gave him control of Jerusalem, Gregory was still against him. Although he was 84 when elected, Gregory IX proved himself a vigorous pope, his mind as sharp as when he was a brilliant student studying law at the University of Paris. He promoted the Franciscan order, strengthened missionary work abroad, and strove valiantly to keep papal finances in check. He was also a firm believer in the Inquisition, and put the Dominican Order in charge of

Above: King John signing the Magna Carta on June 19, 1215, at Runnymede. Innocent III had a bitter struggle with John over the appointment of the archbishop of Canterbury. England was placed under an interdiction which was only raised after John swore fealty to the papacy. There was one benefit in all this for John: Innocent III declared the Magna Carta null and void as it had been extracted under duress.

Left: Initial G from a psalter from San Marco depicting St. Dominic upholding the church and the dream of Pope Honorius III, Innocent III's successor.

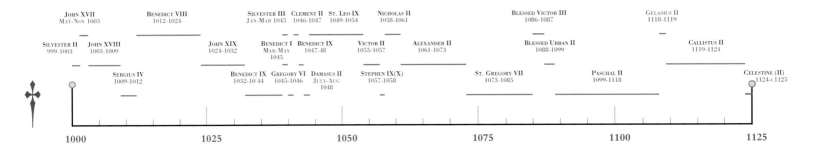

JOHN XVII
MAY-NOV 1003

BENEDICT VIII
1012-1024

SILVESTER III   CLEMENT II   ST. LEO IX
JAN-MAR 1045   1046-1047   1049-1054

NICHOLAS II
1058-1061

BLESSED VICTOR III
1086-1087

GELASIUS II
1118-1119

SILVESTER II   JOHN XVIII
999-1003   1003-1009

JOHN XIX
1024-1032

BENEDICT I   BENEDICT IX
MAR-MAY   1047-48
1045

VICTOR II
1055-1057

ALEXANDER II
1061-1073

BLESSED URBAN II
1088-1099

CALLISTUS II
1119-1124

SERGIUS IV
1009-1012

BENEDICT IX   GREGORY VI   DAMASUS II
1032-10 44   1045-1046   JULY-AUG
1048

STEPHEN IX(X)
1057-1058

ST. GREGORY VII
1073-1085

PASCHAL II
1099-1118

CELESTINE (II)
1124-c1125

1000   1025   1050   1075   1100   1125

it—they proved themselves unforgiving zealots who committed great cruelties in the name of God.

The Inquisition has its roots in the church's desire to destroy heresy. In the Middle Ages it was, initially, the duty of the bishops to suppress enemies of the faith. Gregory centralized this in 1233 with his instructions to the Dominicans to become the sword of the Lord. Particularly sought-out were members of the Albigensian sect in France, a clique that defied the Catholic Church and severely ruffled the feathers of the Vatican. It was to France, in fact, that the first Inquisitors were sent by the pope, and where the framework for their dubious work was laid down.

After arriving at their destination, a month of grace went to all those who wished to confess their heresy and recant. Those who did so were given a light penance; others went to jail; still others were burned at the stake. Cecil Roth, author of a work on the Spanish Inquisition—far more brutal than these Vatican witch-hunts—said that the papal Inquisition was more efficient:

"By the end of the 13th century it had developed a system of great thoroughness, with a hierachy of officials and detailed records, and its arm was notoriously long, so that the very name already struck terror into every wavering heart. Sanctioned by Gregory, in 1252 the use of torture was officially approved in a Papal Bull. It possessed its own prisons, and it wrapped up its affairs in inviolable secrecy. The Inquisitor was maintained by the confiscation of the property of the victim—a particularly forceful argument, in most cases, against acquittal. When a person was arrested, his property was immediately sequestered. The prisoner was not allowed the use of counsel for his defense, and the names of witnesses were concealed from him.

"Its titular object was the salvation of souls, which it hoped to bring about by the imposition of penances sufficient to wash away sin. Sentence, when passed, was not by the Inquisitors alone, but by a larger body containing a number of experts on theological and doctrinal points, including some delegate of the Bishop to whose see the accused belonged. Impenitent heretics were usually burned. The Inquisition itself did not carry out the death penalty, for it was a spiritual body, but handed the victim over to the secular authorities. The public reading and execution of the sentence was an early institution, and soon became a popular spectacle, like anything else which involves the loss of life."

Below: Grandson of Barbarossa and a ward of the papacy in his youth, Holy Roman Emperor Frederick II was finally forced into a crusade following his excommunication by Gregory IX in 1227. It proved a successful venture and he took Bethlehem, Nazareth, and Jerusalem—but by negotiation rather than warfare.

64

| CELESTINE (II) 1124–c1125 | LUCIUS II 1144–1145 | ADRIAN IV 1154–1159 | URBAN III 1185–1187 | HONORIUS III 1216–1227 | INNOCENT IV 1243–1254 |

INNOCENT II 1130–1143   BLESSED EUGENE III 1145–1153   ALEXANDER III 1159–1181   GREGORY VIII Oct–Dec 1187   CELESTINE III 1191–1198   GREGORY IX 1227–1241

CELESTINE II 1143–1144   ANASTASIUS IV 1153–1154   LUCIUS III 1181–1185   CLEMENT III 1187–1191   INNOCENT III 1198–1216   CELESTINE IV Oct–Nov 1241

1125   1150   1175   1200   1225   1250

Above: The Holy Roman Empire and the Papal States in the Middle Ages.

While Gregory laid the cornerstone of a grotesque terror, it was Frederick's defiance of his wishes for a renewed Holy War that was to bring Gregory to grief. In 1230 he signed the Treaty of San Germano with Frederick, which temporarily ended the feuding between them, but in 1239 war erupted again with Frederick, who this time sent his troops to besiege Rome. The old pope died in 1241, aged 98, just as the armies of Frederick were about to attack the city.

Celestine IV, who was elected supreme pontiff after him, did not stay in office long enough for history to adequately judge his contribution to the church. Elected on October 25, he reigned until November 10—his health wrecked by the very conclave he was forced to sit at while he and his fellow cardinals mulled over their choice of successor. He was one of only 14 cardinals alive, and two of those were languishing in Frederick's dungeons. A lackey of the Emperor Frederick, Matteo Orsini, who had become the virtual dictator of Rome, despised the cardinals and made the conditions of their conclave the most hideous

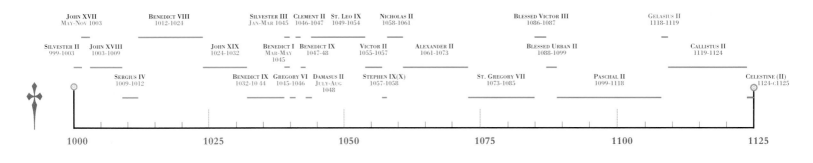

JOHN XVII MAY-NOV 1003	BENEDICT VIII 1012-1024	SILVESTER III JAN-MAR 1045	CLEMENT II 1046-1047	ST. LEO IX 1049-1054	NICHOLAS II 1058-1061	BLESSED VICTOR III 1086-1087	GELASIUS II 1118-1119	

SILVESTER II   JOHN XVIII   JOHN XIX   BENEDICT I BENEDICT IX   VICTOR II   ALEXANDER II   BLESSED URBAN II   CALLISTUS II
999-1003   1003-1009   1024-1032   MAR-MAY   1047-48   1055-1057   1061-1073   1088-1099   1119-1124
                                                            1045

SERGIUS IV   BENEDICT IX GREGORY VI DAMASUS II   STEPHEN IX(X)   ST. GREGORY VII   PASCHAL II   CELESTINE (II)
1009-1012   1032-10 44   1045-1046   JULY-AUG   1057-1058   1073-1085   1099-1118   1124-c1125
                                                         1048

1000   1025   1050   1075   1100   1125

Relative stability came to the Vatican until the appointment of Celestine V (later St. Celestine) in 1294, the Supreme Pontiff widely thought of as the most tragic figure in the history of the papacy.

ever recorded. He ordered them locked up in the foul-smelling dungeon of a ruined palace. One cardinal expired from the brutal treatment and it certainly ruined the health of the man they eventually chose—a pope who had no time to implement any policies, change anything or provide any spiritual guidance whatsoever.

It took the cardinals an exhausting 18 months to choose Celestine's successor—Genoese-born Innocent IV, who was to rule from 1243 until 1254. As with Gregory IX, Innocent IV's rule was characterized by his battles with Frederick, a ruler he wanted deposed at all costs. To this extent he sought allies throughout Europe, determined to launch his own crusade against the man who refused to carry out one for an earlier pope. Born Sinibaldo Fieschi, Innocent IV was elected after numerous squabbles and intrigues, most of them fueled by the emperor of whom he once professed to be a friend. Upon receiving news of his election to pope he hoped that he might forge a working relationship with Frederick, but it was never to be. Frederick said: "My friendship with a cardinal is ever possible: with a pope never!"

Backed by his considerable military strength, Frederick drove the pope into exile in France. There, in 1225, Innocent called a council at Lyons where, once again, Frederick was excommunicated from the church—a futile act that did nothing to diminish his military might. But while there Innocent reached out to noblemen in Holland, in Sicily, in some of the German states, seeking allies to side with Rome against Frederick. The calls mostly fell on deaf ears, although certain English and French princes were considering his proposal for an alliance against Frederick when the Emperor died in 1250. Innocent outlived him by four years. A man of devious nature and not much loved by the clerics who served him, it was Innocent who issued the Papal Bull that sanctioned torture in the dungeons of the Inquisition.

After his death in Naples in December 1254, Innocent was succeeded by Alexander IV, member of the noble house of Segni that had already produced two popes—Innocent III and Gregory IX, his uncle. Nepotism, in the form of his uncle, appointed him cardinal and, in line with previous popes obsessed with Frederick and his ways, he set about gaining papal revenge on the royal house he sprang from. First he excommunicated Frederick's illegitimate son, Manfred, and then entered into an alliance with Henry III of England, promising his son Edmund the kingdom of Sicily if he provided men and arms to go to war against the remaining armies of the Frederick's house of Hohenstaufen. The alliance was a disaster. Papal troops were roundly defeated in Sicily and Manfred's armies marched unopposed over much of central Italy, in the course of which the the Vatican lost most of the Papal States. Alexander IV was exiled to spend the remainder of his life in Viterbo, where he died in 1261, unloved and unmourned.

Frenchman Jacques Pantaleon succeeded him as Pope Urban IV—a

wise choice as he was shrewd, holy, thoroughly decent, and a man, finally, with the clout necessary to polish off the house of Hohenstaufen. He was, however, first and foremost a profound scholar and theologian, whose writings are preserved in the Vatican and are particularly treasured.

Throughout his reign he stayed mostly in Viterbo and Orvieto, following the advice of his aides that the climate in Rome was still unsafe for him. Manfred of Hohenstaufen's minions ruled, even though Urban was able to secure an alliance with a rival Germanic royal house, the Guelphs, to secure more support for papal policy. But the Guelphs did not have the military might necessary to smash the power of Manfred once and for all.

As his predecessors had done, so Urban looked abroad for support, using the tempting offer of papal lands as inducement to offer up men, arms, and supplies. He saw in Charles of Anjou an ambitious man who would repay papal largesse in any way he, Urban, wanted it when the time was ripe. So he gave him the crown of Sicily, ensuring help from his brother, the King of France, when the Vatican would call upon it. This alliance sowed the seeds of the defeat of the house of

Far left and above: The Inquisition was started by pope Gregory IX in his 1231 bull Excommunicamus. He can hardly have realized what it would lead to: indeed, initially it was a preferable way to get heretics to recant than the more usual lynch mobs—and with the Albigensian and Cathar heresies rampant in southern France the church had to be seen to do something. In 1252 Innocent IV approved the use of torture and this would lead to dreadful excesses, for example against the Knights Templar in France.

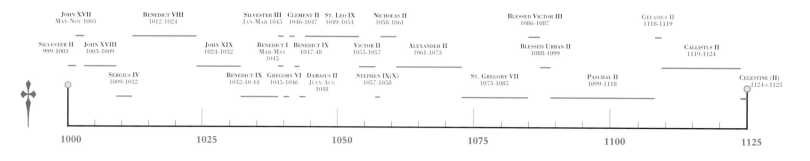

| JOHN XVII | BENEDICT VIII | SILVESTER III | CLEMENT II | ST. LEO IX | NICHOLAS II | | BLESSED VICTOR III | | GELASIUS II |
| MAY-NOV 1003 | 1012-1024 | JAN-MAR 1045 | 1046-1047 | 1049-1054 | 1058-1061 | | 1086-1087 | | 1118-1119 |

| SILVESTER II | JOHN XVIII | | JOHN XIX | BENEDICT I | BENEDICT IX | VICTOR II | ALEXANDER II | | BLESSED URBAN II | | CALLISTUS II |
| 999-1003 | 1003-1009 | | 1024-1032 | MAR-MAY 1045 | 1047-48 | 1055-1057 | 1061-1073 | | 1088-1099 | | 1119-1124 |

| SERGIUS IV | BENEDICT IX | GREGORY VI | DAMASUS II | STEPHEN IX(X) | ST. GREGORY VII | PASCHAL II | CELESTINE (II) |
| 1009-1012 | 1032-1044 | 1045-1046 | JULY-AUG 1048 | 1057-1058 | 1073-1085 | 1099-1118 | 1124-C1125 |

1000   1025   1050   1075   1100   1125

Above: The medieval church was not all about the Inquisition and warfare. Over the centuries huge monuments to the Christian faith were built, such as the glorious cathedral at Chartres, France. This detail shows from left to right: St. Martin of Tours, St. Jerome, and St. Gregory the Great, pope 590-604AD. Bridgeman Art Library, London

Hohenstaufen, which for so long had been a thorn in the side of the papacy.

Urban IV died at Perugia on October 2, 1264, to be succeeded by Clement I— a peculiar choice in many ways as he had formerly been married and had two daughters! This Frenchman, born Guy Foulques, was a well-known lawyer working in the service of the King of France who turned to religion after the death of his wife in 1256. He traveled throughout France as a roving ambassador for Urban who, in turn, promoted Foulques' cause among the cardinals while he was alive, but he never expected to be called forward to assume the supreme post himself. Yet he was a level-headed pope who had no time for nepotism and was true to his word to "rid the land of the Hohenstaufen blight once and for all." To this end he used the armies of Charles of Anjou— now King of Sicily—to fight against Manfred, using a well-honed business acumen to secure loans from Tuscan finance houses to pay for the armies.

Huge battles ensued but Manfred and his family were thrashed only, ironically, to leave Charles of France in a dominant position over future papal affairs! When Clement died he was happy in the knowledge he had killed off the last of the Hohenstaufens—but it was bought at a heavy price to the papal treasury, and an awful lot of blood.

Relative stability came to the Vatican until the appointment of Celestine V (later St. Celestine) in 1294, the Supreme Pontiff widely thought of as the most tragic figure in the history of the papacy. He came to the job in extraordinary circumstances, and departed from it in tragic ones, dying in a fortress prison because of jealousy and fear on the part of his successor.

The origin of his five-month reign lies in the 33-month conclave—the longest in history—that elected him. He was born Pietro

68

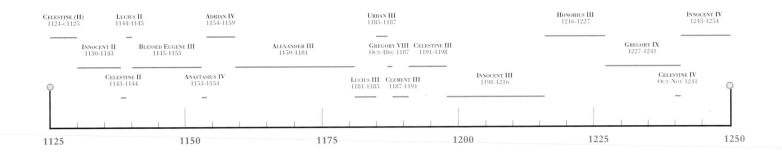

| CELESTINE (II) 1124-c1125 | LUCIUS II 1144-1145 | ADRIAN IV 1154-1159 | | URBAN III 1185-1187 | | | HONORIUS III 1216-1227 | | INNOCENT IV 1243-1254 |

INNOCENT II 1130-1143   BLESSED EUGENE III 1145-1153   ALEXANDER III 1159-1181   GREGORY VIII Oct-Dec 1187   CELESTINE III 1191-1198   GREGORY IX 1227-1241

CELESTINE II 1143-1144   ANASTASIUS IV 1153-1154   LUCIUS III 1181-1185   CLEMENT III 1187-1191   INNOCENT III 1198-1216   CELESTINE IV Oct-Nov 1241

1125   1150   1175   1200   1225   1250

del Morrone around 1210 in the Neapolitan county of Molise and entered a Benedectine monastery as a young man, seeking both spiritual fulfillment and an education. He found the former, but Pietro was singularly lacking in intellect. He left after receiving ordination and took to the hills near Abruzzi where he lived a spartan, ascetic life. He was soon known throughout Italy for his simple but solid faith and for the welcome he gave to strangers seeking the same religious nourishment as himself.

Although he led a simple life, Pietro was a keen follower of church affairs, and he was as perturbed as most people about the length of the conclave. In April 1294 he wrote to a prominent patron of his congregation— Latino Malabranca, dean of the cardinals—informing him that he had had a vision of "divine punishment" for the church if no pope were elected by All Saints Day. On July 5 Malabranca informed the deadlocked cardinals of the vision of the holy man and the effect was extraordinary. After some brief discussions they chose to break with tradition and look outside their ranks— deciding that the 85-year-old hermit should become the supreme ruler of the church! In all their finery and attended by servants and soldiers, the cardinals made the trek up the hillside to his humble home to announce their decision.

Rather than being honored and flattered, the old man was horrified and steadfastly refused to accept the position. But Malabranca went in for some serious arm-twisting. Quickly Pietro acquiesced to the pressure and agreed to become a successor to St. Peter. After being ordained a bishop he was crowned Pope Celestine V on August 29, 1294, in a ceremony stage-managed by King Charles II of Naples. But things went swiftly downhill from then on. It became apparent to the elderly man that he was something of a pawn for both his mentor and the king, who summoned him to Naples, informing him that his court was to operate from there, and not Rome. Under the king's pressure he appointed 12

Above: Boniface VIII was pope from 1294 to 1303 and regularly involved the papacy in European politics, trying to act as mediator in quarrels between the great states. In the end he bit off more than he could chew by fighting with Philip IV of France, whose forces imprisoned him. He escaped but died a broken man shortly afterward.

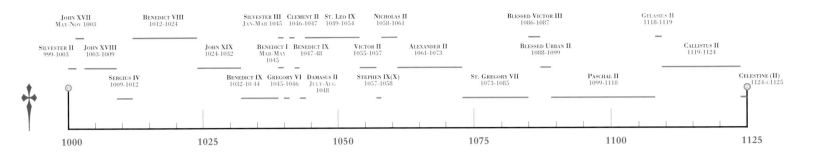

| JOHN XVII | BENEDICT VIII | SILVESTER III | CLEMENT II | ST. LEO IX | NICHOLAS II | BLESSED VICTOR III | GELASIUS II |
| MAY-NOV 1003 | 1012-1024 | JAN-MAR 1045 | 1046-1047 | 1049-1054 | 1058-1061 | 1086-1087 | 1118-1119 |

| SILVESTER II | JOHN XVIII | JOHN XIX | BENEDICT I | BENEDICT IX | VICTOR II | ALEXANDER II | BLESSED URBAN II | CALLISTUS II |
| 999-1003 | 1003-1009 | 1024-1032 | MAR-MAY 1045 | 1047-48 | 1055-1057 | 1061-1073 | 1088-1099 | 1119-1124 |

| SERGIUS IV | BENEDICT IX | GREGORY VI | DAMASUS II | STEPHEN IX(X) | ST. GREGORY VII | PASCHAL II | CELESTINE (II) |
| 1009-1012 | 1032-10 44 | 1045-1046 | JULY-AUG 1048 | 1057-1058 | 1073-1085 | 1099-1118 | 1124-c1125 |

1000   1025   1050   1075   1100   1125

cardinals, who were all royal allies, and found himself surrounded by fortune-seekers and scoundrels, eager to take advantage of his age and lack of sophistication in the rarefied world he now moved in.

His administration, unsurprisingly, fell into chaos. Papal expert John Jay Hughes said: "At 85 he was too old to master the intricacies of curial politics." His lack of education also contributed to his confusion and downfall; his grasp of Latin—the language of the mass and also the papal court—was abysmal, in fact he was so bad at it that Italian came into day-to-day usage instead. "All around him," said papal scholar Charles Wells, "were people seeking to exploit him. The humble and gracious piety that had served him so well in his life as a hermit now worked drastically against him. He was a man simply in the wrong job at the wrong time and should never have been elected in the first place. If he had never had the vision in which he saw catastrophe befalling the church he would have lived his days out in peace and quiet. Instead, it was all to end in poignant tragedy."

In late November Celestine V announced his intention to resign, asking three cardinals to take on the papal affairs while he retired to a cell for his customary Advent fast. The cardinals refused, occasioning panic in those who saw their own fortunes and privileges slipping away if the pliable old man were to be replaced by someone who really knew how to do the job. King Charles, too, was not overjoyed at the prospect of losing so malleable a pontiff and, just as he had stage-managed his coronation, he stage-managed a "spontaneous" demonstration of the people in the streets of major Italian cities, pleading with the Holy Father to stay on. On December 6, in the face of this pressure, Celestine announced that he would continue "unless circumstances intervene."

He soon regretted going back on his decision to quit and confided in Cardinal Benedict Caetani—an expert in papal law—that he truly felt he could no longer go on. "This high office was never meant for such a humble servant of the Lord," he said. Caetani, too, tried to dissuade him, but was forced to admit to the other cardinals that there was nothing that they could do to stop him if he really intended to go. On December 13 he formally proferred his resignation to them and then left to remove his papal vestments, the Ring of the Fishermen and other adornments for the last time. John Jay Hughes wrote:

"He returned to his room in the coarse gray habit of his order to sit on the lowest step of the papal throne where he implored the cardinals (now shedding tears of pity for the poor man as they had wept for joy at his election in July) to elect a successor as soon as possible. A pontificate of five months had demonstrated that personal sanctity alone does not qualify a man to exercize the office of chief pastor in the church."

Celestine V's successor was the very same cardinal he had confided

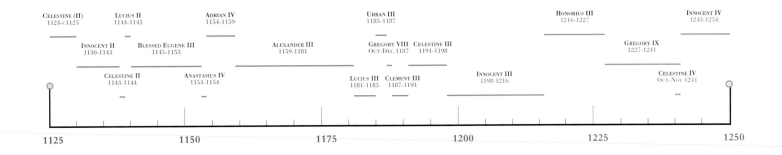

in about his personal dilemma—Benedict Caetani—who, upon election, became Boniface VIII and who was to write the tragic postscript to Celestine's futile reign. A nepotist who made several members of his family cardinals, Boniface VIII was nevertheless supremely intelligent and politically astute. Upon taking office he immediately set about clearing up the administrative mess that had been left behind by Celestine, in particular revoking many major appointments and declaring his independence from King Charles—perhaps the greatest loser in Celestine's abdication.

Caetani was crowned pope among scenes of great splendor in Rome on January 23, 1295. But, great though the challenges were in dealing with the papacy, there was an even more overriding matter—how to deal with the old man who had vacated the job.

This was a unique problem as no pope had ever resigned before. All Celestine wanted to do was retire to a monastery and worship God until he died, but Boniface feared that the old man was unpredictable—that he might be used as a pawn by enemies of the papacy to besmirch Boniface's name or erode papal power. Worse still, he feared that his feeble mind might change yet again, this time seeking to reclaim power and thus causing a schism in the church. Although there was nothing in his character to hint that he would in any way have worked against his successor, Celestine fell victim to Boniface's paranoia.

The new pope refused to allow the old one to slip away to a monastery as he desired and endeavored to put him under surveillance. But Pietro had many friends from his old days and they helped him to get back to his old parish and the monastery he had left. Boniface dispatched papal agents to bring him back to Rome where he had formulated plans to imprison him, but Pietro was one step ahead of them.

He managed to reach the port of Vieste (on the spur of the Italian boot) where he intended to take a ship to Greece and, he hoped, a peaceful life. But he was arrested there on May 10, 1295, and imprisoned—first in a house next to the Papal Palace at Anagni and later in the fortress of Fumone.

It was in a small cell in this fortress that the old man died on May 19 the following year, having written in a letter to one of his supporters that his "punishment" was really nothing to worry about. "I have desired nothing in my life save a cell, and a cell they have given me," he wrote. It would take 21 years for the church to recognize the injustice it had heaped on Pietro; to rectify the calumny he was canonized by Pope Clement V. Ultimately there would be a bitter end for Boniface, the knowing architect of Pietro's woes.

If pride comes before a fall, then it was surely a maxim tailor-made for Boniface. Early on in his reign he took to shouting at his cardinals: "*Ego sum Caesar, ego imperator!*" (I am Caesar, I am Emperor!) He ruled at a time when the papacy was at the height of its powers, at the head of

Left: Louis IX, king of France 1226-1270, was a fervent supporter of the Inquisition and of crusading, leading two crusades in 1249 and 1270, dying in Tunis during the latter. Cannonized in 1297, he is seen here meting out justice from under a tree at Vincennes.

71

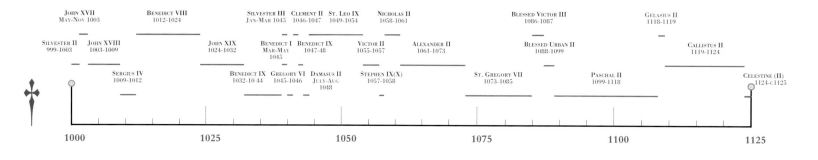

JOHN XVII
MAY-NOV 1003

BENEDICT VIII
1012-1024

SILVESTER III   CLEMENT II   ST. LEO IX
JAN-MAR 1045   1046-1047   1049-1054

NICHOLAS II
1058-1061

BLESSED VICTOR III
1086-1087

GELASIUS II
1118-1119

SILVESTER II   JOHN XVIII
999-1003   1003-1009

JOHN XIX
1024-1032

BENEDICT I   BENEDICT IX
MAR-MAY   1047-48
1045

VICTOR II
1055-1057

ALEXANDER II
1061-1073

BLESSED URBAN II
1088-1099

CALLISTUS II
1119-1124

SERGIUS IV
1009-1012

BENEDICT IX   GREGORY VI   DAMASUS II
1032-10·44   1045-1046   JULY-AUG
1048

STEPHEN IX(X)
1057-1058

ST. GREGORY VII
1073-1085

PASCHAL II
1099-1118

CELESTINE (II)
1124-c.1125

1000   1025   1050   1075   1100   1125

the church rich beyond measure due to centuries of tax collection, bequests, and legacies. Boniface truly believed that this would remain the case for evermore, that he would preside over a papacy that would grow stronger by the day. Nationalist movements, the secular power of governments, and the increasing spread of knowledge would only serve to undermine the church, but Boniface was blind to this. He was only interested in preserving church power and church wealth, and to do so issued a papal bull in February 1296 that was one of the most controversial of the age.

The bull, *Clericis Laicos*, promised automatic excommunication for anyone who imposed a tax on church goods without the permission of the papacy. As the church and its servants were the wealthiest subjects of the age, it was inevitable that such a pronouncement would not be taken without protest. "*Clericis Laicos*," said one papal scholar, "thus set the stage for a power struggle of epic proportions."

Europe's premier power-broker at the time was King Philip IV of France (also known as Philip the Fair) who was engaged in a protracted war against England that became known as the Hundred Years War. Philip needed a continuous flow of money to pay for arms and men. Most of this money—prior to the issuance of *Clericis Laicos*—came from taxes on the church. Philip was enraged at this pronouncement, as was his court, which was surprisingly modern in its outlook, as by this time in his reign Philip had ditched most of the traditionalists who bowed and scraped to the church. They had been replaced instead with advisers contemptuous of the power that Rome still wielded.

In response to Boniface's bull Philip prohibited the export of all goods from Papal States, upon which trade they were heavily dependent, and expelled from France the papal legates who collected church monies for Rome.

Philip knew he had the power to starve Rome into submission and he was right. In July 1297, Boniface was forced to issue a new bull that gave Philip the right to raise taxes for the war from the French clergy. The following month, Boniface completed his U-turn by canonizing Philip's grandfather, Louis IX, as a token of gratitude for Philip once more sanctioning trade and foreign travel.

Having lost both face and power to the king of France, Boniface now found trouble looming on the domestic front. Two cardinals formed an alliance against him, more pertinently two cardinals who had initially been his chief supporters: James Colonna and his nephew Peter—scions of one of the most wealthy and powerful clans in the Papal States. They were numbered among a clique of clergymen rapidly becoming disenchanted with the pontiff's high-handed manner of ruling. This disillusionment spread to the Franciscan "Spirituals," followers of the faith who stood out from their fellow monks because of their ultra-strict interpretations of the vows of poverty. Between them a

"Clericis Laicos thus set the stage for a power struggle of epic proportions."

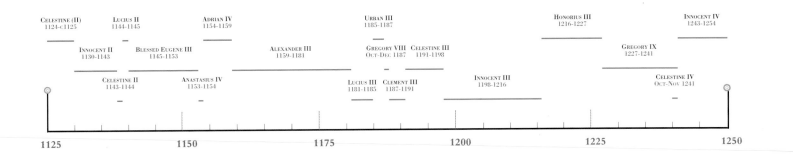

CELESTINE (II)
1124-c1125

LUCIUS II
1144-1145

ADRIAN IV
1154-1159

URBAN III
1185-1187

HONORIUS III
1216-1227

INNOCENT IV
1243-1254

INNOCENT II
1130-1143

BLESSED EUGENE III
1145-1153

ALEXANDER III
1159-1181

GREGORY VIII   CELESTINE III
OCT-DEC 1187   1191-1198

GREGORY IX
1227-1241

CELESTINE II
1143-1144

ANASTASIUS IV
1153-1154

LUCIUS III   CLEMENT III
1181-1185   1187-1191

INNOCENT III
1198-1216

CELESTINE IV
OCT-NOV 1241

1125   1150   1175   1200   1225   1250

whispering campaign started against the pope that was to lead to his ultimate downfall.

The Colonnas, however, were the losers in the short term. After seizing treasure in Rome that was the property of the muddled old pope who preceded Boniface, they were hounded across Italy by a vengeful Boniface who learned of a plot hatched by them to smear his name. Their lands and treasures were seized and the spoils divided up among Boniface's family while the errant cardinals fled to France, placing themselves at the court of King Philip of France, where they were able to drip further poison about Boniface into his ever-receptive ears.

In 1301 new conflict broke out with Philip. Boniface accused him of harassing a bishop in the south of France and revoked his previous concessions to him regarding taxation. But this time Boniface went further—he issued a new bull warning that anyone who went against the will of the church was not a good shepherd and did not belong in the church. "Anyone" in this case read Philip.

Philip retaliated with bellicose words in which he branded Boniface his "high and mighty fatuousness" and pointed out that, as king, he could not be judged by anyone in worldly affairs. He again cut off all exports of gold and valuables from France and placed severe restrictions upon the Catholic clergy. Then Philip went even further, telling his ministers to prepare for war to deal with the upstart pontiff "who considers himself something more than man and God combined."

There were to be no concessions on Boniface's part in the following year. On November 18, 1302, he issued the most inflammatory bull of his reign, *Unam Sanctam*, declaring "it is altogether necessary for salvation for every human creature to be subject to the Roman Pontiff." He also said only he could judge man and that he could be judged only by God. It was another direct affront to Philip, that Boniface considered the pope the master of kings as well as peasants. "It was a serious miscalculation in terms of Realpolitik to fly in the face of the most powerful monarch of the day in this way," said John Jay Hughes.

Yet Boniface—supremely arrogant in his beliefs—genuinely thought an accommodation could still be reached with Philip. To this end, he send a delegate to France to try to placate him, but Philip would have none of it. He declared the pope a sodomite, said he was the murderer of his predecessor, claimed he consulted a private devil, instructed priests to violate the seal of the confessional, and was draining the papal treasury to finance his own love of high living. Further, he claimed that Boniface was not a legitimate pope, and if he was not legitimate then his threats of excommunication—something any person, regardless of status, took with the utmost gravity—were baseless.

Boniface played into Philip's hands in August when he went ahead and excommunicated the king and his advisers. But one of Philip's lieu-

"It is altogether necessary for salvation for every human creature to be subject to the Roman Pontiff."

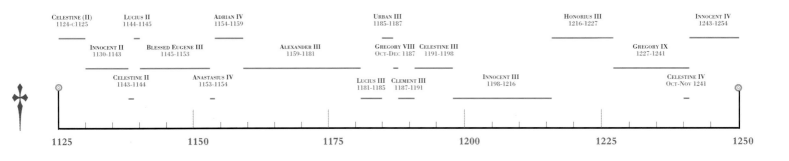

CELESTINE (II)
1124-c1125

LUCIUS II
1144-1145

ADRIAN IV
1154-1159

URBAN III
1185-1187

HONORIUS III
1216-1227

INNOCENT IV
1243-1254

INNOCENT II
1130-1143

BLESSED EUGENE III
1145-1153

ALEXANDER III
1159-1181

GREGORY VIII   CELESTINE III
OCT-DEC 1187   1191-1198

GREGORY IX
1227-1241

CELESTINE II
1143-1144

ANASTASIUS IV
1153-1154

LUCIUS III   CLEMENT III
1181-1185   1187-1191

INNOCENT III
1198-1216

CELESTINE IV
OCT-NOV 1241

1125   1150   1175   1200   1225   1250

tenants, Guillame de Nogaret, had already slipped into Italy with orders from the king to instigate an antipope uprising. The pope was at his residence in Agnani when, on September 8, de Nogaret led a band of armed men carrying papal and French flags through the streets of the town, ransacking the homes of cardinals and crying out: "Long live the King of France and the Colonnas!" They marched on to the papal residence, joined by many of the local townspeople who were also sickened by the manner in which their pope ruled. At the walls of his fortress home the pope was informed his life would be spared if he would restore all treasure and titles to the ousted Colonnas, deliver the (depleted) papal treasury to senior cardinals for safekeeping, surrender, and then publicly resign the office of supreme pontiff. To all of these the pope said a resounding "No." Safe for the moment behind his walls, night fell.

The following day he was captured, but said he would rather die than agree to the demands of his attackers. This gave the mob something of a dilemma: de Nogaret wanted to return him to France, alternatively members of the Colonna clan wanted him executed on the spot. A night of prevarication gave time for loyalist forces in the region to band together to drive the attackers from the town. That night Boniface, clearly disheveled and bruised from the rough treatment he had received, appeared on the balcony of his home to bless his rescuers and forgive those who had joined in the attack against him. He gave instructions to set forth for Rome immediately.

On September 25 he reached the city and ordered celebrations in his honor, but he lived for only another three weeks, by then a man broken in mind and body. He had set out to make the papacy stronger, but had only succeeded in diminishing its power. Although there were some positive aspects to his reign—he made major developments in canon law and was a considerable benefactor to the Vatican library—his own aggrandizment contributed hugely to his downfall. Medieval historian Brian Tierney wrote of him:

"The tragedy of his reign lies in the disproportion between the ends he set himself and the resources of his own personality. All his diplomacy aimed at establishing peace and concord in a Christendom guided and led by the pope. But his inability to comprehend the new forces of nationalism that were stirring into life, his excessive preoccupation with the advance of the Caetani family, his impatient, and irascible disposition, all made the attainment of such an end impossible."

Almost 40 years later the pope had not learned the hard lessons of his predecessors. Clement VI, one-time court chancellor of France, ascended to head the papacy and was the fourth pope to reside at Avignon. Although he was free of the personal ambitions of Boniface, and was genuinely loved by his subjects, he was concerned far more

The tragedy of his reign lies in the disproportion between the ends he set himself and the resources of his own personality.

| ALEXANDER IV 1254-1261 | BLESSED GREGORY X 1271-1276 | JOHN XXI 1276-1277 | NICHOLAS IV 1288-1292 | BLESSED BENEDICT XI 1303-1304 | BENEDICT XII 1334-1342 | BLESSED URBAN V 1362-1370 |

URBAN IV 1261-1264   BLESSED INNOCENT V JAN-JUNE 1276   NICHOLAS III 1277-1280   ST. CELESTINE V JULY-DEC 1294   CLEMENT V 1305-1314   CLEMENT VI 1342-1352   GREGORY XI 1370-1378

CLEMENT IV 1265-1268   ADRIAN V JULY-AUG 1276   MARTIN IV 1281-1285   HONORIUS IV 1285-1287   BONIFACE VIII 1294-1303   JOHN XXII 1316-1334   INNOCENT VI 1352-1362

1250   1275   1300   1325   1350   1375

with personal pleasure—including pleasures of the flesh—than in seriously advancing the cause of the church. Rather like a modern-day politician, he appeared to be all things to all men and his legacy is largely one of unfulfilled promise.

Born Pierre Roger in 1291, he earned a doctorate in Paris after entering a Benedictine order at the age of ten. After rapidly advancing through the French church, including periods as Archbishop of Sens and Rouen, he became a cardinal in 1342 and was appointed pope the following year, following the death of the rather austere Benedict XII.

Benedict had run a gloomy ship that made everyone who came into contact with him despondent, leading the new, pleasure-loving pontiff to declare: "My predecessor did not know how to be pope!" Clement wasted no time in showing just what he thought should be brought to the job—luxury, hedonism, and pleasure. He purchased the city of Avignon directly from Queen Joanna of Naples for 80,000 gold florins and then spent masses of papal treasure in enlarging his palace there. The cellars were stocked with the finest wines; chefs were rated above all other advisers in the curia, and feast days became enormous orgies of excess.

There were also the stories of women. Whispers began to circulate of ladies of dubious moral quality being escorted to the papal apartments at all hours of the day and night to attend to the Holy Father's physical appetite. Also, apart from prostitutes, Clement is widely reported to have had a long affair with his niece, Cecile de Turenne, a leading beauty of her day. Nothing was ever proved and some papal scholars dismiss the reports as the work of gossips and malcontents. But others point to his love of the good life as ample evidence that his libido was hardly likely to be in check if every other sense was indulged to the maximum.

Yet Clement was not an entirely unworthy man; when plague swept through Avignon in 1348 he spent vast amounts of his own wealth—not the treasury's—in easing the suffering of the people. Over 11,000 died, but historians believe it could have been many more but for the generosity of

Below: The enduring image of the medieval church—taking the cross in a war proclaimed by the papacy on Christ's behalf. It is difficult today to understand just how genuine was the devotion behind crusading at this time—but there is no doubt that it attracted people from all walks of life who genuinely believed that it was both necessary and also good for their souls. Of course, there were exceptions: particularly the Fourth Crusade when Crusaders entered Constantinople and sacked it.

75

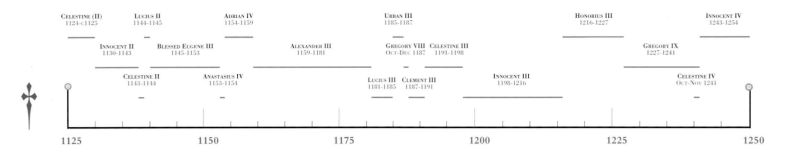

| CELESTINE (II) 1124-c1125 | LUCIUS II 1144-1145 | ADRIAN IV 1154-1159 | URBAN III 1185-1187 | HONORIUS III 1216-1227 | INNOCENT IV 1243-1254 |

INNOCENT II 1130-1143 BLESSED EUGENE III 1145-1153 ALEXANDER III 1159-1181 GREGORY VIII OCT-DEC 1187 CELESTINE III 1191-1198 GREGORY IX 1227-1241

CELESTINE II 1143-1144 ANASTASIUS IV 1153-1154 LUCIUS III 1181-1185 CLEMENT III 1187-1191 INNOCENT III 1198-1216 CELESTINE IV OCT-NOV 1241

1125   1150   1175   1200   1225   1250

the pope in providing food, shelter, and clean straw. Furthermore he proved himself a friend of the Jews, saving them from an ugly pogrom when ignorant townspeople tried to blame them for the Black Death. He also hoped to immortalize his own name with a new crusade against the Turks, but the will was lacking. In his ten-year reign he is remembered for being a mammoth partygiver and little else.

It was left to Gregory XI, born Roger Pierre de Beaufort, to return the papacy to Rome after its exile in Avignon. The son of a noble family, and a nephew of Pope Clement VI, he was crowned in 1370 and reigned for eight years. He was responsible for directing a war with Florence over the governance of the Papal States during the early part of his reign, but it was the move back to Rome for which he is chiefly remembered. Gregory XI entered the city in triumph on January 17, 1377, but his personal stay was brief as violence in the city, although not directly threatening him, nonetheless upset his state of mind. He decamped for Anagni where he died the following year from exhaustion, but his decision to return to Rome was one that was emulated by succeeding popes.

It was with the appointment of Gregory's successor, Urban VI, that the church was once more plunged into great crisis. Bartomeo Prignano was to become the architect of the Great Western Schism that became such a destructive and divisive force for Christianity. The popes had only recently returned to Rome and there was still instability in the city and surrounding areas. After Gregory's death there were fears among the cardinals of a schism, some wanting to return to Avignon, others pleading for renewed efforts to consolidate Rome.

The problem revolved around the cardinals, most of whom were French and pro-French in their outlook. They wanted to move back to France to once again be close to the French court, the dominant assembly in Europe. But the irate Italians wanted none of it. While the conclave to elect Urban was meeting, a mob stormed the building, threatening to put to death all the cardinals should a non-Italian pope be chosen. The choice fell on Prignano, who was not a cardinal at the time but in charge of the papal chancery. The cardinals saw in him someone who might be acceptable to the mob—and pliable to the cardinals. He was the last non-cardinal in Vatican history to be elected pope.

Any illusions that the cardinals may have had about holding Urban VI in their grasp were quickly dispelled. He soon proved himself an uncontrollable eccentric who had a violent and domineering nature. He lashed out at cardinals as well as lesser members of the curia and had a bloated sense of his own achievements and qualities. He was soon being compared to Boniface in his meglomaniac outlook. Not surprisingly, the cardinals soon decamped from Rome. The French contingent went to Anagni where they pronounced that Urban was not the real pope because their election of him had been made under threat of death.

76

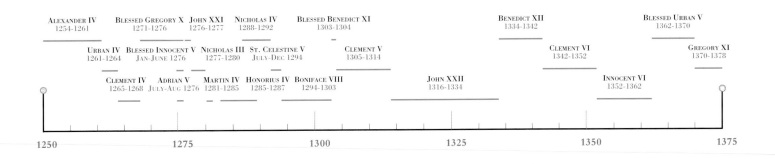

| ALEXANDER IV 1254-1261 | BLESSED GREGORY X 1271-1276 | JOHN XXI 1276-1277 | NICHOLAS IV 1288-1292 | BLESSED BENEDICT XI 1303-1304 | | BENEDICT XII 1334-1342 | | BLESSED URBAN V 1362-1370 |

URBAN IV 1261-1264 · BLESSED INNOCENT V JAN-JUNE 1276 · NICHOLAS III 1277-1280 · ST. CELESTINE V JULY-DEC 1294 · CLEMENT V 1305-1314 · CLEMENT VI 1342-1352 · GREGORY XI 1370-1378

CLEMENT IV 1265-1268 · ADRIAN V JULY-AUG 1276 · MARTIN IV 1281-1285 · HONORIUS IV 1285-1287 · BONIFACE VIII 1294-1303 · JOHN XXII 1316-1334 · INNOCENT VI 1352-1362

1250   1275   1300   1325   1350   1375

They called instead for a new election to choose a pope more suited to their ends. With the blessing of King Charles V of France and Queen Joanna of Naples they were able, on September 20, to elect Robert of Geneva as Clement VII. The Great Western Schism was born.

Urban strove to consolidate his power in Rome, supported by his loyal followers, while many members of the curia decamped to Avignon to give their backing to Clement. Urban moved to try to broaden his authority by creating 29 new cardinals while ordering the hideous torture of six old ones, who he feared were traitors to his cause. Historians believe that the schism could have been healed earlier, were it not for the volatile temper and paranoia of Urban. He saw enemies at every turn, merely fueling the desires of more moderate men to ally themselves with the antipope residing in France.

It was therefore in a state of schism and confusion that the papacy entered the most glittering, if not glorious, period of its long history—the Renaissance.

Below: The spectacular Papal Palace at Avignon, France. Home of the papacy from 1309 (Clement V) to 1377, when Gregory XI returned to Rome, it would also house antipopes Clement VII and Benedict XIII. It would remain a possession of the papacy until annexed by France in 1791.

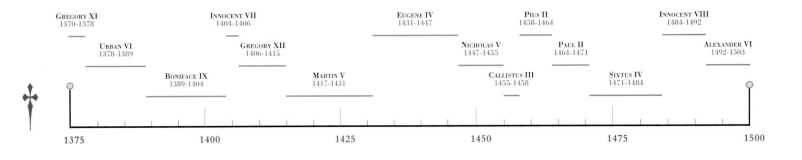

| GREGORY XI 1370-1378 | | INNOCENT VII 1404-1406 | | EUGENE IV 1431-1447 | | PIUS II 1458-1464 | | INNOCENT VIII 1484-1492 |

URBAN VI 1378-1389   GREGORY XII 1406-1415   NICHOLAS V 1447-1455   PAUL II 1464-1471   ALEXANDER VI 1492-1503

BONIFACE IX 1389-1404   MARTIN V 1417-1431   CALLISTUS III 1455-1458   SIXTUS IV 1471-1484

1375   1400   1425   1450   1475   1500

THE RENAISSANCE POPES

Above: The popes of the Renaissance were known for their patronage of art.

In one brutal episode, Migliorati slaughtered a dozen local Roman noblemen, sparking scenes of chaos in the streets that hadn't been seen for hundreds of years. The brutality of his executions revolted a populace who expected better from their church.

THE "REBIRTH" OF EUROPE saw many great spiritual and artistic changes, but for the papacy it was a case of: "*Plus ça change, plus ça la même chause.*" (As things change, so they remain the same.) The 200 years between the fourteenth and sixteenth centuries presented a prime opportunity for the papacy to consolidate, strengthen, reform, and renew. While the period displayed its usual mix of piety and decadence, peace and war, the papacy squandered many opportunities, leading to public disillusion, the Reformation, subsequent loss of territories, and hideous, bloody wars. Only in the last few years did the papacy put its house in order and banish the corruption that had been so blatantly endemic within the Vatican for such a long time.

Pope Innocent VII became pontiff in 1404. Born Cosima Gentili de' Migliorati, he was one of the legitimate popes elected during the Great Schism, the split between personalities that led to the rival line of antipopes decamping to Avignon. Innocent, it was hoped, would be a force to heal this rift, but he was to be ineffectual in this, even though it was his prime brief when the conclave that elected him met to place the tiara of power upon his head. The cardinals hoped he would make a peace overture to Antipope Benedict XIII, but his pride and obstinacy would not allow it.

Innocent VII presided over the papacy at a time of great social and political upheaval in Rome and the mob was growing stronger by the day. Innocent—weak and wooly-minded despite a sharp legal mind honed in the universities of Bologna, Perugia, and Padua—came to rely increasingly on his brutal nephew, Ludovico Migliorati, to put down the violence that was sweeping the city.

In one brutal episode, Migliorati slaughtered a dozen local Roman noblemen, sparking scenes of chaos in the streets that hadn't been seen for hundreds of years. The brutality of his executions revolted a populace who expected better from their church. Soon a mob was descending on the Papal Palace, smashing statues and stoning churches on the way. Innocent was forced to flee Rome to seek sanctuary in Viterbo in 1405, returning quietly to the Vatican in March the following year. "Quiet, unassuming, and unfortunately ineffectual," said papal historian Matthew Bunson, "he made no progress toward resolving the schism."

78

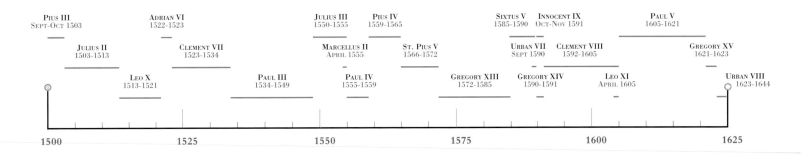

PIUS III SEPT-OCT 1503	ADRIAN VI 1522-1523		JULIUS III 1550-1555	PIUS IV 1559-1565		SIXTUS V 1585-1590	INNOCENT IX OCT-NOV 1591	PAUL V 1605-1621	
JULIUS II 1503-1513	CLEMENT VII 1523-1534		MARCELLUS II APRIL 1555	ST. PIUS V 1566-1572		URBAN VII SEPT 1590	CLEMENT VIII 1592-1605	GREGORY XV 1621-1623	
LEO X 1513-1521	PAUL III 1534-1549	PAUL IV 1555-1559	GREGORY XIII 1572-1585	GREGORY XIV 1590-1591	LEO XI APRIL 1605		URBAN VIII 1623-1644

| 1500 | 1525 | 1550 | 1575 | 1600 | 1625 |

Gregory XII succeeded him, but his reign was brief and undistinguished, save for some valuable hard work toward healing the schism in the church. It was his successor, Martin V, who became the papal superstar of the Renaissance, the first universally recognized pope, who actually ended the Great Schism that so divided and undermined the papacy.

He ascended to the title in 1417, bringing to an end a divisive 39-year split and the end of the antipope line that caused so much division among the faithful. Born Oddone Colonna at Gennazano, he owed his ascension to the ranks of the cardinals to Pope Innocent VII. He was initially loyal to the Roman popes, but switched allegiance during his years as a cardinal to pledge allegiance to Antipope John XXIII, whom he continued to support until 1414.

Martin was chosen by the cardinals because they viewed him as a pliant, bendable man who would do their bidding. But, Martin would prove them very wrong. He came to the highest Catholic office with a twofold plan—to restore the prestige and power of the newly reconciled church, and to revive the Papal States, which were essential as a means of making money for the depleted Vatican coffers.

He gathered an army of cutthroat mercenaries to wage a war against rival claimants to power in the Papal States, putting opponents to death in a brutal and arbitrary fashion. He ordered his soldiers to instigate a ruthless scorched-earth policy that destroyed great tracts of land in order to bring dissenters back into line. Meanwhile, on the diplomatic front, he dispatched many papal ambassadors to different parts of the globe to promote the newly reunified church in an effort to make the flock see that all was well with the Roman line once more.

Martin also moved to dismantle conciliarism, the theory that grew up during the late Middle Ages that supreme church power should rest

Above: The Renaissance—the re-birth of European civilization after the Dark Ages—was a time of learning, of art, of beauty, of the pursuit of man's enlightenment. While the papacy produced many capable and learned men, and great patrons of the arts, the times also gave rise to despots like the Borgias.

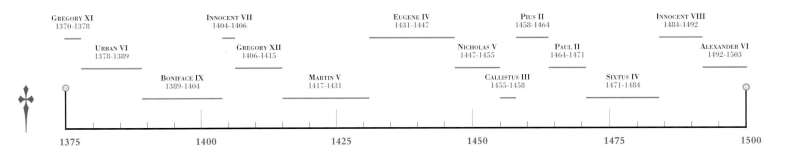

GREGORY XI
1370-1378

INNOCENT VII
1404-1406

EUGENE IV
1431-1447

PIUS II
1458-1464

INNOCENT VIII
1484-1492

URBAN VI
1378-1389

GREGORY XII
1406-1415

NICHOLAS V
1447-1455

PAUL II
1464-1471

ALEXANDER VI
1492-1503

BONIFACE IX
1389-1404

MARTIN V
1417-1431

CALLISTUS III
1455-1458

SIXTUS IV
1471-1484

1375   1400   1425   1450   1475   1500

The roots of the Borgias were in rural Spain, but it was in medieval Italy that they thrived so much that they ended up wielding enormous power. In 1455 His Excellency Don Alonso y Borja, Archbishop of Valencia, was elected pope by his fellow cardinals. At the age of 77 he was rather too old for the greatest and most powerful post in feudal Europe, but the wise men who elected him did not expect him to live long anyway.

in the hands of a council—a committee—instead of being vested solely in the pope. Naturally, conciliarism was a movement much opposed by most pontiffs, who saw supreme autocratic power as their divine right. While submitting to councils that had been ordered by predecessors, Martin laid the foundation stones of the papal Code of Canon Law, which was later to state that it is unlawful for anyone to make an appeal against the pope's judgments.

Although a nepotist, quick to anger and harsh with his enemies—his cardinals feared an audience with him because of his razor-edged tongue—he did restore prestige and power to the church at a time when it was much needed. If he had never existed, scholars debate whether the Great Schism would ever have been healed. It was a pity, therefore, that there was soon to be a dynasty visited upon the papal scene that would make the Dark Ages seem illuminated by comparison.

The name Borgia conjures up the dark side of man's soul like few others, invoking images of depravity, debauchery, distilled evil, ruthlessness, rape, and murder—and rightly so. This clan, sponsored by the papacy, was the worst of the lot, a wicked bunch who lived life beyond all of society's laws and conventions. Cesare's name, particularly, while indelibly linked with the Renaissance—the renewal of European culture and civilization after the veil of the Dark Ages had been lifted from the land—is also forever remembered for the brutality, venality, and wickedness associated with the Borgias.

The roots of the Borgias were in rural Spain, but it was in medieval Italy that they thrived so much that they ended up wielding enormous power. In 1455 His Excellency Don Alonso y Borja, Archbishop of Valencia, was elected pope by his fellow cardinals. At the age of 77 he was rather too old for the greatest and most powerful post in feudal Europe, but the wise men who elected him did not expect him to live long anyway. He had been in Italy for 20 years and the Italians had shortened his name to Borgia. His ascendancy created a papal dynasty, which the cardinals who elected him at the time could never have foreseen, and gave the world one of the most despotic individuals ever to sully mankind's name—Cesare.

Don Alonso, as Pope Callistus III, made Rome his playground for himself and his family. Nepotism was the order of the day, with plum jobs in the church and government allotted to his family members. One of them was Rodrigo, his nephew who, at 25, was made a powerful cardinal and would later follow him and be elected pope. The Italians balked at what they perceived as this Spanish takeover of their most cherished institutions and positions, but there was little that they could do to stop the preferments.

The son of a landowner, Don Alonso became a jurist of some note and consequently was invited often to the court of King Alfonso V of Aragon and Sicily. Pope Martin appointed him Bishop of Valencia in

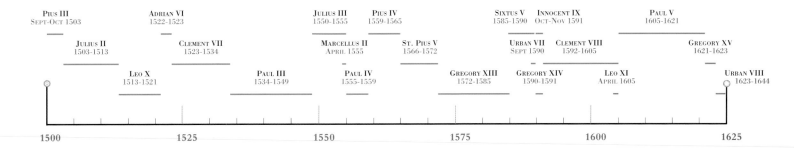

PIUS III	ADRIAN VI		JULIUS III	PIUS IV		SIXTUS V	INNOCENT IX		PAUL V
SEPT-OCT 1503	1522-1523		1550-1555	1559-1565		1585-1590	OCT-NOV 1591		1605-1621
JULIUS II		CLEMENT VII		MARCELLUS II	ST. PIUS V		URBAN VII	CLEMENT VIII		GREGORY XV
1503-1513		1523-1534		APRIL 1555	1566-1572		SEPT 1590	1592-1605		1621-1623
	LEO X		PAUL III		PAUL IV		GREGORY XIII	GREGORY XIV	LEO XI		URBAN VIII
	1513-1521		1534-1549		1555-1559		1572-1585	1590-1591	APRIL 1605		1623-1644

| 1500 | 1525 | 1550 | 1575 | 1600 | 1625 |

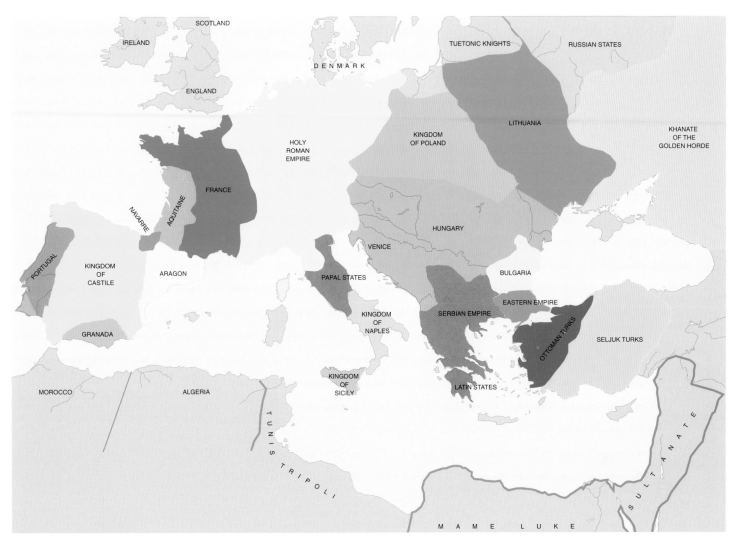

1429, and in 1444 he was made a cardinal by Eugene IV. By luck, when he entered the conclave to choose a new pope after the reign of the great pontiff Nicholas V, he found himself elected, as a compromise pope by the split clergy.

Pope Callistus III is chiefly remembered for two things—his berserk lust to enhance the personal fortunes of his own family, and his call for a crusade against the Turks. Although he was quite moderate in his own tastes, he had no moral qualms about his family feathering their nests thanks to his patronage. Italian society was outraged at what they perceived to be the blatant promotion of his brood. His relatives from Aragon were despised by Roman nobles and it was hardly surprising that, upon his death, they were swept out of the city.

Pius II succeeded in 1458 to bring some semblance of sanity and decorum back to the papacy. Formerly a nobleman, Enea Silvio de Piccolomini, Pius reigned for six years, during which time he wrestled with the problems of the Turks encroaching on Christian lands, but he had little success in mounting a crusade to confront them. A devoted

Above: The map of Renaissance Europe shows the two major threats to Christendom: the Mongols in the east, although the main thrust of Mongol attacks had been in the 13th and 14th centuries, and the Ottoman Turks in the southeast. Bulgaria fell to the Turks in 1371; Serbia at Kossovo in 1389; but, following the defeat of the Ottomans by Tamburlane at Ankara in 1402, Constantinople would hold out until 1453, and the Balkan states would regain their freedom. It would be shortlived: by 1475 the Turks had reimposed their rule on the Balkans; in 1521 they took Belgrade and besieged Vienna for the first time in 1529. At the height of the Reformation, therefore, the Papacy had not only to contend with the schism within the church but also to rally Christendom.

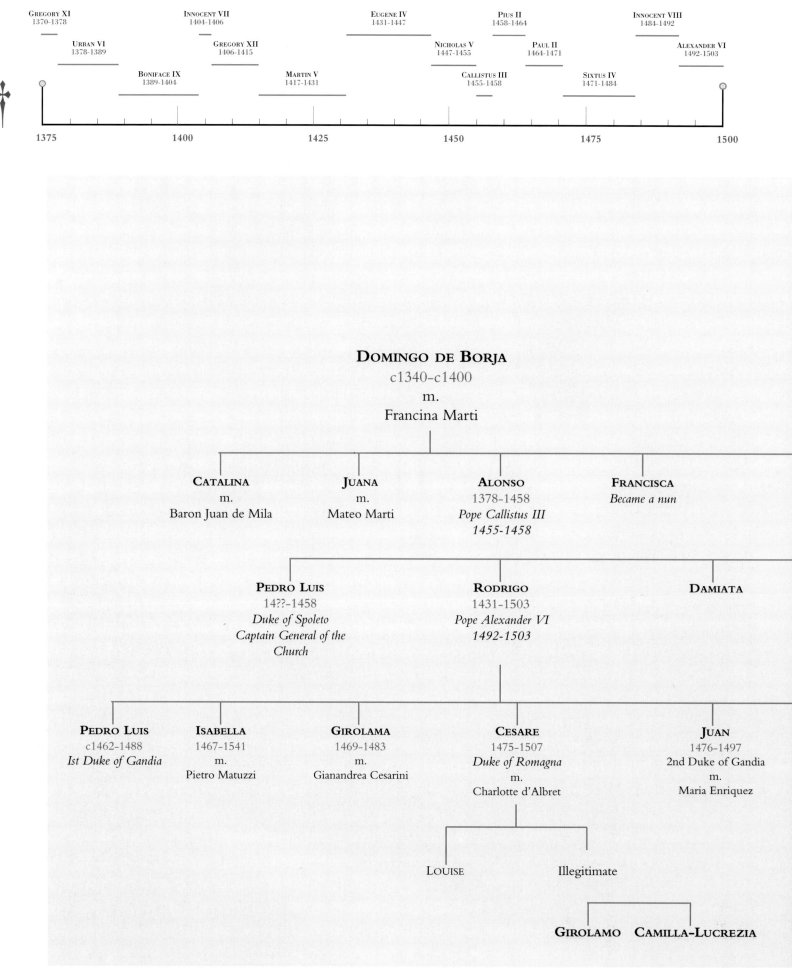

GREGORY XI 1370-1378		INNOCENT VII 1404-1406		EUGENE IV 1431-1447		PIUS II 1458-1464		INNOCENT VIII 1484-1492
URBAN VI 1378-1389		GREGORY XII 1406-1415			NICHOLAS V 1447-1455		PAUL II 1464-1471		ALEXANDER VI 1492-1503
	BONIFACE IX 1389-1404		MARTIN V 1417-1431		CALLISTUS III 1455-1458		SIXTUS IV 1471-1484	

1375   1400   1425   1450   1475   1500

DOMINGO DE BORJA
c1340–c1400
m.
Francina Marti

CATALINA
m.
Baron Juan de Mila

JUANA
m.
Mateo Marti

ALONSO
1378-1458
Pope Callistus III
1455-1458

FRANCISCA
Became a nun

PEDRO LUIS
14??-1458
Duke of Spoleto
Captain General of the
Church

RODRIGO
1431-1503
Pope Alexander VI
1492-1503

DAMIATA

PEDRO LUIS
c1462-1488
Ist Duke of Gandia

ISABELLA
1467-1541
m.
Pietro Matuzzi

GIROLAMA
1469-1483
m.
Gianandrea Cesarini

CESARE
1475-1507
Duke of Romagna
m.
Charlotte d'Albret

JUAN
1476-1497
2nd Duke of Gandia
m.
Maria Enriquez

LOUISE   Illegitimate

GIROLAMO   **CAMILLA-LUCREZIA**

Family tree of the Borgias, showing two
popes—Callistus III (left) and Alexander
VI—and the latter's notorious offspring.

PIUS III SEPT-OCT 1503		ADRIAN VI 1522-1523			JULIUS III 1550-1555	PIUS IV 1559-1565			SIXTUS V 1585-1590	INNOCENT IX OCT-NOV 1591		PAUL V 1605-1621	
JULIUS II 1503-1513			CLEMENT VII 1523-1534			MARCELLUS II APRIL 1555	ST. PIUS V 1566-1572			URBAN VII SEPT 1590	CLEMENT VIII 1592-1605		GREGORY XV 1621-1623
	LEO X 1513-1521			PAUL III 1534-1549		PAUL IV 1555-1559		GREGORY XIII 1572-1585	GREGORY XIV 1590-1591		LEO XI APRIL 1605		URBAN VIII 1623-1644

1500   1525   1550   1575   1600   1625

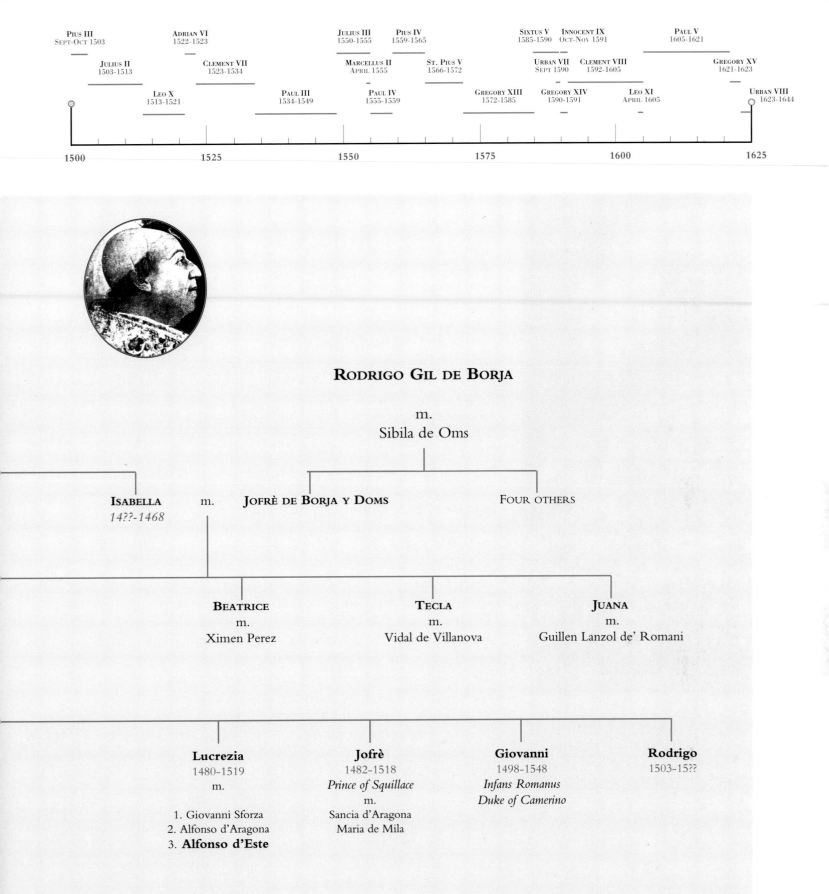

RODRIGO GIL DE BORJA

m.

Sibila de Oms

ISABELLA   m.   **JOFRÈ DE BORJA Y DOMS**   FOUR OTHERS

14??-1468

BEATRICE   **TECLA**   **JUANA**

m.   m.   m.

Ximen Perez   Vidal de Villanova   Guillen Lanzol de' Romani

Lucrezia   **Jofrè**   **Giovanni**   **Rodrigo**

1480-1519   1482-1518   1498-1548   1503-15??

m.   *Prince of Squillace*   *Infans Romanus*

     m.   *Duke of Camerino*

1. Giovanni Sforza   Sancia d'Aragona

2. Alfonso d'Aragona   Maria de Mila

3. **Alfonso d'Este**

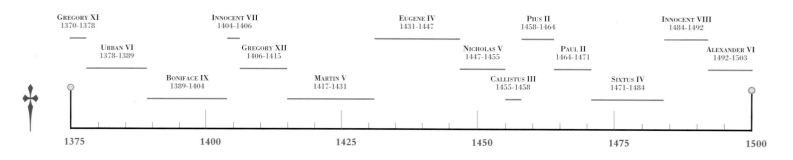

| GREGORY XI 1370-1378 | | INNOCENT VII 1404-1406 | | EUGENE IV 1431-1447 | | PIUS II 1458-1464 | | INNOCENT VIII 1484-1492 |

URBAN VI 1378-1389   GREGORY XII 1406-1415   NICHOLAS V 1447-1455   PAUL II 1464-1471   ALEXANDER VI 1492-1503

BONIFACE IX 1389-1404   MARTIN V 1417-1431   CALLISTUS III 1455-1458   SIXTUS IV 1471-1484

1375   1400   1425   1450   1475   1500

Above: Rodrigo Borgia became Pope Alexander VI in 1492: it was his licentious life as a cardinal and that of his children that would make the family name itself a synonym for corruption, excess, and murder.

humanist who often wrote frivolously of the church and its teachings when he was a young man, Pius denounced them when he was supreme pontiff, asking people to "believe the old man and not the youth." As that young man he no longer cared to be remembered, he had written love stories under the name of Aeneas Silvius, poems, a novel, and a play. However he never dabbled in fiction while pope, instead as Pope Pius II he wrote a weighty tome about the state of the known world, a copy of which rests still in the Vatican library. He died in 1464 on an odyssey eastwards in which he hoped to spread the word of God.

Rodrigo—the truly wicked nephew of Callistus III—succeeded him as Pope Alexander VI and set about turning the papacy into a great power. But there was nothing saintly or indeed remotely religious about Rodrigo. While he was a cardinal and later as pope he enjoyed a long affair with an Italian noblewoman called Vannnozza dei Cattanei, a woman whose wedding he attended but who bore him five children. The most infamous of these children was the notorious Cesare, who would pass into legend as the most hated and bloodthirsty noble of his age.

Rodrigo, it is said, purchased the final votes of the cardinals in Rome necessary to make him pope. Once ensconced, he turned the Vatican into a medieval pleasure palace, complete with whores, drink, obscene banquets, and bizarre sexual practices. He both observed and participated in wild orgies with his invited guests and his licentiousness knew no bounds; in such an atmosphere corruption and not Christ was the principle to be worshiped and revered. Accordingly his favorite children, Cesare and sister Lucrezia, were brought up to revere this corruption and encouraged by their father to abandon biblical teachings in favor of the maxim of taking what they coveted.

Cesare, exonerated by corrupt Papal Bulls, or decrees, did not even have to explain his illegitimacy to the Vatican cardinals when he began his clerical training at the age of 17. He had been the recipient of many Spanish and Italian titles by the time he was 20 by which time he showed all of the debauchery, drunkenness, and corruption of his father. His ruthlessly cruel streak is best illustrated by the murder in 1497 of his own brother, Juan, whom he wanted out of the way so he could claim the wealthy duchy of Gandia in Spain. On the night of June 14 his mother Vannozza held a small party for family members attended by Cesare and Juan. Two days later, on June 16, Juan's body, wildly hacked with a sword and with his hands tied behind his back, was fished from the Tiber as it flowed through Rome. Cesare was never charged with the murder but historians concur that his naked ambition would stop at nothing and that he was the true assassin. A cruel verse of the time aimed at his father went: "It's easy to believe, Sixtus, that you're a fisher of men, Since out of the Waters, You've fished your own son!"

In 1498, when Cesare was 23, he resigned his cardinal's post and set out through bullying, war, and murder to accomplish his aims—power,

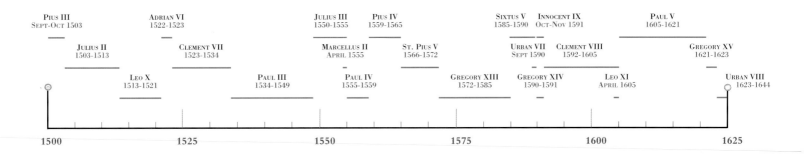

PIUS III SEPT–OCT 1503	**ADRIAN VI** 1522-1523		**JULIUS III** 1550-1555	**PIUS IV** 1559-1565	**SIXTUS V** 1585-1590	**INNOCENT IX** OCT-NOV 1591	**PAUL V** 1605-1621

women, and riches. He claimed one feudal duchy after another for himself, often putting conquered towns to the torch while he allowed his renegade band of followers to rape the womenfolk as a lesson to all men who opposed him. After conquering one town, Cesare, who also reveled in the despoiling of the women of his enemies, ordered that 40 of the prettiest virgins be brought to him. For 48 hours he would not move from his bedchamber until he had violated every one—and some of them more than once; and this while he was in the advanced stages of the sexually transmitted disease syphilis, which it is thought he picked up in Neapolitan whorehouses. Perhaps as an explanation for his great mood swings, author E.R. Chamberlin, in his authoritative book *The Fall of the House of Borgia*, suggests that the pain he suffered through the disease may have contributed to his brutality and madness. He wrote:

"The contrasting contemporary opinions of Cesare Borgia, opinions which saw him alternatively as a blood-maddened fiend and as a level-headed, vigorous man, can be explained and recognized in clinical, simple terms. He was suffering from an advanced form of syphilis, contracted on his first visit to Naples in 1497. The disease achieved epidemic proportions at the turn of the century and was viewed with a horror exacerbated by its mysterious nature. Throughout Cesare's life its effect upon him would rise and fall, compelling him at times to withdraw into total privacy. In the beginning its sores seem to have only affected his groin but later the disfigurement spread to his face. Whether raging or quiescent the disease must have had a profound effect upon a handsome man who was otherwise so attractive to women, and accounts reasonably enough for the bursts of near-fiendish cruelty of which he was capable."

To enable him to maintain a lethal hold on his petrified subjects, Cesare Borgia enlisted the aid of the brutal warlord Don Ramiro de Lorca, a sadistic, domineering bully whose servility to his master knew no bounds, and who went about his bloodthirsty tasks with the blessing of the Holy Father. He traditionally hunted down the enemies of Cesare in places of sanctuary—churches, monasteries, and other consecrated places—and was swift to execute them once they had been found. Once, at Faenza with Cesare watching, he had strung up a miscreant whose rope suddenly snapped as he swung on the gallows. Medieval people took this as a sign that God wanted the criminal spared and, as he ran for the church, the crowd of townspeople aided him in his flight and blocked the doors to de Lorca and his thugs. He fought his way through the crowd, grabbed the wretched man and had him hanged once again, this time from the window of the mayor's palace.

This incident took place in the Romagna, a collection of territories bordering the Adriatic which Cesare wheedled, brutalized and bought

Above: Cesare Borgia, son of Pope Alexander VI, was born in 1476. A cardinal at 17, he was released from his vows in 1493 to marry Charlotte d'Albret, sister of the king of Navarre. He would die in 1507, fighting in Castile, after—it is said—murdering both his brother Juan and his brother-in-law Alfonso.

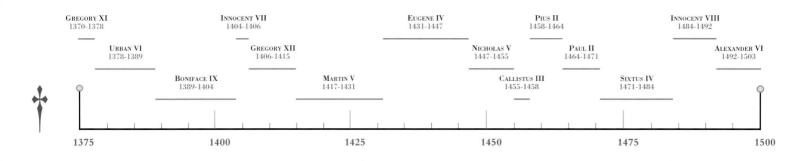

GREGORY XI 1370-1378		INNOCENT VII 1404-1406		EUGENE IV 1431-1447		PIUS II 1458-1464		INNOCENT VIII 1484-1492
URBAN VI 1378-1389		GREGORY XII 1406-1415		NICHOLAS V 1447-1455		PAUL II 1464-1471		ALEXANDER VI 1492-1503
BONIFACE IX 1389-1404		MARTIN V 1417-1431		CALLISTUS III 1455-1458		SIXTUS IV 1471-1484		

| 1375 | 1400 | 1425 | 1450 | 1475 | 1500 |

Above: Julius II was an enemy of Alexander VI and the Borgias. He fled to France in 1494 fearing Borgia assassins and returned only when Alexander died. Bribes gained him the position of pope at the second attempt after Alexander's successor, Pius III, lasted only 10 days after his coronation.

until it was all under his fiefdom—with the sanction of the pope, of course. Once completed, he returned to Rome in triumph and resumed a life of hedonistic pleasure.

While consolidating power in the powerful city-states that sprawled across medieval Italy, he was scheming with his beautiful sister Lucrezia for greater things. They were extremely close—so close, in fact, that for years the legend has persisted that they slept together. Most historians have concluded that this was not the case, although in every other respect concerning human morals and standards of behavior, she was as depraved as he.

She was married three times, each union designed to strengthen the Borgia dynasty throughout Italy in the duchies and city-states. Her third union, to the nephew of the King of Naples, Alfonso of Aragon, was a happy one for Lucrezia, but Cesare wanted her to be unwed one more time so he might gain the prize of Ferrara in a marriage to the powerful duke of the region. The pope had annulled the first marriage and granted a papal decree formally recognizing her divorce in the second, but even he could not grant a second divorce. As an indication of her corruption she agreed to a plot hatched by Cesare to help kill her husband to advance her brother's power.

On July 15, 1500, Alfonso dined with Cesare and Lucrezia and other close friends at an intimate dinner party in Rome at Cesare's lavish apartments. Afterward, as he crossed a square outside, he was set upon by three men. His page and valet were unable to fight off the armed men who left their master seriously wounded. The Vatican guard were turned out to help Alfonso who was carried back to Cesare's residence before he lapsed into unconsciousness. Soon, at Cesare's suggestion, he was recuperating in his home, secure in a tower that was guarded by elite troops, but on August 18 he was left alone, the guards mysteriously called off. When they returned an hour later he was strangled—at the hands of Cesare himself and two hired hitmen. It was the solution to the problem, and soon the Borgia's influence would extend across the Duchy that both Cesare and Lucrezia coveted. Soon she married Aldonso de Este in Ferrara and became a grand duchess, attracting to her court some of the greatest painters, musicians, and craftsmen of the Renaissance age.

Cesare continued his ravages throughout Italy and also undertook an odyssey through France where he was received with trappings befitting royalty instead of mere nobility. In Lyons he showed his gluttony in a 14-hour banquet in which he ate two ribs of beef, six chickens, a side each of veal and mutton, and washed the whole lot down with 16 bottles of finest burgundy.

He wanted to curry favor with French nobility and warlords in case he ever needed to raise mercenary forces for further advances on hitherto independent states and duchies. But by this time he already had

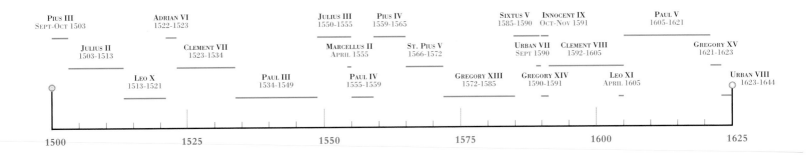

| PIUS III
SEPT–OCT 1503 | ADRIAN VI
1522–1523 | | JULIUS III
1550–1555 | PIUS IV
1559–1565 | SIXTUS V
1585–1590 | INNOCENT IX
OCT–NOV 1591 | PAUL V
1605–1621 |

immeasurable wealth—all of it stolen with the blessing of the pope. Never in history, with the possible exception of Herman Göring the art-loving air force leader of Hitler's Luftwaffe, has an individual stolen so much and lived so high on the hog because of it.

While his sister flourished in Ferrara, Cesare crowned himself the Duke of Romagna and settled in a magnificent palace at Cesena, some 60 miles away. His court consisted of the brutal (mostly Spanish) followers who had been with him from the beginning. He even had an official poisoner in his ranks who dispensed potions to his enemies! He amused himself with grotesque orgies; one of his favorite pastimes was to strew hot chestnuts over a marble floor and laugh uproariously as naked courtesans crawled around suspended lighted candles to retrieve them. He staged fertility contests and routinely terrorized local nobles into turning over their virgin daughters for him to defile.

There was another side to him—his penchant for beautiful and luxurious things. Inside his palace he collected one of the finest Renaissance libraries ever to be compiled under one roof—although all the works therein were looted from other castles, palaces, and monasteries from all over Italy.

Although he read little of these masterworks and had consistently shown throughout his life that whoring, murder, theft, and intrigue were the closest things to his heart, he nevertheless was philanthropic when it came to erecting bridges and other public works; possibly, because—as with so many public figures throughout history—he wanted to leave his mark long after his wretched mortal remains had rotted away.

To this end he hired Leonardo da Vinci to repair the shattered fortress walls of so many of the city-states that had been damaged in his attacks, and praised the genius for his artistic rendering of siege fortifications for the region of Piombino. From his book-lined palace and away from his limited philanthropy, he continued to subdue cities and regions that appealed to him and whose plunder he needed to fuel his extravagant lifestyle.

The end for Cesare, and ultimately that of the Borgia influence on Italy, came with the death of his protector and benefactor, the pope. On August 11, 1503, Alexander died, great black tumors having broken out all over his body in the hours before his death. A priest attending to him for the last rites said: "Today he is descended to the hell from whence he was born." Truly, there were none to

Never in history . . . has an individual stolen so much and lived so high on the hog because of it.

Below: Michaelangelo, the personification of the Renaissance, whose remarkable painting on the ceiling of the Sistine Chapel is a testament to both his skill and his faith.

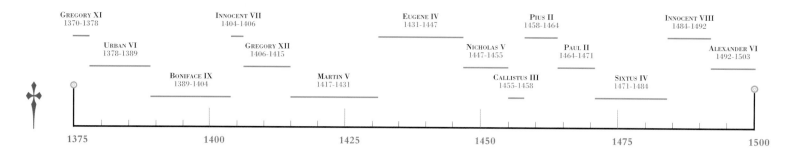

GREGORY XI 1370-1378		INNOCENT VII 1404-1406		EUGENE IV 1431-1447		PIUS II 1458-1464		INNOCENT VIII 1484-1492
URBAN VI 1378-1389		GREGORY XII 1406-1415		NICHOLAS V 1447-1455		PAUL II 1464-1471		ALEXANDER VI 1492-1503
BONIFACE IX 1389-1404		MARTIN V 1417-1431		CALLISTUS III 1455-1458		SIXTUS IV 1471-1484	

1375   1400   1425   1450   1475   1500

Below: St Peter's was designed by Bramante, who died in 1514 and for 30 years construction of the basilica effectively ceased. In 1547, however, Paul III turned to Michaelangelo, now age 72, and the Vatican's chief architect, to continue the job: Michaelangelo reverted to Bramante's design. He would not live to see its completion, dying in 1564.

weep for the Holy Father who abused his seat of power to turn Italy into an adventure playground for the warlord Cesare.

Coincidentally, Cesare fell ill at exactly the same time as his wicked father, prompting suspicion among some Romans that Cesare had poisoned the old man and had then inadvertently partaken of the lethal poison himself, but the probable cause of both illnesses was a virus transmitted by foul water or air in those less-than-sanitary times.

As Cesare fought for his life a contemporary writer branded the late pope "avaricious . . . he caused by poison the death of many cardinals and prelates, even among his intimates. His cruelty was great and

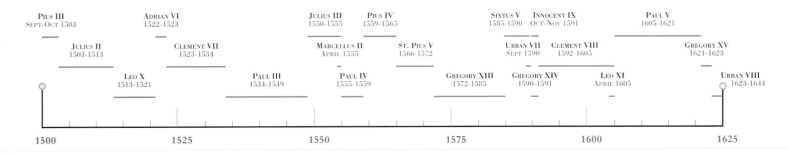

PIUS III SEPT-OCT 1503	ADRIAN VI 1522-1523		JULIUS III 1550-1555	PIUS IV 1559-1565		SIXTUS V 1585-1590	INNOCENT IX OCT-NOV 1591	PAUL V 1605-1621	

JULIUS II 1503-1513   CLEMENT VII 1523-1534   MARCELLUS II APRIL 1555   ST. PIUS V 1566-1572   URBAN VII SEPT 1590   CLEMENT VIII 1592-1605   GREGORY XV 1621-1623

LEO X 1513-1521   PAUL III 1534-1549   PAUL IV 1555-1559   GREGORY XIII 1572-1585   GREGORY XIV 1590-1591   LEO XI APRIL 1605   URBAN VIII 1623-1644

1500   1525   1550   1575   1600   1625

there was in him no religion nor keeping of his troth . . . In one word, he was more evil and more lucky than ever for many ages peradventure had been any Pope before."

Anarchy usually followed the death of the Holy Father in medieval times and the death of Rodrigo was no exception—except this time three columns of troops descended on the city. Troops from Spain, Italy, and Catholic-led generals in Italy took the pope's demise as the opportunity to grab land and power.

Cesare, recovering in his luxury apartment, his body racked with syphilis, malaria, and the mystery fever that killed his father, was enraged that he was not fit enough to take charge and try to restore his crumbling power—crumbling because the cardinals that were to elect the new pope had had their fill of the Borgias and all their evil ways. They were determined to distance the Vatican from the clan.

Cesare's physicians tried desperate measures to cure his fever—which included dunking him up to ten times per day in ice cold baths—but all they succeeded in doing was ripping great diseased chunks of skin and flesh from his ravaged body. Even as he was mourning his father from his sickbed he dispatched his emissaries with keys to his father's private chambers—he had to get his hands on secreted papal treasures because, with the death of his protector, money was surely to be in short supply.

The cardinals were able at last to elect an honest man, Pope Julius II, after their original choice, Pius III, lasted just ten days before he succumbed to a serious illness. Cesare's days were now numbered. Although Pope Julius offered Cesare back his fiefdom in the Romagna, he did so only because he did not relish the alternative option of the Kingdom of Venice—a state often at odds with the Holy See—taking over the territories. Julius would have been content to have a loyal Cesare holding together the fracturing states. But Cesare, used to pulling the strings of power for so long in Rome, was not used to living as a

Above: Lorenzo de' Medici, known to history as Lorenzo the Magnificent, as seen in an engraving after Vasari. Florentine bankers, the Medici family was one of the great Italian Renaissance families, producing two popes—Leo X and Clement VII—and a queen of France, Catherine de Medici. Lorenzo was a patron of such famous artists as Botticelli, Michaelangelo, and Leonardo.

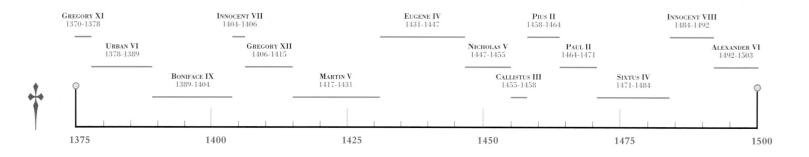

GREGORY XI 1370-1378		INNOCENT VII 1404-1406		EUGENE IV 1431-1447		PIUS II 1458-1464		INNOCENT VIII 1484-1492
URBAN VI 1378-1389		GREGORY XII 1406-1415			NICHOLAS V 1447-1455		PAUL II 1464-1471		ALEXANDER VI 1492-1503
	BONIFACE IX 1389-1404		MARTIN V 1417-1431			CALLISTUS III 1455-1458		SIXTUS IV 1471-1484	

1375   1400   1425   1450   1475   1500

Above: Pope Leo X, the second son of Lorenzo the Magnificent and a great patron of the Renaissance. He made Rome a place of great beauty and learning, but it was at the cost of ignoring the rise of Lutherism which would split in two the "Catholic" Church in the coming years, and see the papacy lose control of half its flock.

subordinate bound to the Catholic church. Advisers to Julius warned him that Cesare would become a problem and the wise old pope began making peace overtures towards the Venetians, hoping that they would bind the states to the coat-tails of the church. In November 1503 Cesare was under arrest on the pope's orders, charged with many murders and the robbery of personal property and estates, which he was ordered to hand back to the rightful owners or the church.

In 1504, fearful that his influence could rise again to form an army that might march anew on Italian cities, he was banished to Spain. There, for two years he was a prisoner near Valencia, the city from where the clan had found its first roots of power within the church. In October 1506 he escaped and headed for Italy where he intended to revive his splendid military victories and once again build up his empire. The pope was greatly alarmed at news of his escape but Cesare was never again to rise to the great military heights that had once been his trademark. By the beginning of March 1507 he was broke, his health frail and his supporters few. Nevertheless he rode out to the castle of Viana in Spain, having decided to pursue his fortunes there instead. The city was on the Castille-Navarre frontier and Cesare intended to take it with a force supplied by his former French allies. He had 1,000 cavalrymen, 5,000 infantrymen, and some heavy artillery. But in the chaos of battle he was speared by a lance under the arm and toppled into the midst of a bloodthirsty mob who trampled, stabbed, and beat him to death.

Cesare was buried in Viana in the church of Santa Maria where the epitaph on his gravestone read: "Here, buried in a little earth, lies one who held the world in fear, one who held peace and war in his hands. Oh, you that go in search of things deserving praise, if you would praise the worthiest, then let your journey end here nor trouble to go further." The pithy words may have been true in part, but for most of the ancient and modern worlds, he is remembered solely as a prime scoundrel, a sexual deviant, and as bloodthirsty thief. The writer Niccolo Machiavelli, himself an intriguer of the first rank, admired the ruthless Cesare so much that he used him as his role model in his work *The Prince*.

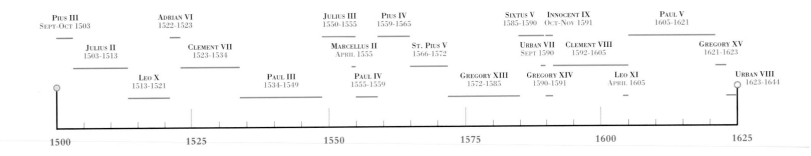

PIUS III SEPT–OCT 1503	ADRIAN VI 1522–1523		JULIUS III 1550–1555	PIUS IV 1559–1565		SIXTUS V 1585–1590	INNOCENT IX OCT–NOV 1591		PAUL V 1605–1621	
JULIUS II 1503–1513	CLEMENT VII 1523–1534		MARCELLUS II APRIL 1555	ST. PIUS V 1566–1572		URBAN VII SEPT 1590	CLEMENT VIII 1592–1605			GREGORY XV 1621–1623
LEO X 1513–1521	PAUL III 1534–1549		PAUL IV 1555–1559		GREGORY XIII 1572–1585	GREGORY XIV 1590–1591	LEO XI APRIL 1605		URBAN VIII 1623–1644

| 1500 | 1525 | 1550 | 1575 | 1600 | 1625 |

There was to be no peace for the mortal remains of Cesare. Two centuries after he was buried the Bishop of Calahorra ordered that his bones should be removed and the grave destroyed, offended as he was that holy ground should be used as the repository for the remains of someone so foul. The bones were buried in the road outside—unconsecrated ground. In his book *The Borgias*, Ivan Cloulas writes:

"A few bones buried beneath the church steps and a couple of gracefully carved pilasters from the tomb that are now part of the high altar—that is all that is left on Spanish soil of the one who for so many years made the world tremble at his name."

The arrival of Julius began to lift the stain of the Borgias from the papacy, but there was little of the peacemaker in him—or, indeed, the humble priest. In fact, even as a cardinal, he was father to three children and his warlike tendencies became legendary. He became so well-known for bloodthirsty wars that a contemporary historian noted of him: "Beneath the dress and the name and the rosary, there is nothing of the priest in Julius." He was one of those popes who coveted the power of the Papal States and was more often seen on a horse leading armies to fight in bloody battles than he ever was in church. With such zeal he won back the lost territories of Rimini, Ravenna, and Faenza before turning toward the arts.

Julius became the patron of Bramante (architect of parts of the Vatican), Michaelangelo, and Raphael, sitting for the latter in a famous portrait. He was known throughout the land as the "Warrior Pontiff," but he was possessed of a sharp intellect married to a keen eye for beauty. He intended for his trio of classical artists to transform the papal buildings into works of supreme beauty—which, of course, is what they accomplished. Furthermore, worldly though he undoubtedly was, history owes him a great debt as the man who, in 1506,

Below: Martin Luther was not a lone voice crying out against the decadence of the papacy: the religious revival had been well in evidence at the end of the 15th century. This meant that there was much public support for the Professor of Theology, who challenged the sale of indulgences (certificates guaranteeing that the purchaser would not be punished in purgatory) by Friar Johann Tetzel when he nailed his famous 95 theses to the door of Wittenberg castle's church. Luther was a portent of the growing dissatisfaction with Rome but the popes were too shortsighted to heed his warnings, and this dissatisfaction quickly became organized dissent, leading ultimately to the Reformation.

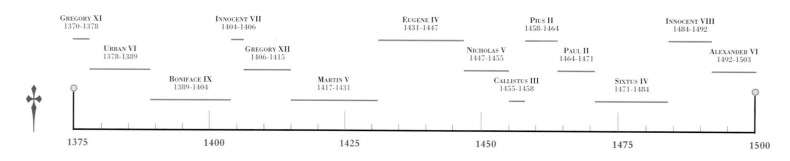

GREGORY XI 1370-1378		INNOCENT VII 1404-1406			EUGENE IV 1431-1447		PIUS II 1458-1464		INNOCENT VIII 1484-1492
URBAN VI 1378-1389			GREGORY XII 1406-1415			NICHOLAS V 1447-1455		PAUL II 1464-1471		ALEXANDER VI 1492-1503
	BONIFACE IX 1389-1404			MARTIN V 1417-1431			CALLISTUS III 1455-1458		SIXTUS IV 1471-1484	

| 1375 | 1400 | 1425 | 1450 | 1475 | 1500 |

Above: Martin Luther, an unlikely reformer, but one whose message still rings down the ages. The division of the church-into Roman Catholics and Protestants would lead to centuries of warfare, and allow the state to disentangle itself from the church..

laid down the cornerstone of the Basilica of St. Peter's, the greatest shrine to Catholicism in the world. He did little in the way of church reforms—except banishing nepotism briefly from the Vatican—but is regarded by papal historians as one of the more important popes.

There followed Leo X, a man who single-handedly did more to erode the power and status of the Church of Rome than even Henry VIII did with the formation of the Church of England. Essentially a pious, educated man with a great thirst for knowledge, he was interested in the glory of the papacy and the splendor of Rome—without paying any heed to the changing society over which he presided.

The second son of Lorenzo de' Medici the Magnificent, Leo X grew up in opulence and splendor at the court of his famous family. After much wandering around Europe following the exile of the Medici family from Florence in 1494, he returned to Rome where he was the closest aide to Pope Julius II. A cardinal from the age of 13, he swapped his vestments for armor and was a fierce warrior.

There were many pressing issues for him to address as pontiff. There was a groundswell of dissent growing amid the artisan classes at what was perceived as the profligacy of the papacy—not helped by the fortunes Julius II had squandered in pursuit of his wars or the lavishness with which Leo X set the tone for his pontificate. "Let us enjoy the papacy which God has seen fit to bestow upon us!" he cried at his coronation . . . and indeed the celebrations were the most lavish that any pope has ever presided over, costing fully one-seventh of all the treasure that Julius II had bequeathed him!

Although he himself refrained from Bacchanalia and women, Leo's court was nowhere near as restrained. There were great hunting parties, masked balls, banquets, and pageants—all of which strained the purse strings of the papacy and fueled a growing resentment against the hierarchy of the church. This wasn't only a simmering resentment in Rome—cardinals in far-flung places, seeing the splendor which the new pope tolerated and encouraged, began to build their own lavish palaces which were modeled on the pope's. This, too, did not escape the notice of the peasantry. E.R. Chamberlin wrote in his book *The Bad Popes*:

"From the very beginning Leo had need of money, if for no better reason than to hold his own in the fantastic orgy of spending in which his fellow nobles in Rome indulged. The city now presented a curious contrast in public squalor and private luxury. To the eyes of the pilgrims who still flocked in their thousands it was a shabby, inhospitable city. But within the palaces, designed by men whose names were destined to be immortal, an almost oriental splendor was maintained at a cost that might have made Nero look thoughtful."

While Leo encouraged excess, he was also a great patron of the arts

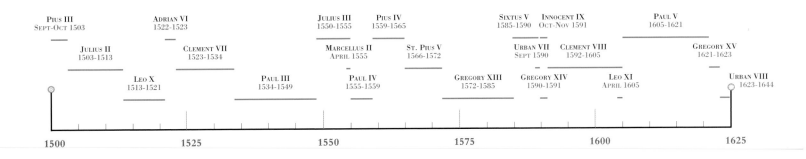

PIUS III SEPT–OCT 1503		ADRIAN VI 1522–1523		JULIUS III 1550–1555	PIUS IV 1559–1565		SIXTUS V 1585–1590	INNOCENT IX OCT–NOV 1591		PAUL V 1605–1621	
JULIUS II 1503–1513		CLEMENT VII 1523–1534		MARCELLUS II APRIL 1555	ST. PIUS V 1566–1572		URBAN VII SEPT 1590	CLEMENT VIII 1592–1605		GREGORY XV 1621–1623
LEO X 1513–1521		PAUL III 1534–1549	PAUL IV 1555–1559		GREGORY XIII 1572–1585	GREGORY XIV 1590–1591		LEO XI APRIL 1605		URBAN VIII 1623–1644

1500   1525   1550   1575   1600   1625

and unstinting in his support of those Renaissance artists first brought into the Vatican by his predecessor to work on St. Peter's and assorted papal palaces. Yet all this was breaking the bank and he was forced to turn to moneylenders who gave increasing amounts to him with exorbitant interest rates often in excess of 40 percent. "It would be easier for a stone to fly in the air than for this pope to keep together a thousand ducats," wrote a Florentine nobleman of the time. So   Leo X took to selling off papal offices and honors, even artificially creating a further 30 new cardinals, despite there being no need for them. The grateful holy men were only too happy to accept their new titles as "Princes of the Church" and paid up a whopping half-a-million gold ducats between them for the privilege.

It was left to a dissident holy man to speak for the uneducated masses in a document that has gone down in history. Martin Luther was a German theologian who became sickened by the corruption of the church and its willy-nilly dispensation of honors. His most famous protest was the publication of 95 Theses which he nailed to the door of Wittenberg church in Saxony in 1517. This was a revolutionary act in a Europe bound heart and soul to the power of Rome, but one that struck a chord and found great sympathy and support among the oppressed masses. It was not an act of dissent that sat well with Leo X, who could think only of confrontation instead of reconciliation, excommunicating the errant priest with all the fury he could muster. This was an act of folly, because it merely strengthened public anger against the church and left Leo's successors to struggle with the full wrath of the Reformation, the movement that blew through the old ideals of the medieval church and took with it much of the power and prestige of the papacy.

Leo X died on December 1, 1521, leaving the Vatican finances in a state of chaos and the church ill-prepared for the tumultuous changes yet to come. Following the short reign of Adrian VI, Clement VII was elected by the cardinals in 1523. Romans of the day called him "sour face," because of his look of perpetual scorn, but he was every bit as aristocratic as his patron Leo X had been. Born the bastard son of Giulliamo de Medici it was only the patronage of Leo—waving aside his illegitimacy—that allowed him to become a high-ranking cleric in the first place. "He

Although he himself refrained from Bacchanalia and women, Leo's court was nowhere near as restrained. There were great hunting parties, masked balls, banquets, and pageants—all of which strained the purse strings of the papacy and fueled a growing resentment against the hierarchy of the church.

Below: One of the key features of the Reformation was the translation of the Bible so that all could read it: this is Luther's bible.

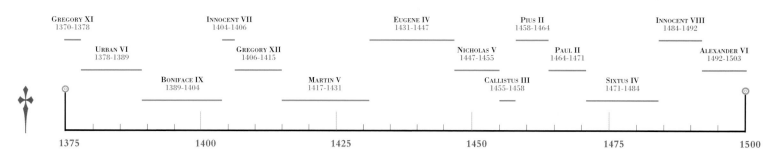

GREGORY XI 1370-1378		INNOCENT VII 1404-1406		EUGENE IV 1431-1447		PIUS II 1458-1464		INNOCENT VIII 1484-1492
URBAN VI 1378-1389		GREGORY XII 1406-1415		NICHOLAS V 1447-1455		PAUL II 1464-1471		ALEXANDER VI 1492-1503
BONIFACE IX 1389-1404		MARTIN V 1417-1431		CALLISTUS III 1455-1458		SIXTUS IV 1471-1484	

1375   1400   1425   1450   1475   1500

Above: Reformation and Counter-Reformation: the religious battleground of Europe.

Right: Printing played a major role in the dissemination of new ideas and was used by both reformers and the papacy. This is an engraving of Pope Gregory I by Anton Wierix (c1552-c1624) published in 1580. Private Collection/Bridgeman Art Library

was a rather morose and disagreeable person, reputed to be avaricious, by no means trustworthy and naturally disinclined to do a kindness," was how Francesco Guicciardini, a Florentine scholar, described him. Yet he became pontiff with high hopes vested in him by the people—Adrian before him was immensely unpopular. But if they thought he would be more humble, they were sorely mistaken.

Clement loved jewelry and baubles, commissioning many famous craftsmen of the time to fashion ever-more extravagant trinkets for him. Because he was so easily distracted by the pleasures of the papacy, he ignored foreign policy and the mounting dangers facing the Vatican and Rome. With the treasury almost bankrupt—thanks to Leo's excesses—he was urged to borrow more to strengthen both the state and the church. But, with a reputation for never being able to make up his mind, he did neither.

The crunch for him came in his vacillating dealings with Henry VIII of England, who wanted to annul his marriage to Catharine of Aragon on the grounds that her pervious marriage with his brother had

94

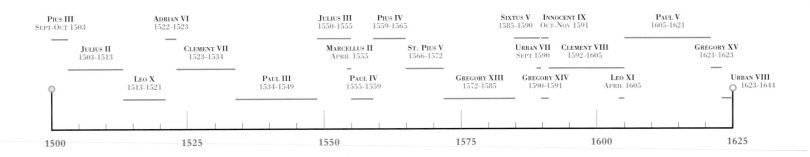

| PIUS III | ADRIAN VI | | JULIUS III | PIUS IV | | SIXTUS V | INNOCENT IX | | PAUL V |
| SEPT-OCT 1503 | 1522-1523 | | 1550-1555 | 1559-1565 | | 1585-1590 | OCT-NOV 1591 | | 1605-1621 |

| JULIUS II | CLEMENT VII | MARCELLUS II | ST. PIUS V | URBAN VII | CLEMENT VIII | GREGORY XV |
| 1503-1513 | 1523-1534 | APRIL 1555 | 1566-1572 | SEPT 1590 | 1592-1605 | 1621-1623 |

| LEO X | PAUL III | PAUL IV | GREGORY XIII | GREGORY XIV | LEO XI | URBAN VIII |
| 1513-1521 | 1534-1549 | 1555-1559 | 1572-1585 | 1590-1591 | APRIL 1605 | 1623-1644 |

| 1500 | 1525 | 1550 | 1575 | 1600 | 1625 |

been consummated, technically making his union with her incestuous. Clement was all for pleasing Henry who had been bestowed with the title "Defender of the Faith" by Pope Leo X for his defence of the papacy in the face of the scurrilous attacks by Luther. But he faced an angry opponent in Catharine's nephew, Charles V, the Holy Roman Emperor. Pope Clement at first agreed to Henry's wish to revoke the marriage, then backtracked, causing outrage both in Rome and London and leading, ultimately, to the English Reformation and the birth of the Church of England. Yet his problems did not stop there.

Clement found himself in a vise between the corrupt King Francis I of France and Charles V over his handling of the Henry VIII question and of the individual desires of both continental rulers to seize territories in Italy. Clement made the mistake of telling the far-more powerful Charles that he was a neutral pontiff . . . while conducting secret talks for an alliance with Francis. Charles learned of his deception, and a later treaty between France and Clement, and declared: "I shall go to Italy and revenge myself on those who have injured me, particularly on that fool of a pope. Martin Luther, perhaps, was not so far wrong."

In May 1527 the sword of Charles descended with bloody fury upon the eternal city. Spanish and German armies moved through Rome like the Visigoths of old, plundering, raping, looting, and murdering. The entire Swiss Guard protecting Clement was murdered as they fought to secure his safety. As he remained, effectively, under house arrest in the papal fortress—Castel Sant' Angelo —in the city, his enemies began a five-month sack of Rome with cruelty that knew no bounds. Nuns were raped and murdered, or dragged naked to auctions where the mercenaries bought and sold them like cattle. Priests were put to the sword in their hundreds and the great palaces and churches were robbed of all treasures before being desecrated and defiled.

By June the city was a smoking ruin, the air heavy with the stench of corpses. The bloodlust continued until autumn when Clement formally surrendered from the fortress and went into exile in the Umbrian hill town of Orvieto, and later Viterbo, for two years. His final humiliation before Charles came in 1529 when he was forced to crown him emperor in a coronation in Bologna. He was now a servile puppet of Charles and duly forbade Henry of England from divorce, paving the way for his future excommunication from the church and sewing the seeds of the English Reformation. In return Charles ordered his armies to seize Papal States in the north of Italy that had been taken by the French, and restored them to the Vatican.

There was little or nothing that he could do, now, to stem the tide of Protestantism that began sweeping Europe. Scandinavia, Germany, Holland—everywhere the power of the Universal Church was being destroyed. The only consolation for "Sour Face" was that he had managed to create many new bishoprics in South America, guaran-

In May 1527 the sword of Charles descended with bloody fury upon the eternal city. Spanish and German armies moved through Rome like the Visigoths of old, plundering, raping, looting, and murdering.

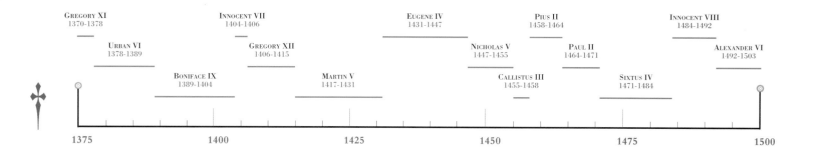
teeing there, at least, an unbroken Catholic domination for centuries to come. So negative and so weak was he regarded that a verse of the day ran: "His reign was rich in seeking every way, in change of mind and trying to be wise. In ifs and buts and nos and ayes. With nothing ever done . . . but always much to say." He died on September 25, 1534, mourned by very few of his countrymen indeed.

Successor to Clement was Paul III in 1534, who was known as "Cardinal Petticoat" throughout his reign. Paul, born Alessandro Farnese, enjoyed his patronage as a cardinal at the elbow of the notorious Alexander VI— who, during his reign, was enjoying ravaging his sister Giulia Farnese. Romans knew of the goings-on in the notorious papal household, coining the phrase for Alessandro when the pope made him a cardinal. He bore the epithet with humor when a Prince of the church—but could be roused to fury when he heard it in his position as Supreme Pontiff.

Still, with a Borgia as patron, his climb up the slippery pole to power was guaranteed. He first became papal treasurer and familiarized himself at length with the intricate workings of the Vatican finances. Never a clergyman—during these times it was within the papal power to appoint cardinals who were laymen—he thumbed his nose at convention, keeping a mistress who bore him three sons and a daughter! But he claimed to have received a visitation from God during the reign of Leo X and turned his life around completely. He became dean of the College of Cardinals after being ordained in 1519, and shared the imprisonment of Clement during his ruinous reign in the fortress of Castel Sant'Angelo.

He was elected pope on October 13, 1534, and made it his task to try to combat the mounting threat of the Protestant Reformation that had so undermined the rule of the previous papal incumbent. Paul, despite his libidinous early life, proved himself a worthy pontiff, committed wholeheartedly in trying to restore the crumbling authority of the Universal Church. He is credited with the Catholic Reformation, or Counter-Reformation, which sought to check the Protestant revolution. Paul was generally sickened by the corruption that his predecessors had done so little to stop, but was unmovable in his belief that watering down the tenets upon which Catholicism was founded was not the answer. The Great Schism had sapped all reforming efforts, turning the church in on itself instead of putting itself in order.

Above: Clement VII was another Medici, the bastard son of Giulano de' Medici, who was brought up by Lorenzo the Magnificent following his father's death. Made Archbishop of Florence by his cousin Leo X, Clement VII played a dangerous game siding with each of the big political players of the day—Francis I of France and Holy Roman Emperor Charles V—something that put him and the Papal States in the firing line. This culminated in the sack of Rome in 1527 and the pope's imprisonment by the emperor.

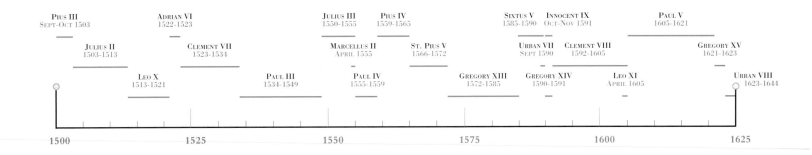

| PIUS III SEPT–OCT 1503 | ADRIAN VI 1522–1523 | | JULIUS III 1550–1555 | PIUS IV 1559–1565 | | SIXTUS V 1585–1590 | INNOCENT IX OCT–NOV 1591 | | PAUL V 1605–1621 |

JULIUS II 1503–1513 · CLEMENT VII 1523–1534 · MARCELLUS II APRIL 1555 · ST. PIUS V 1566–1572 · URBAN VII SEPT 1590 · CLEMENT VIII 1592–1605 · GREGORY XV 1621–1623

LEO X 1513–1521 · PAUL III 1534–1549 · PAUL IV 1555–1559 · GREGORY XIII 1572–1585 · GREGORY XIV 1590–1591 · LEO XI APRIL 1605 · URBAN VIII 1623–1644

1500   1525   1550   1575   1600   1625

In 1545 he called the Council of Trent in Northern Italy, a forum to promote the reforms of the church that he saw necessary if it was to survive the withering onslaught of Protestantism. Naturally, prelates who had lived a gilded existence under the old order were virulently opposed to any changes which might rob them of status or luxuries, but Paul was not to be dissuaded from his mission.

The work of the council concentrated on eliminating papal abuses, dogmatic definition, and restoring papal credibility to a disillusioned flock. In fact, the Council of Trent was to meet for 20 years under successive pontiffs, but the cornerstones of change were firmly laid down by Paul III. One of the most important decisions it took was to commission the writing of a Catholic Catechism, the first time the church sought to present the truths of Catholicism in a comprehensive and systematic way. It was completed in 1566 and was intended to serve as a guide for clergy in instructing the faithful.

Another of his main goals was to promote the rise of religious orders, such as the Jesuits—pious, humble, devoted servants of Christ who would dedicate themselves to the church in a stark contrast to the flamboyance and high living of the papal court as the people of his time understood it. The Jesuits, or Society of Jesus, with their vows of poverty, chastity and obedience, were seen not only as living symbols of the eternal faith, but also deployed as missionaries and messengers to spread the word and act as a bulwark against the watered-down teachings of Protestantism.

In his crusading zeal Paul III confirmed the excommunication of Henry VIII in 1538, reasoning to dissenting cardinals that Catholicism would not brook such an effrontery as divorce ever. It is a tenet that survives to this day. He was also, though, protective of the great artists that had come to Rome under previous pontiffs and the world owes the painting of *The Last Judgment* in the Sistine Chapel to him. He died in 1549, a bitter man because of the defection of his son to the Emperor Charles V and the loyalties of two papal duchies he took with him. Yet the church was a better institution upon his demise and his memory is cherished in the hallowed halls of the Vatican.

It was obviously too good to last. In seemingly traditional papal style, his successor reverted to the pleasures of the flesh with alacrity. He was Julius III, supreme pontiff from 1550 to

Below: Henry VIII's showdown with Rome over the question of his divorce seriously weakened the church. Clement was regarded in the end, in a popular doggerel of the day, as a pope who had a lot to say—but rarely, if ever, did anything.

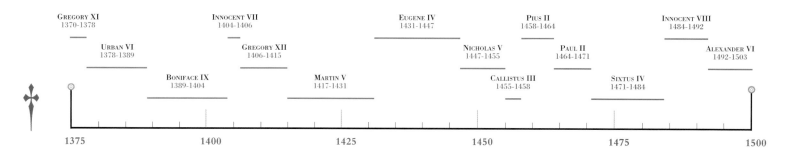

| GREGORY XI 1370-1378 | | INNOCENT VII 1404-1406 | | EUGENE IV 1431-1447 | | PIUS II 1458-1464 | | INNOCENT VIII 1484-1492 |

URBAN VI 1378-1389 — GREGORY XII 1406-1415 — NICHOLAS V 1447-1455 — PAUL II 1464-1471 — ALEXANDER VI 1492-1503

BONIFACE IX 1389-1404 — MARTIN V 1417-1431 — CALLISTUS III 1455-1458 — SIXTUS IV 1471-1484

1375   1400   1425   1450   1475   1500

Above: Michaelangelo's Sistine Chapel roof was started in 1509 under the aegis of Julius II.

1555. A Roman, born Giovanni Maria Ciocchi del Monte, he was a brilliant law graduate from the universities of Perugia and Siena and enjoyed his cardinal success under the patronage of Pope Julius II. Appointed an archbishop in 1511, he shot rapidly up the ladder of promotion becoming in succession a bishop, governor of Rome, vice-legate of Bologna, and finally a cardinal in 1536. He played a major role as a reformer at the opening of the Council of Trent—but paid little heed in later years at any serious attempts at reforming his own character!

Julius III was interested in reforms in a superficial sense. He realized that disciples needed to see changes in the church, but he was all for making them cosmetic. While he promoted the Jesuits like his predecessor and sought to chisel away much of the privilege enjoyed by lesser members of the church, he ensured that the papal court lived as high on the hog as ever. And he was opportunistic, claiming the credit for the accession of the Catholic Mary Tudor to the throne of England in 1553, although experts concur he did nothing in the way of bringing the English throne briefly under the auspices of the Universal Church.

As he lacked the will to carry out major reforms, he turned, as had popes before him, to the artists who imprinted their very souls upon the image of Renaissance Rome. He made Michaelangelo the chief architect of St. Peter's and the famous choirmaster Palestrina was given the title of chief choirmaster. These, and others too numerous to mention, were, naturally, always at the table of the pleasure-loving, homosexually inclined Holy Father.

It was in Parma that Julius met a youth called Innocenzo, with whom he became infatuated. The boy was a street-urchin with a reputation for being a vagabond, but there was something about his angelic features and curly hair that captivated the pope. Soon the boy was,

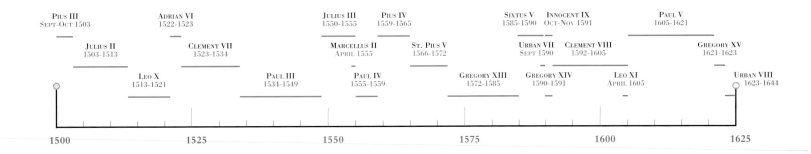

Pius III SEPT-OCT 1503		Adrian VI 1522-1523		Julius III 1550-1555	Pius IV 1559-1565		Sixtus V 1585-1590	Innocent IX OCT-NOV 1591		Paul V 1605-1621
Julius II 1503-1513		Clement VII 1523-1534		Marcellus II APRIL 1555	St. Pius V 1566-1572		Urban VII SEPT 1590	Clement VIII 1592-1605		Gregory XV 1621-1623
Leo X 1513-1521		Paul III 1534-1549		Paul IV 1555-1559		Gregory XIII 1572-1585	Gregory XIV 1590-1591	Leo XI APRIL 1605		Urban VIII 1623-1644

1500   1525   1550   1575   1600   1625

allegedly, being smuggled into the Papal Palace at night, and courtiers remarked on the forlorn expression upon the face of the Holy Father whenever his favorite friend was not around. All Rome buzzed with the gossip—even more so when the pontiff declared him a cardinal!

Julius, however, did not live long to savor his obsession. He died in 1555 from gout caused by . . . excess.

There followed a brief reign by Marcellus II from April to May 1555, when Paul IV was elected as one of the most severe of all pontiffs. Born into a wealthy Neapolitan family, he advanced through the ranks of the clergy in Rome thanks to an uncle who was a cardinal. A bishop, a papal legate, and a papal nuncio, he resigned all offices in 1524 to become a devout servant of God, existing on the most spartan of diets and spending upwards of 14 hours a day in prayer. He was made a cardinal in 1536 and six years later found a worthy management tool to, literally, whip into line dissenters to the papacy—the recently re-formed Inquisition.

"Even if my father were a heretic I would gather the wood to burn him," he once proclaimed. He was 79 when the cardinals appointed him and, although he gave approval for the torturers of the Inquisition to do their worst, he was personally devoid of the worldly temptations that lured so many before him into sins of the flesh. A puritan through and through, the only vice he indulged in was vengeance. "No one knows how to hate like our Holy Father," was a popular maxim of the day, and it was true. He issued decrees and laws, making Rome virtually a city under martial law, and imprisoning dissenters he judged guilty of heresy—generally, anyone who disagreed with him or spoke out against him—in the Castel Sant'Angelo.

Julius used the Inquisition as a tool of terror and no one was safe from it, not even the respected Cardinal Morone, a humble and pious cleric who spoke out against him. He was hideously tortured within its walls. Julius also turned his venom on

Below: Don John of Austria, in 1571 at the Battle of Lepanto, produced one of the decisive moments of Renaissance Europe. For a brief period the fleets of Spain, Genoa, and Venice forgot their emnity and combined to destroy the Ottoman fleet and stop Turkish expansion in its tracks. This last major sea battle fought by galleys was a triumph for the natural brother of Philip II of Spain.

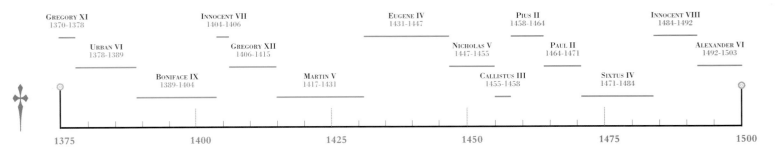

Above: The daughter of Tudor monarch Henry VIII, Queen Elizabeth I of England spent much of her reign combating the threat of Catholic invasion. In 1570 Pius V excommunicated her and ordered her deposition from the throne. This action was no longer the threat it had been, worked against Catholics in Britain, and did not sit easily with other, Catholic, monarchs who believed in the divine right of princes.

the Jews, ordering them to wear distinctive clothing, and he instructed judicial authorities to expel itinerant monks and holy men from Rome, saying only those in recognized orders were allowed to walk the streets of the Eternal City. Moreover, he instituted the Index of Forbidden Books and declared Elizabeth I of England "unfit" to be queen because of her Protestantism. Such extremism, of course, served to undermine the reforming zeal of the previous pope and hastened the advance of Protestantism in nations that hated the Roman Church and its excessiveness.

While he was busily shaping society the way he thought it ought to be, Paul ensured that his own clan lived a luxurious life. The Carafa clan was an influential brood even before their most famous son, Giapetro, Paul IV, ascended to the papacy. He bestowed many riches and honors upon his family, including making his worthless nephew Carlo a cardinal and chief political adviser in the office of Cardinal Secretary of State. Carlo ran amok in the Papal Palace, putting virtually every member of the Carafa family, and far-flung acquaintances and near relatives, onto the Vatican payroll. Even the pope could not ignore the systematic abuse of power forever, and in January 1559, with the mob growing ugly in the streets at the seemingly endless aggrandizement of his family, he stripped them of all titles and banished them forever from Rome. Carlo and another nephew were later put to death by Paul's successor for murders committed during their uncle's papal tenure.

When he died in August 1559 the papacy was as moribund and corrupt as it had ever been—yet that did not stop crowds literally dancing in the streets over his demise. Despised by the mob, they tore down statues of him and went on to storm the dungeons of the Inquisition, setting free the prisoners and hurling the instruments of torture into the Tiber.

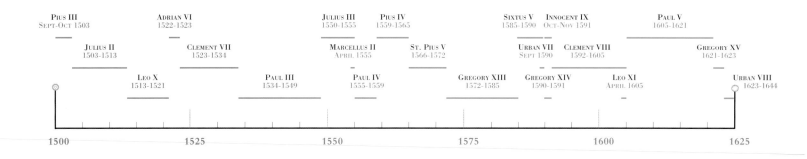

| PIUS III | ADRIAN VI | | JULIUS III | PIUS IV | | SIXTUS V | INNOCENT IX | | PAUL V |
| SEPT-OCT 1503 | 1522-1523 | | 1550-1555 | 1559-1565 | | 1585-1590 | OCT-NOV 1591 | | 1605-1621 |

| | JULIUS II | CLEMENT VII | | MARCELLUS II | ST. PIUS V | | URBAN VII | CLEMENT VIII | | GREGORY XV |
| | 1503-1513 | 1523-1534 | | APRIL 1555 | 1566-1572 | | SEPT 1590 | 1592-1605 | | 1621-1623 |

| | LEO X | PAUL III | PAUL IV | | GREGORY XIII | GREGORY XIV | LEO XI | | URBAN VIII |
| | 1513-1521 | 1534-1549 | 1555-1559 | | 1572-1585 | 1590-1591 | APRIL 1605 | | 1623-1644 |

| 1500 | 1525 | 1550 | 1575 | 1600 | 1625 |

Succession fell to Pius IV, born Giovanni Medici, but not a member of the notable House of Medici, who was elected in 1559 to reign for six years. Pius was not a very apt name for this particular pope to choose. Like Paul III, he indulged in pleasures of the flesh and fathered three children in his lifetime—in between gorging himself on enormous banquets until he was so fat he could hardly walk! In fact, when he developed something of a phobia about his weight later on in life it became a regular pastime for Romans to watch him as he struggled, puffing and panting around the streets of the ancient city, in an attempt to get fit.

A student of medicine and law, he entered the church as a young man and rose through the ranks before being appointed a cardinal. His election as pope was not unanimous and the cardinals wrangled for months before coming to their majority decision.

If the Princes of the Church were unsure of the wisdom of their choice, the Roman populace was not. Pius was a man of great charm and easy going, far different from his stern predecessor. He won great public acclaim by organizing the arrest, trial, and execution of the Carafa nephews who did the bloody bidding of Paul IV, and releasing still more heretics condemned by their patron to dungeons both inside and outside Rome.

Pius's weaknesses included his predisposition to the same old practices that clogged the arteries of the church and prevented efficient daily running of it—nepotism. He choked the Vatican with friends and relations, most of whom were content with enjoying the gilded cage rather than working toward the all-important Catholic Reformation. By the time Pius became pontiff, all of Scandinavia had broken with Rome, as had large chunks of Germany, Britain, of course, and there was disquiet still with church practices in his own country. However, he did make one lasting contribution to the church, reconvening the Council of Trent which confirmed Catholicism as the one true faith, promised further reforms, and made all ecclesiastical office holders take a declaration of faith, a measure to reduce corruption that stayed in place until the 1960s.

Below: Clement VIII reigned 1592-1605 and left the papacy stronger than when he took office. Ascetic and pious, during his pontificate the millions of Orthodox Poles joined the Catholic Church, a major victory for the Counter-Reformation, although his hopes for the reversion of England, following Elizabeth I's death in 1603, and Sweden, following the accession of Sigismund III of Poland in 1593, came to nothing. He also had to recognize Henry IV of France—a reformed Protestant—and with him the Edict of Nantes which allowed the Huguenots of France religious freedom.

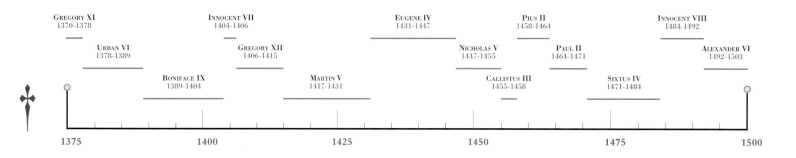

| GREGORY XI | INNOCENT VII | | EUGENE IV | PIUS II | | INNOCENT VIII |
| 1370-1378 | 1404-1406 | | 1431-1447 | 1458-1464 | | 1484-1492 |

URBAN VI 1378-1389 · GREGORY XII 1406-1415 · NICHOLAS V 1447-1455 · PAUL II 1464-1471 · ALEXANDER VI 1492-1503

BONIFACE IX 1389-1404 · MARTIN V 1417-1431 · CALLISTUS III 1455-1458 · SIXTUS IV 1471-1484

1375   1400   1425   1450   1475   1500

Pius was a zealot when it came to cleaning up the morals of the Vatican. He demanded lists from servants in the curia of any who left the Holy City after nightfall. He ordered doctors not to treat patients who would not receive the sacrament of penance. He quizzed all the cardinals one by one, extracting from them promises of piety in their future conduct.

It did not stop his need, though, for more and more money to keep up the sybaritic lifestyle of the courtiers, hangers-on, and relations who crammed into the Vatican at his behest. Finally he was forced to raise taxes again and again on the hapless citizens of the Papal States—condemning himself to the kind of hatred they displayed towards Paul IV when he died on December 9, 1565. Yet his funeral itself was lavish, one of the biggest ever staged for a supreme pontiff.

With the next pope, Pius V, the terror of the Inquisition was once more visited upon the citizens of Rome, and none knew better how to apply it—for he headed the heretic-hunters under Paul IV. Although he was later to be canonized by the church for his undeniable contribution to the Catholic Reformation and the total lack of nepotism and corruption within his court, to the citizenry it seemed as if the clock had been turned back on them yet again.

It was as Michele Ghislieri, a Dominican monk, that he became Grand Inquisitor under Paul IV. He had a particular distaste for Jews and Protestants, believing them to be the source of the decline in the power of the church.

Utterly devout, righteous, and pious, he was born into a poor family and worked as a shepherd before joining an ultra-strict Dominican order at the age of 14. He proved himself an able scholar and was ordained a priest in 1528. By the time he had worked his way through the church to be elected pope he was 62 and looked much older—contemporary portraits show him to be emaciated, with a long white beard, bald, and somewhat wizened. He continued to wear the coarse Dominican cloth under his papal finery, spent many hours alone at prayer each day, and totally banished nepotism from his court. "People were captivated by him," wrote the German Protestant historian Ludwig von Ranke. "When they saw him walking barefoot and without head covering in a procession, with an expression of deep devotion on his face, it was said that Protestants had been converted by the mere sight of him."

Pius was a zealot when it came to cleaning up the morals of the Vatican. He demanded lists from servants in the curia of any who left the Holy City after nightfall. He ordered doctors not to treat patients who would not receive the sacrament of penance. He quizzed all the cardinals one by one, extracting from them promises of piety in their future conduct. He examined in depth the curia and papal finances, putting an end to the squandering that had drained the papacy in successive reigns. Pius was not a toothless tiger either—one cardinal he found guilty of moral laxity was ordered to spend the rest of his life in a Jesuit monastery receiving spiritual care therein from the brotherhood. Lowlier priests were made to attend weekly lectures given by him on philosophy and theology, and were instructed to attend mass at least three times each week.

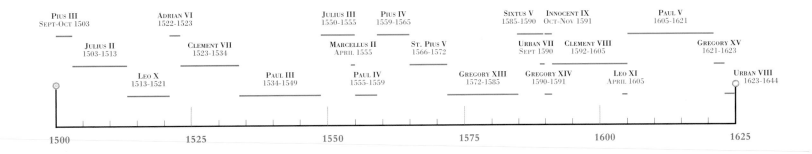

| PIUS III | ADRIAN VI | | JULIUS III | PIUS IV | | SIXTUS V | INNOCENT IX | | PAUL V |
| SEPT-OCT 1503 | 1522-1523 | | 1550-1555 | 1559-1565 | | 1585-1590 | OCT-NOV 1591 | | 1605-1621 |

| JULIUS II | | CLEMENT VII | | MARCELLUS II | ST. PIUS V | | URBAN VII | CLEMENT VIII | | GREGORY XV |
| 1503-1513 | | 1523-1534 | | APRIL 1555 | 1566-1572 | | SEPT 1590 | 1592-1605 | | 1621-1623 |

| LEO X | | PAUL III | | PAUL IV | | GREGORY XIII | GREGORY XIV | | LEO XI | | URBAN VIII |
| 1513-1521 | | 1534-1549 | | 1555-1559 | | 1572-1585 | 1590-1591 | | APRIL 1605 | | 1623-1644 |

1500   1525   1550   1575   1600   1625

He worked hard to fulfill the pledges of the Council of Trent and published the Roman Catechism, the written beliefs of the Catholic Church, that would stay in effect until a new one was published in 1994 by Pope John Paul II.

His efforts at checking Protestantism were largely ineffective. He dismissed Elizabeth I of England from the church and called her reign unlawful; the fact that these were mere words with nothing to back them up illustrated how much the power of Rome had declined. On the other hand, in Germany he allowed some prelates to hold more than one office, a bid to exclude Protestants from benefices, especially in northern Germany where the Protestant faith was strongest. He was also notably successful in one other field, stemming the advance of Islam. He negotiated an alliance with papal rivals Spain and Venice in a "Catholic League" and lived to see a massive defeat of the Turks at the battle of Lepanto.

Although the populace feared the Inquisition and were saddened that Pius V had reinstated it, the practice itself must be viewed in the context of the times. Pius and his contemporaries lived in a world of religious absolutes and anyone dismissing them or defaming them would be seen in the same light as a drug pusher or child molester in today's society. "A generation which is witnessing widespread demands for the execution of illegal drug dealers is hardly well-positioned to condemn people who used the ultimate penalty against the purveyors of ideas considered, in their day, to be equally dangerous to society," said American author John Jay Hughes, an expert on the papacy.

Pius V believed in the moral righteousness of his crusade to stamp out corruption and halt the spread of Protestantism. That the men who languished in the dungeons of the Inquisition were often cultured and of noble birth cut no ice with him. Additionally, there was often just as much persecution carried out by the Protestants to salve the conscience of the Inquisitors. All knew the story of the 40 Spanish and Portuguese Jesuits who, when traveling to Brazil as missionaries in 1569, were captured by a Huguenot—Protestant—admiral who first tortured them and then drowned them as "heralds of papist superstitions."

For the church, Pius's reforming zeal cannot be understated. He was made a saint in the eighteenth century, his expulsion of Jews and Protestants from Papal States notwithstanding. Papal expert Ludwig von Pastor said of him:

Above: Pope Gregory XIII, best known today for the reforms of the calendar published in 1582, was an important figure in the Counter-Reformation. A significant lawyer, he attended the Council of Trent and played a major role in drafting its decrees. He became pope in 1572 and promoted Catholic colleges and learning, as well as missionary work by the Jesuits. His outlook—and that of many Catholics of the period—was typified when he had the bells rung and Te Deums sung on hearing of news of the St. Bartholemew's Day Massacre of Huguenots in France.

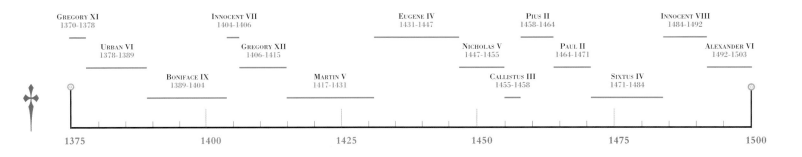

GREGORY XI
1370-1378

INNOCENT VII
1404-1406

EUGENE IV
1431-1447

PIUS II
1458-1464

INNOCENT VIII
1484-1492

URBAN VI
1378-1389

GREGORY XII
1406-1415

NICHOLAS V
1447-1455

PAUL II
1464-1471

ALEXANDER VI
1492-1503

BONIFACE IX
1389-1404

MARTIN V
1417-1431

CALLISTUS III
1455-1458

SIXTUS IV
1471-1484

1375   1400   1425   1450   1475   1500

The civil service virtually broke down, authorities were not paid and anarchy became the order of the day. Many noble families were at the forefront of the terror, disgruntled by the loss of lands and the burden of taxation which weighed down on them. It led to bands of armed brigands instigating a reign of terror that cost many lives and caused much resentment among the masses.

"By his unflagging zeal the dead letter of Trent became a living force and changed the whole appearance of the church. It is with deep emotion that one may see today in the church of St. Maria Maggiore, among the relics of the great pope, the printed copy of the Tridentine decrees which he used. This little book became in his hands the lever by means of which he uprooted from its bed a whole world of disorders."

He died on May 1, 1572, age 68. The people who feared him so much at the beginning of his reign wept in the streets upon his death, grateful at the cleansing he had carried out at the Vatican.

It was left to Gregory XIII, recognized as the last of the great Renaissance popes, to carry on his work. Best known for his reforms of the modern calendar, he entered the priesthood late, spending his youth as a student then law professor, fathering a son who would later become a governor of the papal fortress Castel Sant' Angelo. It was in 1539 that he underwent his own personal renaissance, forswearing forever the pleasures of the flesh. Three years later he was ordained into the priesthood and worked his way into the Vatican by reason of his legal knowledge. Popes Paul III and IV were so impressed with his acumen that they entrusted him with much notary work on their behalf. He finally was appointed papal legate to Spain where he won the respect and admiration of King Philip—a bond that served him well because Philip influenced the cardinals in their decision to appoint him pope on May 14, 1572.

Easygoing, kindly, and devout, he had been a prime force behind the negotiations at the Council of Trent and was determined that the Vatican should not slip back into the bad old ways. He saw education as the key to the church's future and founded many teaching seminaries, colleges and missionary schools, instructing all to spread the word of the Universal Church as far as the New World and the Far East. Fascinated on an intellectual level with the calendar—Rome kept time on the inaccurate Julian calendar that had been in place since 46BC and was notoriously out of sync—he formed a committee that came up with the Gregorian Calendar, shaving six hours off of the Julian system.

He also initiated the system of sending permanent papal ambassadors, known as apostolic nuncios, to all the Catholic courts in Europe. These envoys were charged with a dual responsibility: to oversee the spiritual needs of the church in the country of their posting and to defend the land interests, or temporal power, of the Papal States against any monarch with an eye to acquiring them for himself. With certain adaptations, the nuncio system operates to this day.

Such educational and spiritual projects—he built 23 colleges in Rome alone—were coupled with large papal expenditure on the political front. He strengthened the Catholic League that had polished off the Turks, but at great cost. Soon he was faced with the dilemma that

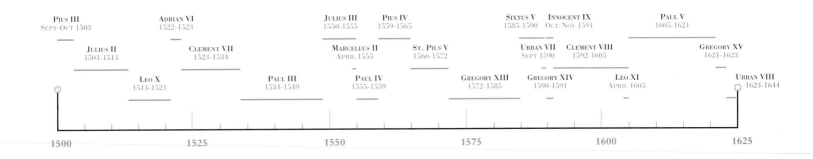

| PIUS III | | ADRIAN VI | | | JULIUS III | PIUS IV | | | SIXTUS V | INNOCENT IX | | PAUL V | |
| SEPT–OCT 1503 | | 1522–1523 | | | 1550–1555 | 1559–1565 | | | 1585–1590 | OCT–NOV 1591 | | 1605–1621 | |

| | JULIUS II | | CLEMENT VII | | | MARCELLUS II | ST. PIUS V | | | URBAN VII | CLEMENT VIII | | GREGORY XV |
| | 1503–1513 | | 1523–1534 | | | APRIL 1555 | 1566–1572 | | | SEPT 1590 | 1592–1605 | | 1621–1623 |

| | | LEO X | | PAUL III | | PAUL IV | | GREGORY XIII | GREGORY XIV | LEO XI | | URBAN VIII |
| | | 1513–1521 | | 1534–1549 | | 1555–1559 | | 1572–1585 | 1590–1591 | APRIL 1605 | | 1623–1644 |

| 1500 | 1525 | 1550 | 1575 | 1600 | 1625 |

had confronted virtually every Holy Father that had gone before him: how to consolidate and spread the power of the church while there was no money left in the bank.

He turned to the Papal States to raise taxation levels, but it was a policy that led to disaster. The civil service virtually broke down, authorities were not paid, and anarchy became the order of the day. Many noble families were at the forefront of the terror, disgruntled by the loss of lands and the burden of taxation that weighed down on them. It led to bands of armed brigands instigating a reign of terror that cost many lives and caused much resentment among the masses. These bandits roamed in bands sometimes thousands strong, turning whole cities into playgrounds of pillage, rape, and murder. But Gregory was in a financial morass, creaking under a burden of debt with no perceived way out of it. His reign of the Papal States was described by one historian as "execrable" but it was due more to fiscal constraints than any malice toward the population. It would be left to another pope to destroy the anarchy swamping the Papal States, long after Gregory had passed away in 1585.

Below: St. Peter's Square: the expenses of the papacy—including the building programs of various pontiffs—led to increased taxation of the Papal States and Gregory XIII's financial problems.

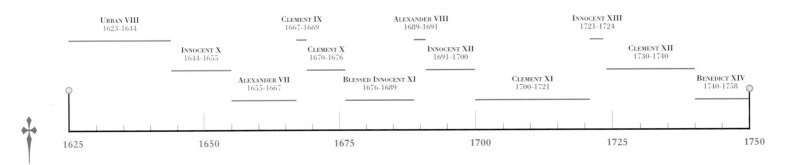

URBAN VIII 1623-1644		CLEMENT IX 1667-1669		ALEXANDER VIII 1689-1691		INNOCENT XIII 1721-1724
INNOCENT X 1644-1655		CLEMENT X 1670-1676		INNOCENT XII 1691-1700		CLEMENT XII 1730-1740
ALEXANDER VII 1655-1667		BLESSED INNOCENT XI 1676-1689		CLEMENT XI 1700-1721		BENEDICT XIV 1740-1758

1625   1650   1675   1700   1725   1750

THE POPES OF THE AGE OF ENLIGHTENMENT

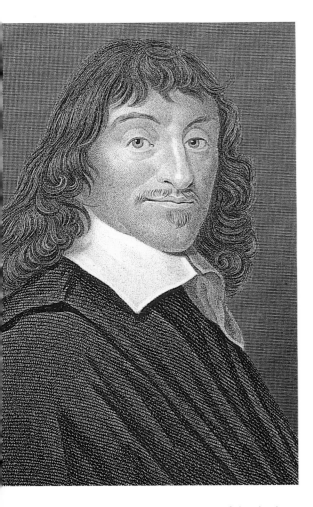

Above: Rene Descartes, one of the thinkers of the new age, who would call into question man's—and the church's—role on earth and lead him into conflict with a papacy eager to keep hold of the reins of power.

GREAT CHANGES were to sweep the world at the advent of the seventeenth century. New, radical ideas were being espoused by writers and thinkers. Soon words like "democracy" and "rights of man" would be uttered on the lips of citizens now quick to question the divine right of their rulers and churchmen. For the papacy it was to be a period of challenge and doubt, a struggle to maintain papal supremacy in the face of writers such as Rene Descartes, scientists such as Isaac Newton, philosophers such as Francis Bacon and John Locke. With supreme faith in "rational man," they set the educated classes to questioning spiritual authority, the dogma of the church, its role in a society that they believed man alone, not God, could shape. In the light of such forces it was no wonder the papacy felt power slipping away.

The Age of Enlightenment did not have a very auspicious dawn in Rome. Leo XI, appointed by the cardinals on April 1, 1605, reigned for a mere 27 days before he succumbed to a cold caught while settling into the papal palace. A member of the famed Renaissance family of the Medicis, he was a nephew of Leo X and served for some years as the ambassador to Rome of Grand Duke Cosimo of Florence. It was in this service that he came under the patronage of Pope Gregory XIII who made him Bishop of Pistoia in 1573. A year later he was made the influential Bishop of Florence and a cardinal nine years later. A supremely well educated man, there were great hopes for him before the chill struck him down.

He was succeeded by Paul V, who managed to keep healthy enough to reign from 1605 until 1621. A member of the elite Borghese family, Paul was a law student in Perugia and Padua before taking his legal knowledge into the Vatican. He was an expert in Canon law and rose steadily through the curia until he was appointed a cardinal in 1596. He was the choice for pope at the conclave following Leo XI's untimely end because of his strong legal brain and his devotion to the cause of consolidating papal power. To this end he upset many bishops upon his appointment by ordering them out of Rome—where they had a habit of

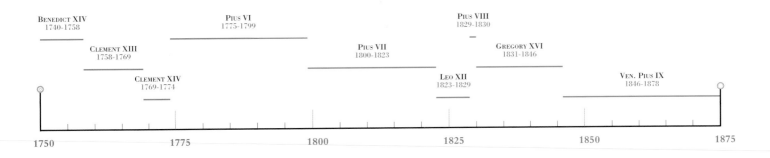

BENEDICT XIV 1740-1758	PIUS VI 1775-1799		PIUS VIII 1829-1830	
CLEMENT XIII 1758-1769		PIUS VII 1800-1823	GREGORY XVI 1831-1846	
CLEMENT XIV 1769-1774		LEO XII 1823-1829	VEN. PIUS IX 1846-1878

| 1750 | 1775 | 1800 | 1825 | 1850 | 1875 |

lingering around the papal court to enjoy its splendors—and back to their parishes where he knew the fight had to be carried on for the hearts and minds of the flock. He also canonized a large number of saints, many of the them popular figures like Ignatius Loyola, something he hoped would make the peasantry realize he—and therefore the church—was at one with them.

He learned the hard way that papal power was not what it used to be when he tried to regain control of some Papal States. France stepped in, then Spain, and the pope was forced to realize that spiritual, not temporal, power was now the way of the future. He tried his best to prevent the outbreak of the Thirty Years War, which raged between German Protestant princes and European powers between 1618 and 1648. Mainly a dynastic and territorial squabble, it was nevertheless a bloody and destructive war that Paul failed to stop. That he even tried to do so was a measure of his compassion, because he had no time for Protestants, princes or not.

After his death in January 1621 Gregory XV was appointed by *acclamatio*, the spontaneous unanimous decision of the cardinals in the conclave. He reigned for just two years, but in this time the Bologna native founded the Sacred Congregation of the Propagation of the Faith, a mission-control for overseeing and directing all missionary work overseas. He modernized the secret ballot procedures for voting in a pope and canonized several saints, including Teresa of Avila.

Modernism was not something that duly concerned Urban VIII, Gregory XV's successor, who reigned from 1623 to 1644. Urban, born Maffeo Barberini, brought back into the papal palaces nepotism, splendor, and living large. He was a great patron of the arts and he salted away a goodly portion of Vatican treasure to finance his lavish ways.

He was, in many ways, a curious character. He spoke out fiercely

Above: Isaac Newton (1642-1727), the British scientist who discovered the basic laws of gravity. Typical of the new age of enlightenment, the Unitarian Newton and so many other rational thinkers were Protestants. The struggle of the catholic rationalists to be heard created the impression that the papacy was against change at any price.

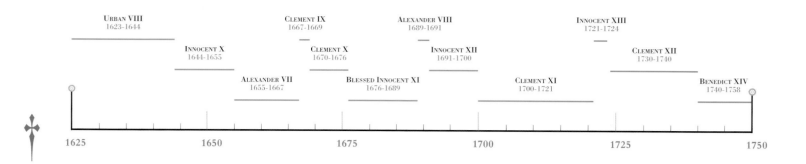

URBAN VIII 1623-1644		CLEMENT IX 1667-1669		ALEXANDER VIII 1689-1691		INNOCENT XIII 1721-1724	
INNOCENT X 1644-1655		CLEMENT X 1670-1676		INNOCENT XII 1691-1700		CLEMENT XII 1730-1740	
ALEXANDER VII 1655-1667		BLESSED INNOCENT XI 1676-1689		CLEMENT XI 1700-1721		BENEDICT XIV 1740-1758	

1625   1650   1675   1700   1725   1750

Above: Pope Urban VIII, a high-living nepotist whose reign was overshadowed by the bloody Thirty Years War.

Right: The battleground of the Thirty Years War was Germany and the conflict was a continuation of the regular strife between the emperor and the princes, but with massive religious overtones. The Treaty of Westphalia, which ended the war, was not to the liking of the papacy in the form of Innocent X, who felt that it was too concessionary to the French and Protestants.

against the slave trade, the first pontiff to do so, calling the shipment of human beings "a crime against God." But as pontiff he was obliged to sentence his friend, the astronomer Galileo, to imprisonment for his theories on the movements of the galaxy as they contradicted accepted clerical teachings. He was intellectual enough to know that, as he sentenced him—with a warning to the Inquisition that he was not to be tortured—he was making the church take a huge backward step. It was not until 1992 that Pope John Paul II made a formal apology for the trial.

Ill-advised by his power-hungry nephews, he went to war with the duke of Parma between 1642 and 1644 in a bid to regain papal lands that might finance the high living he so enjoyed in Rome. To make cannon for his assaults on the fortifications of Parma he stripped the famed Pantheon of bronze—an act that outraged Romans. They were even more outraged when he lost the war, lost several thousand men, and lost almost the entire papal treasury! The scene of dancing and rejoicing in the streets upon his death in 1644 is a chapter in the history of the papacy the Vatican does not dwell on.

Another five popes followed before Alexander VIII was appointed in 1689. The church still had not come to grips with the erosion of its influence over society. If one pope lived piously and frugally, the next was lavish and extravagant. If one sought to expand the church's teachings, another merely tried to seize papal lands again to raise money. It was a struggle for the right path that was to dominate the papacy for the next 200 years.

Alexander shared many of the faults of Urban VIII and nepotism was to rule at his court. Two of his nephews received exalted positions as cardinals and secretary of state, while other benefices—which always translated into land or money—were bestowed on cousins, nieces, and other far-flung relations. But he was not without ability, even though he came to power at the age of 79. He achieved a reconciliation with the King of France over territories in France that were restored to the papacy, and quashed movements sprouting in Rome that questioned the primacy of the papacy. He reduced a crushing tax burden on the population of Rome, improved social conditions, and procured from many European notables priceless manuscripts, which he donated to the Vatican library. Although he was a confirmed nepotist, he nevertheless lived quite frugally.

Innocent XII, who followed, had been a Jesuit scholar and was, in consequence, a supremely devout and humble man. He reigned from 1691 until 1700, but in that time he fought fiercely against nepotism, finally issuing a decree that only one relative should be allowed entry to

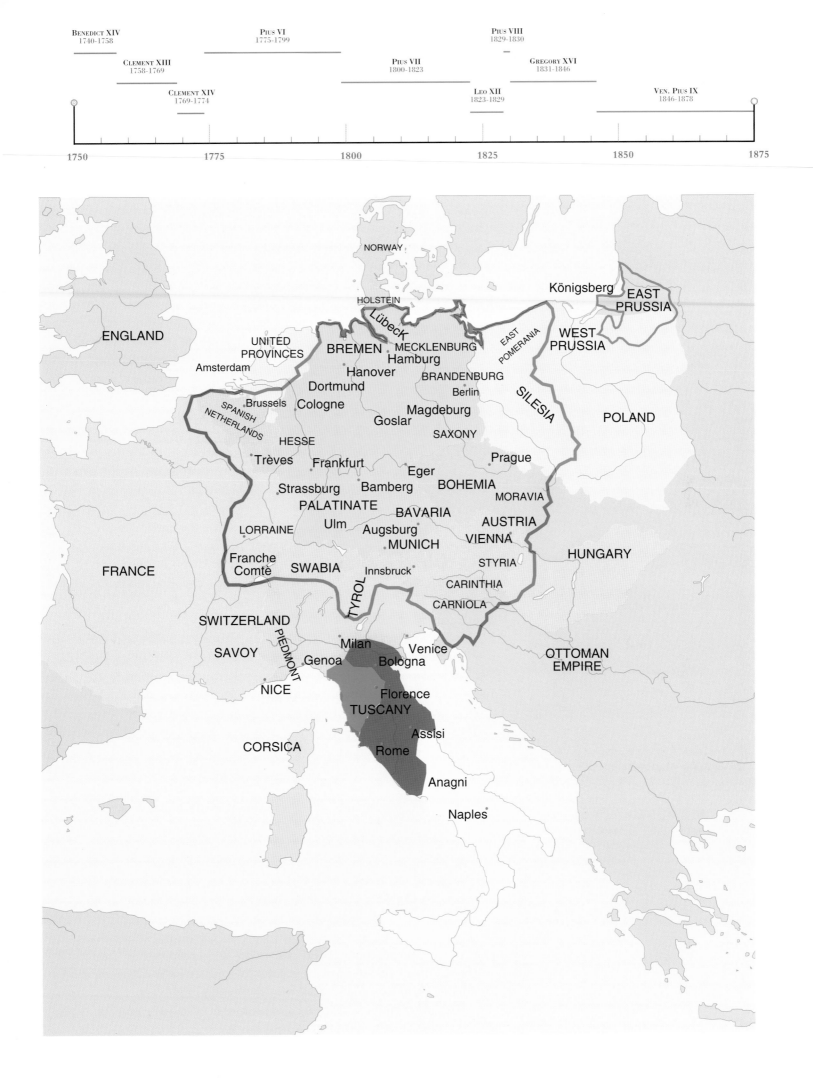

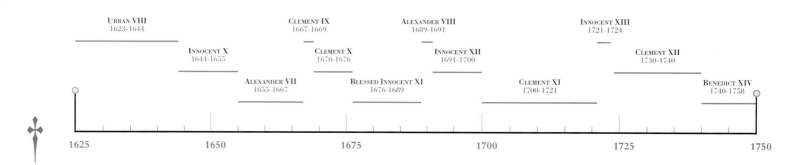

URBAN VIII 1623-1644		CLEMENT IX 1667-1669		ALEXANDER VIII 1689-1691		INNOCENT XIII 1721-1724	
INNOCENT X 1644-1655		CLEMENT X 1670-1676		INNOCENT XII 1691-1700		CLEMENT XII 1730-1740	
ALEXANDER VII 1655-1667		BLESSED INNOCENT XI 1676-1689		CLEMENT XI 1700-1721		BENEDICT XIV 1740-1758	

1625   1650   1675   1700   1725   1750

Above: Clement IX (1667-1669) had a short reign before dying of a stroke. Appointed because he was acceptable to the two strongest Catholic powers of the day, France and Spain, his main interest was to recover Crete from the Turks. Despite initial successes, the expedition fell to pieces when the French contingent abandoned the operation.

the papal inner circle. "The family of the pope should not profit from lands or titles," he declared. He also launched a cleanup of the curia and set about tax reforms, which earned him great favor with the public.

In Benedict XIII, who was appointed pope in 1724, the papacy found a truly saintly man. Born into the famous Orsini family, which had produced many popes down the years, he was drawn to the religious life at an early age, entering into a Dominican order when he was 16. Pietro Francesco Orsini proved himself a brilliant scholar and achieved a professorship when he was just 21. He held various church posts before being elected a cardinal in 1672. He became pope after a nine-week conclave and set about living in the Vatican's palaces in the style of the humblest parish priest. He was repelled by the grandeur and the pomp, the extravagant habits of the papal court which stronger willed men than he had been unable to break.

He wore a hair shirt under his vestments and acted at all times with utter piety. James Elmwood, a papal writer, said:

"He was intent on being a broom but few of the cardinals and bishops wanted to be swept. Had he had good advisers he could have done so much more. As it was, he ended up being surrounded by corrupt men who turned his goodness in on himself to the point where he was rendered ineffectual."

The pope spent his days at prayer, visiting the sick and the needy, and hearing confessions personally in St. Peter's. While he busied himself with this minor reform of the curia or that minor reform of the cardinals—forbidding them, for instance, to wear wigs—Cardinal Niccolo Coscia, in charge of the treasury, was milking it rotten. He organized a system of selling offices for cash, which was then divided up between him and a coterie of equally corrupt bishops and cardinals who were his lieutenants. Vatican historians concur that the saintly Benedict knew nothing of the scheming until his death—and by then it was too late. Clement XII took charge, like so many of his predecessors, of a papacy tottering on the verge of bankruptcy once more.

In 1730 Clement, born Lorenzo Corsini in Florence, was nearly eighty when he was appointed by the cardinals. Two years into his ten-year reign he went completely blind and spent most of the remainder of his term conducting affairs from his bed. Nevertheless, he took a keen interest in reviving papal finances—through taxation, the revival of the city lottery which gave a portion of profits to the papacy, and a reduction of the Vatican budget. He also won wholesale public approval for his prosecution of the rogue treasurer Coscia, who finally ended up in the firm clutches of the Inquisition for his swindles.

Clement, too, was shown the blunt edge of papal power in dealing with the Papal States. Spain wanted territory and men and decided to

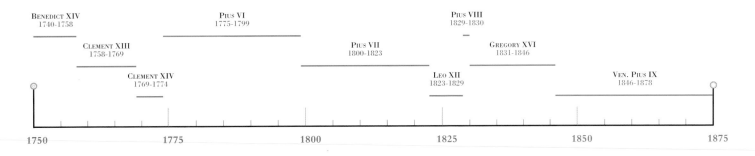

BENEDICT XIV 1740-1758		PIUS VI 1775-1799			PIUS VIII 1829-1830	
CLEMENT XIII 1758-1769				PIUS VII 1800-1823		GREGORY XVI 1831-1846
	CLEMENT XIV 1769-1774				LEO XII 1823-1829	VEN. PIUS IX 1846-1878

| 1750 | 1775 | 1800 | 1825 | 1850 | 1875 |

take them. Rome protested and the protests were ignored, leaving Clement ashamed and rioters in the streets. To appease them he made humiliating concessions to the aggressors and built what has become one of the most famous landmarks of modern Rome—the Trevi fountain—from his own purse. As to furthering papal power, he died before getting a chance to be a shaper of any solid destiny.

In his successor, Benedict XIV, the papacy received the first man who recognized the power of the enlightenment. Rather than try to stop it, in some areas he embraced it, becoming a firm friend of the great thinker Voltaire and ordering curia officials to exercise restraint in adding new works to the Vatican's Index of Forbidden Books. Curiously, however, he did not include Voltaire's works among those to be left off, considering his outpourings acceptable to his ears but not to the masses! Benedict, born Prospero Lorenzo Lambertini, was a cheerful, uncomplicated fellow who was moderate in outlook and tolerant of many opinions. Leaders as diverse as Frederick the Great, King of Prussia, and Britain's Horace Walpole were welcomed at his court. He extended courtesies to Protestant countries and reasoned that the papacy must be accommodating as changes were all around and that the hierarchy "ignored them at its peril."

To keep his bishops up-to-speed on papal policy, he revived the practice of sending out encyclicals, or circular letters, to them wherever they were in the world, informing them of current theological practices, doctrinal updates, and a plethora of church-related issues. It was his way of trying to keep those in the remotest parts of the world informed about the great issues that were abroad in the new, enlightened times. Vatican historians, consequently, regard him as one of the best of the eighteenth century pontiffs, a man whose passing in May 1758 plunged most of Europe into mourning.

Clement XIII, supreme pontiff from 1758 until 1769, spent most of his reign trying to protect the Jesuit Orders from attacks by the ruling houses of Europe. The Jesuits were both feared and hated—feared because of their talent and independence, hated for their unswerving devotion to Rome. Many saw them as underminers of a national will, although this was due more to paranoia than fact. They were libeled as being slave traders, corrupters of children, inciters of revolution and dissent in countries where they established missions. Portugal was first to kick them out with France threatening to do the same unless they radically changed their ways. The pope refused, aghast at what he saw as further attacks on the church, but worse was to come. Representatives of most of the European monarchies came to Rome to petition him for change, which he refused to sanction. He died of a massive stroke on February 2, 1769.

It was left to the next pope, Clement XIV, finally to suppress the Jesuits. A Franciscan monk, the pope was under no illusion that he was

Frederick the Great (Above) and Horace Walpole of Britain (Below)—one an autocratic monarch, the other an enlightened elected leader. They were emblematic of the powers in Europe that would shape destinies of peoples far more than the church in the coming years.

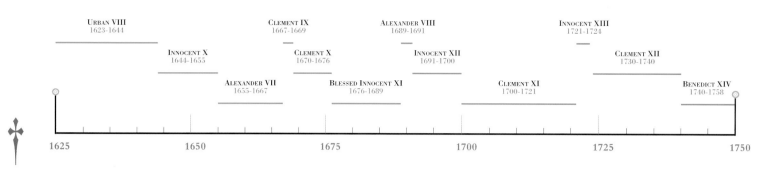

URBAN VIII 1623-1644		CLEMENT IX 1667-1669		ALEXANDER VIII 1689-1691		INNOCENT XIII 1721-1724	
INNOCENT X 1644-1655		CLEMENT X 1670-1676		INNOCENT XII 1691-1700		CLEMENT XII 1730-1740	
ALEXANDER VII 1655-1667		BLESSED INNOCENT XI 1676-1689		CLEMENT XI 1700-1721		BENEDICT XIV 1740-1758	

| 1625 | 1650 | 1675 | 1700 | 1725 | 1750 |

elected to stamp out the Jesuit order once and for all—enormous pressure from the monarchies had been put on the cardinals in the conclave to elect him for expressly that purpose. For the monarchies the Jesuits represented a throwback to a different age, an age of consummate papal power. Things had changed; they were used to having the civil authorities in their lands having a say in appointing bishops and other officials of the church. The Jesuits supported and obeyed only the pope. They were elitist and secretive and that angered the Catholic kings who thought their word the last in all matters. Finally the pope, against his own wishes, gave in and disbanded the order on May 19, 1769. Papal historian John Hughes called it a bitter blow for the papacy. In his book *Pontiffs Who Shaped History* he writes:

"While the Jesuits were not blameless in the troubles which came upon them, their suppression was a grave injustice, and for the papacy a disaster. For the pope to dissolve, at the behest of jealous Catholic monarchs, the one religious order, which, more than all others, upheld a high view of papal independence, was an act of craven weakness. The loss to Catholic missionary works in the New World especially, and to Catholic education, was enormous. Ironically, the two countries in which the society's suppression was never promulgated, thus permitting it to maintain a shadow existence until its restoration by Pius VII in 1814, were ruled by non-Catholic sovereigns; the Protestant King of Prussia and the Orthodox Czar of Russia. Both regarded the continued existence of Jesuit schools as a matter of national self-interest."

Another papal scholar, J. Kelly, said: "The reign of Clement XIV saw the prestige of the papacy sink to its lowest level for centuries." There was even worse to come.

Pius VI ascended to the papacy upon Clement's death in 1774. He reigned through a turbulent period of world history which saw the French Revolution, the rise of Napoleon, and the defeat of the British in America. He was a deeply cultured man, fond of high-living but cautious with the papal purse strings as he knew that rough times lay in store for the papacy. The strong-arm tactics that the monarchies had exerted on his predecessors showed him that papal power was a dwindling force in the new age.

He began his reign with a series of public works in Rome, carrying out extensive improvements to the Vatican and to public museums. It was not long, however, before he had to turn his attention to more pressing matters—the spread of anti-papal secularism from France and the Holy Roman Empire promoting the theory that the state alone should be supreme arbiter of church power. The two biggest secular movements, Febronianism and Josephism, had

BENEDICT XIV
1740-1758

PIUS VI
1775-1799

PIUS VIII
1829-1830

CLEMENT XIII
1758-1769

PIUS VII
1800-1823

GREGORY XVI
1831-1846

CLEMENT XIV
1769-1774

LEO XII
1823-1829

VEN. PIUS IX
1846-1878

1750   1775   1800   1825   1850   1875

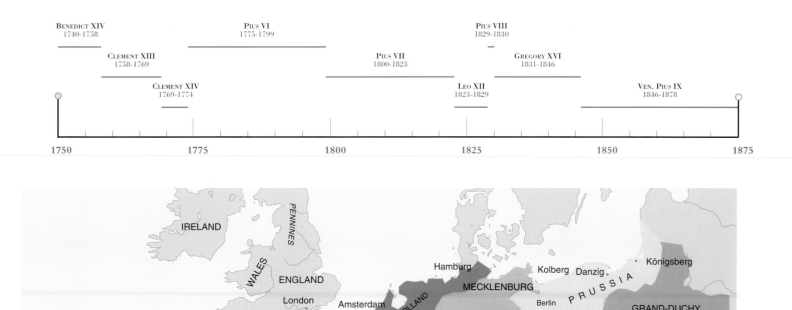

strong support in Austria, France, and Germany. As Pius grappled to deal with this, another powder keg went off—the French Revolution. Overnight the existing order of things was turned on its head as the church struggled to find a role, wedged between representing the oppressed people and the established Catholic monarchy. The anti-church revolutionary government in France laughed in the face of Pius's attempts to forge diplomatic contacts. Two thousand priests were executed in the terror instituted by Robespierre, and many more imprisoned. It led Pius to institute a decree condemning the Civil Constitution and the Revolution.

In 1796 the brilliant French military upstart Napoleon Bonaparte marched into Papal States in the north of Italy with his citizen army,

Above: Europe under Napoleon.

Left: Robespierre was the leader of the terrors of the early French Revolution, which led thousands of Catholic priests to the tumbrel. He would himself meet death on July 28, 1794 at the guillotine.

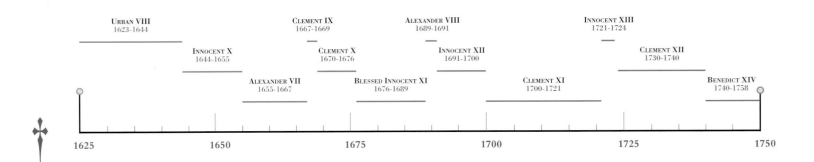

URBAN VIII 1623-1644		CLEMENT IX 1667-1669		ALEXANDER VIII 1689-1691		INNOCENT XIII 1721-1724	
INNOCENT X 1644-1655		CLEMENT X 1670-1676		INNOCENT XII 1691-1700		CLEMENT XII 1730-1740	
ALEXANDER VII 1655-1667		BLESSED INNOCENT XI 1676-1689		CLEMENT XI 1700-1721		BENEDICT XIV 1740-1758	

| 1625 | 1650 | 1675 | 1700 | 1725 | 1750 |

Above: Napoleon, the warlord of the new age, whose conquests made him the mightiest force on the continent of Europe and whose prejudices led him to try to humiliate Rome at every turn.

plundering great works of art and seizing huge tracts of land. While Pius skillfully halted the armies with a fragile peace, they stayed put and were a permanent threat to Rome.

That threat became reality in 1797 when a French general, visiting the city, was killed by a berserk member of the pontifical guard protesting the occupation of papal lands. On February 15, 1798, Napoleon sent in his troops, deposed Pius, and sent him into exile in a monastery in Florence. The scenes of his leaving moved even non-believers to tears of admiration. Romans knelt in the rain before his carriage, a silent, somber mass who wept as the Holy Father passed by, never to return. Napoleon's puppets in Rome proclaimed a republic and later schemed to kidnap the pope, which they carried out in the spring of 1799, carting him over the Alps to Valence, France, where he died in August of that year, still refusing to recognize the authority of Napoleon over him or his countrymen.

Calling a conclave to elect a new pontiff presented a great problem. Napoleon had seen to it that no pontiff could be elected in Rome, so the cardinals chose Venice, mercifully still free from French troops. The conclave took three months to elect a new pope, but when they did, they chose the right man for the job. In Luigi Barnaba Chiaramonti, to become Pius VII, the cardinals found a man of principle, devotion, and spectacular skill. In the worst days of humiliation and imprisonment that were to befall him under Napoleon, he showed true courage and determination, never faltering and never bending.

Trained as a professor of theology, he ascended to the papal throne during one of the worst crises that had ever faced it. Napoleon was master in France and exerting his influence everywhere. He had brought the French Church under his will, sacking the Bourbon bishops who served the ancien regime, as well as those of the Constitutional Church, formed in the first heady days after the revolution. Napoleon proposed to the new pope, who arrived in Rome in July 1800, that if Pius would recognize his actions and give his appointments the approval of the Holy See, he would endeavor to return papal lands to him. Pius faced stiff opposition from conservatives within the Vatican who objected to a pact with the man they saw as the devil incarnate, the persecutor of clerics, and the thief of valuable church property. Napoleon grew angry at delays and threatened in the end to break away completely from Rome, citing Henry VIII of England as an example of what he intended to do if his terms were not met. Pius knew that, effectively, he would be turning over control of the French church to the French state, but there was little he could do. The Concordat was signed in 1801—and broken a year later when Napoleon published his "Organic Articles," a declaration of stringent state control way beyond what he agreed originally with the pope.

The articles stipulated that papal communications with the church

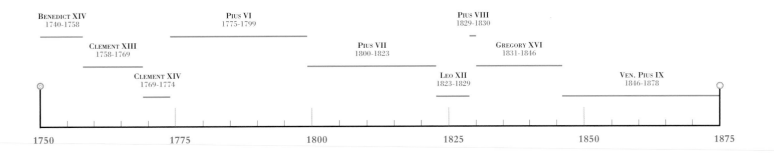

BENEDICT XIV 1740-1758		PIUS VI 1775-1799		PIUS VIII 1829-1830	
CLEMENT XIII 1758-1769		PIUS VII 1800-1823		GREGORY XVI 1831-1846	
CLEMENT XIV 1769-1774		LEO XII 1823-1829		VEN. PIUS IX 1846-1878	

| 1750 | 1775 | 1800 | 1825 | 1850 | 1875 |

were to be subject to government scrutiny at all levels. Seminaries were to be under state control too, bishops administered by local prefects, and police spies were instructed to report any breaches of the regulations.

In an effort to further appease Napoleon, the pope agreed to travel to Paris in 1804 to crown him Emperor of the French. Pius wrestled with his conscience on this, but thought that a face-to-face meeting might make Napoleon soften the Organic Articles or allow other concessions. During his time in Paris the pope was repeatedly subjected to numerous small humiliations, including being given a room in a palace overlooking the execution spot where many priests were put to death during the revolution. Napoleon also degraded him by actually crowning himself at the ceremonies over which he presided. But the pope remained steadfast on his refusal to recognize the civil marriage of Napoleon to his consort Josephine, and a religious ceremony was carried out before the coronation. Despite all the problems, Pius's stay in Paris was not wholly negative: from the French people at least, if not from their emperor, he received tributes and adoration the like of which he had never enjoyed in Rome. He did not return to the Vatican until April 1805.

Napoleon had not finished yet with His Holiness. His grandiose schemes of conquest would, he informed Pius, require the blessing of the papacy. Napoleon harbored dreams of subduing both England and the vastness of Imperial Russia, both nations with a church that did not adhere to Rome. The emperor thought Pius would be swift to back him in a crusade to bring "the voice of St. Peter to the heretic lands." Pius merely informed him that there were millions of Catholics at liberty to practice their religion in these countries and that he wanted no part in becoming an enemy of such rich and powerful empires. Napoleon's revenge on his intransigence was swift; he sent troops in 1808 to occupy Rome, aiming his cannon at the pope's personal apartments in the Quirinal Palace. He also expelled 15 cardinals he considered to be most hostile to French interests.

The pope was nothing if not brave. He did not flinch in the face of such intimidation, but his own courage was blunted by the man who held all the weapons and most of the territories of continental Europe. In May 1809 Napoleon annexed all the Papal States to France to, as he termed it, "end for all time the Abusive confusion of temporal and spiritual power." The French tricolor was hoisted above the Castel Sant'Angelo and Rome was declared a "Free Imperial City" with the pope allowed to remain as spiritual head, but stripped of all temporal power. The pope reacted in the only way he could—he issued a papal bull that excommunicated the Emperor and those servants who had helped him "rob the patrimony of Peter."

In the early hours of July 6, as Napoleon faced the Austrian troops massing at Wagram, the pope was spirited out of Rome on his orders in

Above: Pope Pius VII, a devout and humble man, who was degraded by Napoleon in Paris and later imprisoned by him. But he never backed down and lived to see his tormentor defeated at Waterloo.

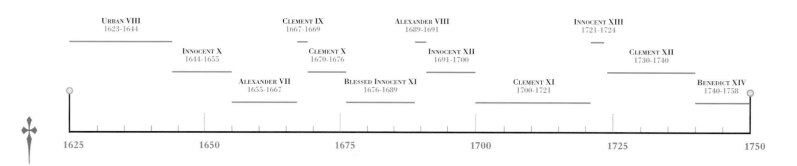

| URBAN VIII | CLEMENT IX | ALEXANDER VIII | INNOCENT XIII |
| 1623-1644 | 1667-1669 | 1689-1691 | 1721-1724 |

| INNOCENT X | CLEMENT X | INNOCENT XII | CLEMENT XII |
| 1644-1655 | 1670-1676 | 1691-1700 | 1730-1740 |

| ALEXANDER VII | BLESSED INNOCENT XI | CLEMENT XI | BENEDICT XIV |
| 1655-1667 | 1676-1689 | 1700-1721 | 1740-1758 |

| 1625 | 1650 | 1675 | 1700 | 1725 | 1750 |

Above: Josephine, mistress to Napoleon. Pius VII's refusal to recognize their union was another cause of great fury to the emperor.

a sealed coach and taken first to Grenoble and then to the episcopal palace at Savona, not far from Genoa. He was to remain there under house arrest for the next three years. "All over the world," said John Jay Hughes, "the ordinary business of the Church ground to a halt." As bishops and priests died there was no-one to elect new ones. All the pope's mail was censored, his visits were restricted and any attempts at carrying on as the way the cardinals intended when he was elected was simply out of the question.

Napoleon, in the meantime, schemed, bullied and cajoled the clergy in France and the conquered lands to set about electing senior church officials without papal approval. When Pius was asked to give a second-hand blessing to this, and refused, Napoleon in 1812—shortly before his ill-fated attack on Russia that was to seal the fate of his Grande Armée—declared the powers of the papacy suspended indefinitely. On May 21, as the warlord drew up his final plans for the assault on Russia, he gave orders for the pope to be transferred under conditions of great secrecy to Fontainbleu, outside Paris, where he intended to have a final showdown with him after he had taken Moscow.

The 12-day journey was a wretched one for Pius, who was suffering acutely from a bladder infection. Indeed, at one halt on the journey, a Benedictine abbot gave Pius the last sacraments. He recovered, at least temporarily, from his harrowing ordeal, although his health was never to be the same again.

As for his tormentor—the unthinkable happened. A combination of Russian arms, great distances, savage weather, and poor supply lines conspired to hand the Emperor the biggest military defeat he had ever experienced. It was a beaten and perplexed Napoleon, not a triumphant one, who returned to Fontainbleau in January 1813 to confront the pope. Yet the bully in him would not let up when it came to the church. Over a period of days he threatened and abused Pius constantly, browbeating him into signing a new set of agreements called the Concordat of Fontainbleau which, among other things, packed the College of Cardinals with French representatives eager to do Napoleon's bidding.

Still the old pope would not give up. In the short term his health improved dramatically and within a year he had written a stinging letter to Napoleon saying the concordat was no longer valid because he had been pressured into agreeing to it. The Emperor kept the letter secret, worried now more about the foreign armies converging on Paris than he was about the papacy.

In January 1814 he ordered the pope to be removed to Savona, fearful that anyone breaching the city would take him. The journey was not like the one that took Pius to Fontainbleau—this time the streets of every town and village he passed through were wild with excitement. "It showed," said historian Piers Milford, "how much Catholics had been upset with Napoleon over his treatment of the Supreme Pontiff."

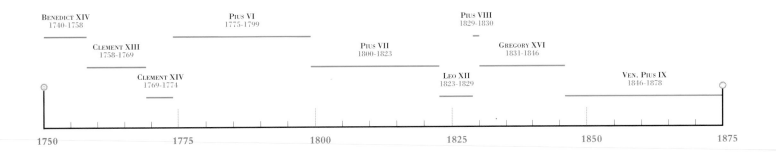

BENEDICT XIV 1740-1758		PIUS VI 1775-1799		PIUS VIII 1829-1830	
CLEMENT XIII 1758-1769			PIUS VII 1800-1823	GREGORY XVI 1831-1846	
	CLEMENT XIV 1769-1774		LEO XII 1823-1829		VEN. PIUS IX 1846-1878

| 1750 | 1775 | 1800 | 1825 | 1850 | 1875 |

Less than three months later it was Napoleon's turn to journey painfully, forced out of Paris and into exile. This time it was he who rode in darkness, whose carriage had its wheels muffled, who dared not look out upon a vengeful population. Although he would return once more for a last attempt at domination of the European mainland, he was for the time being a beaten and broken despot.

On May 24, the pope re-entered the Eternal City and was borne up the Corso in his carriage, pulled by the sons of the Roman nobility, as was customary. He went straight to St. Peter's where he prayed for his deliverance from his enemies, and where he uttered a prayer of forgiveness for his chief tormentor. He had nine years of life left, time in which he sought to restore some of the prestige of the church. Among the people he was regarded as a hero, as a ruler without armies and might who had bravely stood up to Napoleon. Such heroism was recognized as the 1814 Congress of Vienna formed to redraw the boundaries of post-Napoleonic Europe. Except for the papal conclave around Avignon, all the papal territories were returned to the Vatican.

Below: Napoleon's attack on Russia sealed the fate of his Grande Armée which perished in the great retreat from Moscow. It also hastened his end because he was never again able to drum up the support he once enjoyed among the populace.

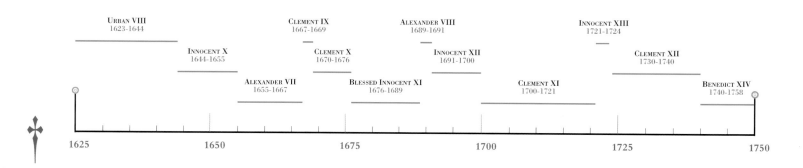

URBAN VIII
1623-1644

CLEMENT IX
1667-1669

ALEXANDER VIII
1689-1691

INNOCENT XIII
1721-1724

INNOCENT X
1644-1655

CLEMENT X
1670-1676

INNOCENT XII
1691-1700

CLEMENT XII
1730-1740

ALEXANDER VII
1655-1667

BLESSED INNOCENT XI
1676-1689

CLEMENT XI
1700-1721

BENEDICT XIV
1740-1758

1625   1650   1675   1700   1725   1750

Above: Pope Leo XIII, architect of a coherent modern social doctrine for the church. He also sought to spread the word of Christ abroad with missionaries, at a time when the power of Rome was waning.

With the lands secure, Pius set about rebuilding the religious orders that had suffered so much under Napoleon. He appointed all the bishops and other high officials of the church whose posts had remained dormant during the long years of his exile. He concluded friendly concordats with states that had suffered under Napoleon—and he showed the true meaning of the Christian maxim of forgiveness when he allowed Napoleon's mother, an uncle, and two brothers to live peaceably in Rome when no other capital in Europe would take them. After Napoleon was defeated at Waterloo and was exiled to St. Helena by the British, Pius even appealed for humanity in Napoleon's treatment there.

Pius has gone down in history as a pope who displayed the greatest qualities of humanity, bravery, and goodness. When he died, a week after his 81st birthday on August 20, 1823, the mourning around the world was genuine and deep. French politician Etienne Pasquier said of him: "His reign was filled with the most terrible vicissitudes; this beautiful figure is one of the most remarkable of the great epoch through which he lived."

In the late 19th century the papacy faced a territorial challenge that succeeded where all before had failed. The Papal States—including the Patrimony of Peter—began to fall to King Victor Emmanuel as he sought to bring about the unification of Italy as a single state. In 1870 Rome itself fell to his armies, bringing an end to all the church's temporal power. When the territories fell to Victor Emmanuel, Pope Pius IX, the longest-reigning pope in history—from 1846 until 1878—declared both himself and the Vatican "inviolable."

"I am a prisoner in the Vatican," he said, and for the next 59 years every pope followed his example. It led to a perpetual state of tension between the church and the Italian state which would not be resolved until 1929 when Mussolini and the Papcy signed the Lateran Treaty, which brought about the establishment of the church's sole remaining territorial foothold—the Vatican City.

The pope, whose reign would span the passing of the old century into the new, was Leo XIII, born Gioacchino Vincenzo Pecci near Rome in March 1810. The son of a minor noble family, he reigned from 1878 to 1903 and, despite his advanced age when he took up the post, he proved himself a worthy pontiff who did much to improve papal relations with the rest of Europe while formulating a coherent social doctrine for the church. He resisted vigorously an anti-Catholic campaign by Prussia's Iron Chancellor Bismarck, warned of the dangers of socialism without religion, and promoted Catholic missions overseas. He was also wise enough to see that the days of absolute monarchy were over. Accordingly, he issued many encyclicals which sanctioned Catholics working for civil authorities instead of kings routinely imbued with the "divine right" to rule.

One thing Leo and his advisers in the curia were not keen on was the separation of "church and state," the cardinal sin of the French revo-

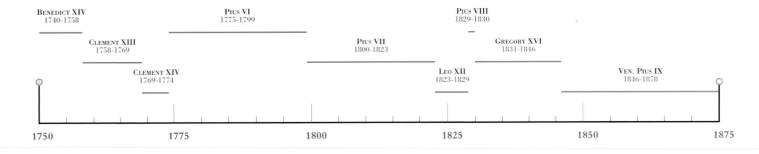

BENEDICT XIV 1740-1758		PIUS VI 1775-1799			PIUS VIII 1829-1830	
CLEMENT XIII 1758-1769			PIUS VII 1800-1823		GREGORY XVI 1831-1846	
	CLEMENT XIV 1769-1774			LEO XII 1823-1829		VEN. PIUS IX 1846-1878

| 1750 | 1775 | 1800 | 1825 | 1850 | 1875 |

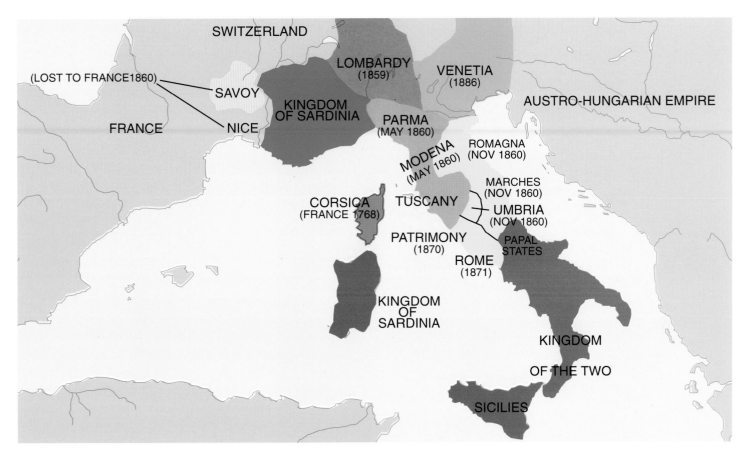

lution. The church had never forgiven the revolutionaries for preaching a doctrine that removed its influence from many spheres of national life, not the least of which was education. The issue of church and state was to raise itself again during Leo's pontificate—but this time in North America.

The massive immigration of Catholics into what was predominantly a Protestant country, meant that the American Catholic Church was under very different circumstances than those in Europe. The Americans insisted that separation of church and state was a necessity because ideas, feelings, and attitudes were so much different in the New World. At first Leo was happy to let the American Church have its head, as long as the ideas—including "harmonizing Catholicism with modernist thought"—did not spread across the Atlantic. When "Americanism," as it was termed, began appearing in pamphlets and literature in Europe, draconian measures against the reformed were handed down. Leo's orders to desist meant that theological teaching in the American Catholic Church was crippled for half a century. It also meant the American Church leaders were in the wilderness, unheard at a time when they needed all the papal support they could get. As a consequence many Protestants seeking conversion in America were denied, although many new dioceses were created.

Leo, despite his shortcomings, is recognized as the first of the

Above: The Risorgimento, the unification of Italy, saw the end of the Papal States.

Below: Prussia's Iron Chancellor, Otto von Bismarck, the greatest statesman of his time, but a thorn in the side of the papacy.

Above: President Woodrow Wilson, who successfully negotiated the formation of the League of Nations, included many of Pope Benedict's peace proposals in his plan.

Above right: The papal position in the Great War was strictly one of neutrality, but its involvement was considerably reduced by its position of emnity towards the Italian crown which had disposessed it of its Papal States. Benedict XV was not deaf to the German promise to return Rome to the papacy if it won, and the Allies denied the papacy a part in the peace settlement of 1919.

Below right: The League of Nations was supported by the papacy; it was the first attempt globally to bring nations under one umbrella to prevent future wars.

"modern" popes, who fought hard to get Catholics to embrace a rapidly changing world while preserving the essential moral leadership provided by the church. His encyclicals are regarded by Vatican scholars as works of genius, and essential for understanding the church today. When he died in 1903 the world had just 11 years of peace left.

Truly, the age of enlightenment could be said to have vanished forever in 1914 when the guns of the Great War broke out and would not be silenced for five bloody years. It was upon the unfortunate shoulders of Benedict XV that the burden of leadership would fall during this terrible bloodletting. Benedict, born Giacomo della Chiesa, was a devout churchman who was made a cardinal just three months before his election to the papal throne in September 1914, one month after the German invasion of Belgium.

The Great War was a different war than those that had taken place in Europe before and it was terrible from every aspect. Not only were the horrors of wholesale industrial slaughter deployed on every front, but for the church it was doubly tragic to see Catholic nations marching against Catholic nations, while each claimed God was on their side. Benedict adopted a policy of strict neutrality on the surface while instructing his legates and ambassadors in the warring nations to constantly seek out ways of trying to forge a peace treaty. The Vatican, under his leadership, went to extreme lengths to ease the suffering of millions of refugees, but there was never any chance of a negotiated peace; too many young men had died hideous deaths for the allied powers to back down, and while Germany's defensive line in the west stayed strong, they were not interested in a negotiated peace. Benedict came close with a seven-point peace plan he mooted in 1917, but only the humanitarian President Woodrow Wilson of the United States gave it any real backing. It was only the success of the allied sea blockade, the arrival of American troops in France, and the starvation of ordinary Germans in their major cities, that brought the Kaiser's representatives to the Armistice table in 1918.

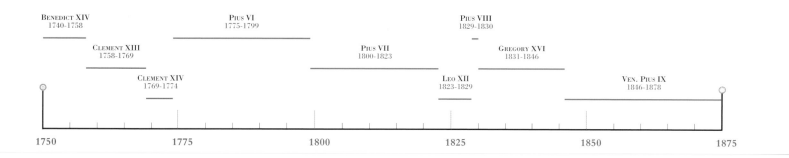

BENEDICT XIV
1740-1758

PIUS VI
1775-1799

PIUS VIII
1829-1830

CLEMENT XIII
1758-1769

PIUS VII
1800-1823

GREGORY XVI
1831-1846

CLEMENT XIV
1769-1774

LEO XII
1823-1829

VEN. PIUS IX
1846-1878

1750   1775   1800   1825   1850   1875

The seven points that the pope formulated were later incorporated in his famous 14-Point Plan which led to the foundation of the League of Nations, but Benedict received little credit for it, and the victorious powers were petty when it came to establishing the new peace for Europe; because Benedict had adopted a strictly neutral pose he was forbidden from attending the peace talks at Versailles. It was left to this humble and pious man to labor for world peace for the rest of his days. He harnessed virtually all papal missionary work to the new task of bringing aid and relief to the survivors of the Great War across the globe, calling what had happened to the young men of the world "an abomination."

Although the Great War overshadowed every aspect of his reign, he nonetheless was credited with 12 major encyclicals and was successful in establishing a papal prsence in Britain for the first time in 300 years. Historian Nancy Ballard's summation of his pontificate sums him up well:

"He made it the duty of the Church in this most violent of centuries to seek peace at all costs. His failing was a failure of the human spirit, not God's will. Benedict was a pope worthy of his office and a statue to him still stands in Istanbul, a Moslem nation, because of his efforts during that horrendous conflagration we call the Great War."

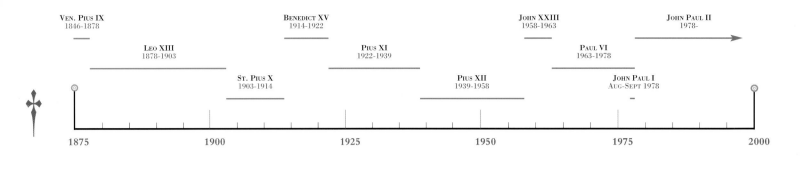

VEN. PIUS IX
1846-1878

LEO XIII
1878-1903

ST. PIUS X
1903-1914

BENEDICT XV
1914-1922

PIUS XI
1922-1939

PIUS XII
1939-1958

JOHN XXIII
1958-1963

PAUL VI
1963-1978

JOHN PAUL I
AUG-SEPT 1978

JOHN PAUL II
1978-

1875   1900   1925   1950   1975   2000

MODERN POPES

Above: Pope Pius XII was a controversial leader of the Catholic faith during the dark days of the war. Critics say his pre-war time in Germany made him too sympathetic to the Nazis and that he did not speak out forcefully enough against the Holocaust. Supporters say he walked a fine line between caring for his flock and trying not to make their lives untenable in those countries under Nazi occupation.

THIS CENTURY HAS PRESENTED THE PAPACY with more problems than any other in terms of moral dilemmas—the bloodletting of the Great War, the convulsions of Fascism and Communism, worldwide unemployment, collapsing empires, resurgent nationalism, and a spiritual malaise that seemed to seep into every country as modern living combined with disillusionment caused many to question the leadership of the papacy. No pope was confronted with harder choices, and remains more controversial in this century, than Pius XII, born Eugenio Pacelli, who reigned during the darkest days of World War II, with all the attendant horrors of the Holocaust and Gestapo repression. Did he do enough to save the Jews? Could he have done more? Did the pope know of the death factories of Auschwitz and Treblinka and do nothing about them, intent, instead, on saving Catholic lives throughout the occupied lands of Europe? These are questions that have vexed Catholics for a long time and are likely to continue to do so.

Pius was born into a much-revered Roman family on March 2, 1876. Extremely intelligent, he received degrees at two universities before his ordination as a priest in 1899. His keen intelligence was not lost on the Vatican hierarchy and in 1901 he was enlisted by the prominent Cardinal Gaspari to help him with the massive codification of canon law. There followed several high positions within the Vatican, culminating in his promotion to archbishop in 1917 and his posting to Bavaria as a papal nuncio in 1917.

This was a time when the young men of Europe were dying in hundreds of thousands on the barbed wire of the western front. And Germany was the cause of this monstrous, seemingly unstoppable war that brought the world the full terrors of the machine gun, high explosive, flame-throwers, and poison gas. Most of the world thought the German leadership reprehensible, but Pius found nothing but decency and goodness in the people of Bavaria. Later, he was made nuncio to the entire republic after the 1918 armistice and collapse of the Kaiser's monarchy.

He established important treaties with Bavaria and Prussia during his 13-year tenure in Germany, developing a fondness for the German people that would mark his time there as the happiest in his life. He was elected to the College of Cardinals in 1929 and the following year appointed by Cardinal Gasparri as the powerful Secretary of State. In this capacity he traveled all over the world as the roving ambassador of Pope Pius XI. But it was his dealings with Nazi Germany that gave a clue as to how he would perform in later life as pope.

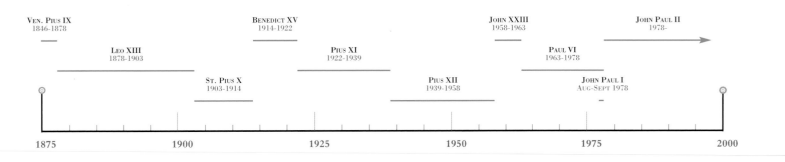
Adolf Hitler's budding Third Reich made no bones about where its destiny lay. The persecution of the Jews, "living space" in the east, the contempt for (but also some admiration of) organized religion—all were outlined in *Mein Kampf*, Hitler's monotonous political manifesto which became the Nazi bible.

There can be little doubt that the super-intelligent Cardinal Pacelli did not perceive in this new racist state the seeds of something terrible. He decided that to work with Nazi Germany, and thus protect the Catholics within its borders, was better than to condemn it outright. So he established a concordat with the new Nazi state in 1933, which guaranteed the status of the Catholic Church within Germany and the inviolability of the Vatican State. He saw the treaty as the duty of the papacy, to protect the rights of the faithful in hostile times. Critics, naturally, saw it as a way for Hitler to win credibility for a regime that most civilized people viewed with distaste and despair. After the war, when the full controversy of his silence in the face of Nazism was raging, Pius said of the concordat with Hitler:

"Although the Church had few illusions about National Socialism, it must be recognized that the concordat in the years that followed 1933 brought some advantages, or at least prevented, worse evils. In fact, in spite of all the violations to which it was subjected, it gave German Catholics a judicial basis for their defence, a stronghold behind which to shield themselves in their opposition to the ever-growing campaign of religious persecution."

By his own admission, then, it was at best a pact with the devil. It was in 1939 that the highest papal office beckoned. A third ballot during a one-day conclave gave him the majority he needed to become Supreme Pontiff. Elected by his fellow cardinals who recognized his supreme diplomatic skills, Pius was to have just six months of peace left before the bloodiest war in history was unleashed by Hitler.

Pius decided before he became pope to campaign vigorously against Communism while trying to work within the framework of Nazism. At least, he reasoned, Hitler allowed the churches to stay open while Stalin brooked no such leniency. The only religion Communism allowed was the religion of the state. Consequently, Pius was not alone as the war clouds gathered over Europe to decide that the menace from Moscow was a far greater threat than the one in Berlin.

When Hitler unleashed his panzers against Poland in 1939, Pius broke his silence to condemn him. At his Christmas address that year he used the occasion to call for conciliation between the warring nations— his Five Peace Points which he outlined as: the Christian Spirit that should exist between nations; the founding of an international tribunal to negotiate for a peace; recognizing the rights of all nations to exist; the

Above: Adolf Hitler, one of mankind's greatest tormentors who paid lip service to the Catholic Church, but persecuted many churchmen who dared to speak out against him.

By his own admission, then, it was at best a pact with the devil

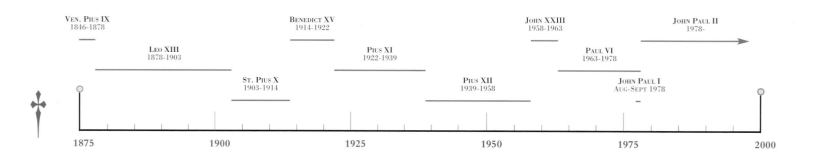

VEN. PIUS IX
1846-1878

BENEDICT XV
1914-1922

JOHN XXIII
1958-1963

JOHN PAUL II
1978-

LEO XIII
1878-1903

PIUS XI
1922-1939

PAUL VI
1963-1978

ST. PIUS X
1903-1914

PIUS XII
1939-1958

JOHN PAUL I
AUG-SEPT 1978

1875   1900   1925   1950   1975   2000

Above: The papacy was determined to work from within the German state: here a 1930s' election poster making clear the church stood on the side of the Nazis.

"Humanity owes this vow to the hundreds of thousands of people who, through no fault of their own, sometimes only owing to nationality or descent, are doomed to death or slow decline."

recognition of all minority rights; and genuine world disarmament. No one listened, of course, and, safe from the shells and the round-ups, the persecutions, and the horrors, Pius was henceforth to maintain a silence on the war that his critics say bordered on the criminal.

But was it? It would be easy to say that he should have done more, but supporters argue that his very neutrality—coupled with genuine and laudable efforts which included the sheltering of Jews in Rome—saved more lives than speaking out would have cost. Jesuit historian Robert Graham said:

"In both world wars publicists and even officials in some countries called on the pope to throw the weight of his religious authority behind their cause—for instance, by expressly condemning certain enemy atrocities, and even by declaring their war a just one and excommunicating enemy leadership. In the circumstances a moral judgment would have served only propagandistic political ends and compromised the Holy See's true religious influence for peace." Indeed, when Hitler turned Poland into the world's biggest killing ground—slaughtering the Catholic intelligentsia as well as setting up the extermination camps which would destroy six million Jews—Pius remained silent, explaining to the future Paul VI:

"We ought to speak words of fire against such things, and the only thing that prevents us from doing so is the knowledge that if we should speak, we would be making the condition of these unfortunate ones more difficult."

He even stopped speaking out against the communists. His silence was explained away by many as ignorance—ignorance of the human atrocities of Treblinka, Auschwitz, and Majdanek where hell on earth had truly been created by the Nazis. It was the excuse that wartime leaders such as Roosevelt would cite after the war—that they simply did not believe the reports from survivors and resistors of the Nazi terror that such places existed. But in the early 1970s a former Polish ambassador to the Vatican shattered that myth once and for all. Kazimierz Papee revealed how he personally delivered to the pope the information on human beings being slaughtered at a phenomenal rate.

Papee was the Polish representative to the Holy See during the darkest days when the ovens of the death camps were operating at full capacity. In December 1942 he handed over to a papal aide the following memorandum:

"The Polish embassy has the honor of communicating to the State Secretariat of His Holiness the following information emanating from official sources;

124

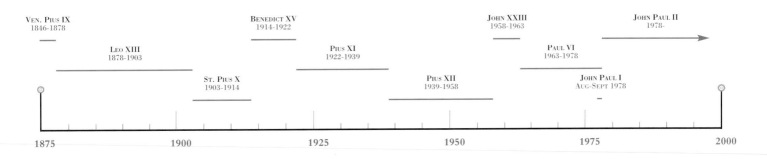

VEN. PIUS IX
1846-1878

LEO XIII
1878-1903

ST. PIUS X
1903-1914

BENEDICT XV
1914-1922

PIUS XI
1922-1939

PIUS XII
1939-1958

JOHN XXIII
1958-1963

PAUL VI
1963-1978

JOHN PAUL I
AUG-SEPT 1978

JOHN PAUL II
1978-

1875   1900   1925   1950   1975   2000

"The Germans are liquidating the entire Jewish population of Poland. The first to be taken are the old, the crippled, the women and children; which proves that these are not deportations to forced labor, and confirms the information that these deported populations are taken to specially prepared installations, there to be put to death by various means while the young and able-bodied are killed through starvation and forced labor.

"As for the number of Polish Jews exterminated by the Germans, it is estimated that it has passed a million. In Warsaw alone there were, in the ghetto in mid-July 1942, approximately 400,000 Jews; in the course of July and August 250,000 were taken east; on September 1 only 120,000 ration cards were distributed in this ghetto, and on October 1 40,000 cards. The 'liquidations' are proceeding at the same rate in the other cities of Poland."

Papee says this was the seventh, and by far the most definitive, communication about the Holocaust that was sent through him to the pope. Three days after receiving it, on Christmas Eve 1942, Pius made a public reference to what was happening to the Jews in his Christmas message to the Catholics of the world. He spoke for 45 minutes, but of the massacres taking place, limited his comments to:

"Humanity owes this vow to the hundreds of thousands of people who, through no fault of their own, sometimes only owing to nationality or descent, are doomed to death or slow decline."

Was this short message the best the Vatican could come up with to stop the greatest mass murder of all time? Papee admits:

"He WAS in a very difficult position. He was, and one must appreciate this, surrounded by Fascism; he had very little freedom of movement. But it is not possible he did not see my communication. The Holy Father saw all such communications. It would simply not have been possible to withold them from him."

Pius's supporters point out the terrible consequences of stepping over the line. Pius knew that the Nazis would have marched into the Vatican in a heartbeat if they felt he was a threat to them. He saw the awful power of the Nazi state when all Jews in the Netherlands were packed off to Auschwitz for extermination in 1942 as a direct retaliation for an outspoken attack on Hitler by the Dutch bishops.

They also point out that, far from being a cold and calculating figure left unmoved by the plight of the defenseless in the conquered lands, Pius was utterly despairing of their fate. D'Arcy Osborne, British minister to the Holy See and a non-Catholic, said:

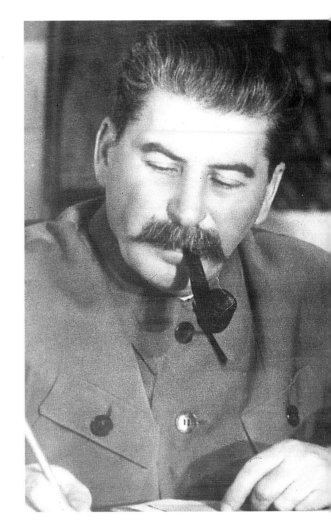

Above: Pope Pius XII regarded Josef Stalin's communism was as a far greater evil—certainly at the outset of the war—than Hitler's Nazism.

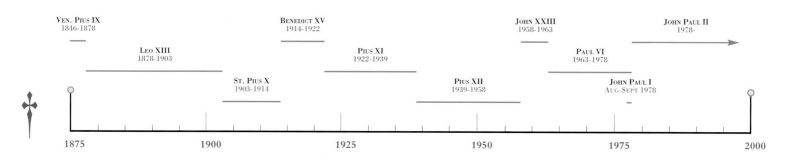

VEN. PIUS IX 1846-1878		BENEDICT XV 1914-1922		JOHN XXIII 1958-1963		JOHN PAUL II 1978-
LEO XIII 1878-1903		PIUS XI 1922-1939		PAUL VI 1963-1978	
	ST. PIUS X 1903-1914		PIUS XII 1939-1958		JOHN PAUL I AUG-SEPT 1978	

1875   1900   1925   1950   1975   2000

This Page and Right: The horrors of the Holocaust—the mass extermination of the Jews in occupied Europe plumbed new depths of human depravity. Here lie sprawled the dead of Dachau and Buchenwald concentration camps. There is still debate about whether the papacy should have spoken out more forcefully against this genocide, and horror that Catholic priests should aid fleeing Nazis reach South America at the war's end.

"It is a matter of dispute as to what extent Pope Pius XII was aware of Bishop Hudal's activities. Among the senior members of the Vatican hierachy there were some who asserted that he was a major influence on the pope, and that Hudal's arguments in support of Nazi Germany found a ready audience with the pontiff."

"So far from being a cool (which, I suppose, implies cold-blooded and inhumane) diplomatist, Pius XII was the most warmly humane, kind, generous (and incidentally saintly) character that it has been my privilege to meet in the course of a long life. I know that his sensitive nature was acutely and incessantly alive to the tragic volume of human suffering caused by the war and, without the slightest doubt, he would have been ready and glad to give his life to redeem humanity from its consequences. And this quite irrespective of nationality or faith. But what effectively could he do?"

Yet Pius was not entirely ineffective. He gave shelter to hundreds of thousands of Jews in Vatican property, and the Jewish writer Pinchase Lapide estimates as many as 800,000 Jews were saved from extermination by his efforts. The Vatican, Castel Gandolfo, and over 150 churches, convents, and priests' homes all over Rome were used as secret hiding places for the Jews. He even, in 1943, ordered the smelting of sacred golden objects to pay a ransom for the lives of some captive Jews held by the Gestapo. But it is the silence on the death camps, the most terrible places on earth, that galls papal critics the most. Was the protection and primacy of the papacy really worth it if these outrages were not condemned by one of the most influential men on the planet? It is a dilemma and a controversy that will rage long after the last Holocaust survivor has passed away.

After the liberation of Rome in 1944, when Pius came out to embrace and bless the soldiers of the victorious allied army, he could look forward to tasks other than trying to reconcile warring enemies. He wrote memorable encyclicals and dispatched papal nuncios with a new zeal around the world to bolster the church. He also turned against the communists he reviled so much, excommunicating Italian Catholics who joined the Communist Party and, in retaliation for political persecution of the church in communist Eastern Europe, he excommunicated the political leaders of Hungary, Romania, Czechoslovakia, Poland, and Yugoslavia, while promoting and strengthening the Catholic hold on countries in South America, promising more funds for the Catholic universities there.

There was, however, one further disturbing legacy of his pro-German position which was exploited by factions close to him at the war's end, and that was the controversial part the Vatican and its officials played in spiriting wanted Nazi war criminals away to safe havens in South America and other far-flung countries. While no one suggests that the pope ordered his underlings to provide the funds and paperwork for such a rat-run to operate, there is no doubt that his aides felt they were operating in the spirit of what their pontiff would have wished. The aiding and abetting of the escape of wanted murderers with the blood of millions on their hands has rankled with Jewish leaders the world over since.

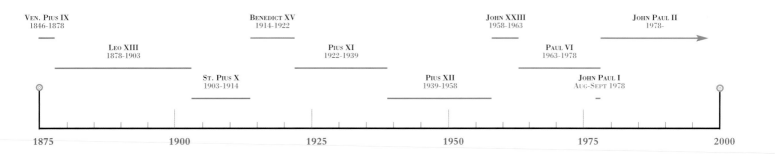
Josef Mengele, the perverted camp doctor of Auschwitz who chose which of the inmates would live and die, was assisted by the Vatican in his getaway. So was Franz Stangl, the demented commandant of Treblinka, where just 40 people out of 900,000 survived the gas chambers. And so was Adolf Eichmann, the greatest Nazi criminal of them all, the architect of the "Final Solution of the Jewish Question in Europe"—the monster who made the trains run on time and the gas ovens operate to maximum capacity.

At the core of this rat-run was Bishop Hudal, Rector of the Anima, the German-Roman Catholic Foundation in Rome from 1923 until 1955. Such eminent Nazi hunters as Simon Wiesenthal, and Nazi historians as Gitta Sereny, name him as the man who helped the big ones get away. He dished out Red Cross passports, Vatican passports designed for refugees, and provided food and shelter for the one-time "supermen" when they were on the run. Hella Pick, in his award-winning biography of Simon Wiesenthal, says:

"It is a matter of dispute as to what extent Pope Pius XII was aware of Bishop Hudal's activities. Among the senior members of the Vatican hierachy there were some who asserted that he was a major influence on the pope, and that Hudal's arguments in support of Nazi Germany found a ready audience with the pontiff. Others claim that the Vatican did not take Hudal very seriously. Whatever the truth of Hudal's standing in the Vatican, there can be no doubt about his own perverted political beliefs which led him to help men like Stangl and Eichmann. He belonged to the faction of the Roman episcopate which advised two successive popes, Pius XI and Pius XII, that they should recognize Hitler's legitimacy, and that Nazi Germany had to be supported as a bulwark against the menace of Bolshevism."

This torn pope, this man of God who did what he considered his best in dark times, reigned until 1958, but his health was in decline from 1954 onwards. A small, some say unscrupulous, circle of cardinals began to exert more power over the direction of the papacy, not always consistent with the pope's views. These included ever-more outspoken attacks on the communist powers, at a time when western governments were balanced on the knife-edge of the Cold War.

Following him to power is the Holy Father regarded as the best pope of modern times, and one of the best loved. He reigned from 1958 to 1963, modernizing the church, striving to create a dialogue with the Soviet Union and other "enemies," mending bridges with the Jews so long branded "Christ killers" by reactionaries in the church, appointed observers to the World Council of Churches, and increased the number of cardinals around the world to "internationalize" the word of Rome.

Born Angelo Giuseppe Roncalli to a peasant family in Bergamo,

Below: Josef Mengele, the brutal camp doctor of Auschwitz who escaped to freedom at the war's end with the aid of Catholic Church officials.

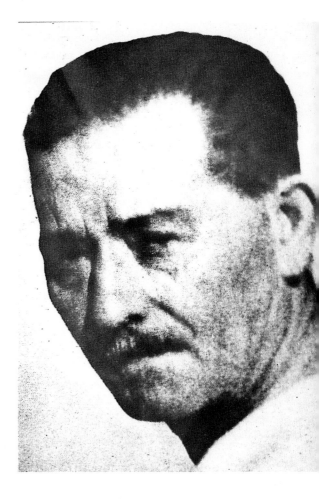

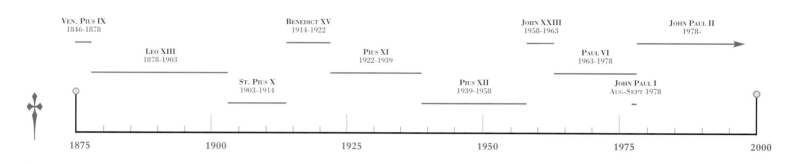

VEN. PIUS IX
1846-1878

BENEDICT XV
1914-1922

JOHN XXIII
1958-1963

JOHN PAUL II
1978-

LEO XIII
1878-1903

PIUS XI
1922-1939

PAUL VI
1963-1978

ST. PIUS X
1903-1914

PIUS XII
1939-1958

JOHN PAUL I
AUG-SEPT 1978

1875   1900   1925   1950   1975   2000

Above: September 1, 1939— the Nazis attack Poland. Here are the remains of the old city of Warsaw after divebombers of Hitler's Luftwaffe had pounded the old city into brickdust.

"I am happy to be here even though there may be some present who do not call themselves Christians, but who can be acknowledged as such because of their good deeds. To all I give my paternal blessing."

Italy, in 1881, he studied at a seminary before ordination in 1904. He served as a military chaplain during the Great War—Italy was on the side of the Allies—and at the end of the war became a director of a hostel for students as well as taking on the directorship of spiritual affairs at the seminary where he was educated. He progressed to become an archbishop and a papal emissary to Bulgaria, Turkey, and Greece, finishing up as nuncio to France in 1944. It was in the Balkans that he played an active role in helping to save the Jews. He forwarded Immigration Certificates issued by the Palestine Jewish Agency to Vatican diplomats who, in turn, gave them to individuals seeking sanctuary from Hitler's death squads. In February 1944 the Grand Rabbi of Jerusalem, Isaac Herzog, wrote to him, saying:

"I want to express my deepest gratitude for the energetic steps that you have undertaken and will undertake to save our unfortunate people. You follow in the tradition, so profoundly humanitarian, of the Holy See, and you follow the feelings of your own heart. The people of Israel will never forget the help brought to its unfortunate brothers and sisters by the Holy See and its highest representatives at this saddest moment of our history."

In 1953 he was appointed a cardinal and became Patriarch of Venice, preferring to be a "pastor" rather than "meeting after meetings in Rome. I am not really good at administration." He was warmly received in Venice, riding in a boat along the Grand Canal to the tumultuous roars of the population. He made it clear that he wanted to be a father to the whole human flock, regardless of whether they were communist or not—a line he would continue to pursue after he had become pope. He told the Venetian city council on his first meeting with them:

"I am happy to be here even though there may be some present who do not call themselves Christians, but who can be acknowledged as such because of their good deeds. To all I give my paternal blessing."

When Pius XII died on October 9, 1958, Roncalli hardly expected to be made pope at the age of 76. However, 24 of the 51 cardinals who went into the conclave were older than he was! After almost three days he was elected and he chose the name John, the first pope to do so for over six centuries. His immediate concern was the modernizing of the church, which he intended to start with Vatican Council convened for 1962, claiming it would show to the world the church's "vigor of life and truth." In it he called for compassion towards the Communists "separated from the Apostolic See—people who may not be Christians but who nevertheless are reasonable men, and men of natural moral

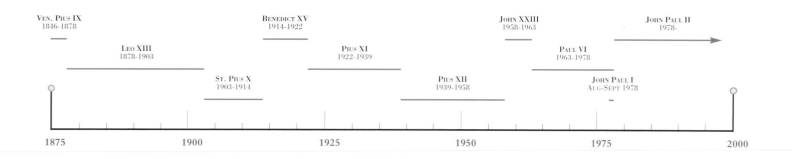

1875　　　　　1900　　　　　1925　　　　　1950　　　　　1975　　　　　2000

integrity." The council did away with much petty bureaucracy from Rome that so infuriated church officials around the world.

He is also credited with laboring hard behind the scenes during the Cuban Missile Crisis of 1962 when the world was dragged perilously close to the brink of nuclear war. As Kennedy and Kruschev played brinkmanship over the siting of nuclear warheads in the Caribbean, John displayed the value of papal diplomacy at its best. He was endlessly urging a peaceful solution to the crisis, so much so that, when it was finally resolved, he received private messages of thanks from both leaders—and a collective sigh of relief from the inhabitants of a frightened world.

John, however, was already a sick man, plagued by intestinal pains. He died in June 1963 and the world was plunged into mourning. His death was reported on the front pages of every major newspaper around the world and there was a palpable sense in every capital and village, among believers and non-believers, that the world had lost a very good man indeed. Cardinal Suenens, who knew him well, gave a fitting epitaph when he said: "At his departure he left us closer to God, and the world a better place in which to live."

The papal decrees that John worked for were to be put into practice by his successor Paul VI, who reigned from 1963 until 1978. There were changes to the Latin Mass, changes to the trappings of papal life and the court—many of the ceremonies and privileges positively medieval—and changes to the administration of the curia. The ancient

As Kennedy and Kruschev played brinkmanship over the siting of nuclear warheads in the Caribbean, John displayed the value of papal diplomacy at its best.

Below: The liberation of Rome in 1944. The pope was one of the first to meet and bless the Allies upon their entry into the city.

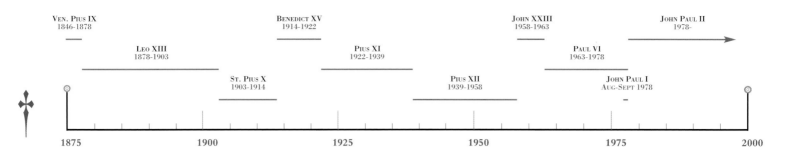

VEN. PIUS IX
1846-1878

BENEDICT XV
1914-1922

JOHN XXIII
1958-1963

JOHN PAUL II
1978-

LEO XIII
1878-1903

PIUS XI
1922-1939

PAUL VI
1963-1978

ST. PIUS X
1903-1914

PIUS XII
1939-1958

JOHN PAUL I
AUG-SEPT 1978

1875   1900   1925   1950   1975   2000

No fewer than six books claim that the pope was murdered, poisoned to give the appearance of having succumbed to a heart attack or a blood clot in the lungs. Many of the conspiracy theorists believe that he died because he was intent on clearing up the Vatican Bank, mired in corruption and scandal, and linked with the Mafia.

Pontifical Noble Guard, for instance, was abolished and a further 144 cardinals, many of them far younger men than the ancients who elected John, were created to further "internationalize" the church. Cardinals were to be retired at 80 and bishops and priests at 75. There was much grumbling within the ranks of the papacy about his reforming zeal, and more than one historian has said that it was only the pope's diplomatic skills that prevented a new schism from tearing the church asunder as it entered the final years of the most tumultuous century known to man.

Until the reign of the present pontiff, John Paul II, John was the most traveled pontiff of all, and was known to followers as the "pilgrim pope." In one of his journeys to the devoutly Catholic Philippines, he was saved from a knife-wielding assassin by the future Archbishop Marcinkus, later to head the Vatican Bank. Deeply spiritual to the end, the war in Vietnam, Middle East terrorism, Northern Irish factionalism, and the terrorist murder of Italian premier Aldo Moro, a close friend, all weighed heavily on him. He suffered a heart attack after the murder of Moro and died shortly afterward at Castel Gandolfo on August 6, 1978.

There followed one of the shortest pontifical reigns in history, and some say the most mysterious. John Paul I was elected pope in August 1978 and remained as Holy Father for just 33 days before his death. During his brief tenure he showed much promise and was adored by Romans who dubbed him the "Smiling Pope" for his continuous mirth and jollity. The Smiling Pope had little to enjoy about his reign, for if some recent investigations into his life are to be believed, he died at the hands of an assassin, killed because he planned to clean up the mess of the Vatican Bank, a scandal in its own right just waiting to break.

John Paul was born Albino Luciani in Forno di Canala in October 1912 to poor parents. Unassuming, modest, with a finely honed sense of humor and the common touch, he was appointed Patriarch of Venice in 1969 and became a cardinal four years later. Elected on the third ballot of the first day as pope, he put his no-nonsense stamp on papal affairs from the outset, dispensing with the tiara because he found it too "pompous." He was a supreme pontiff who had charisma recognized around the world, but his was to be a reign unfulfilled.

On Friday September 29, 1978, Sister Vincenza, an aging nun, brought a flask of coffee up to him in his apartments as she had done every year for 12 years. Forty minutes later the acting head of the Catholic Church, Cardinal Jean Villot, instructed the pope's private secretary, Irishman Fr. John Magee, to lie about the time and circumstances of the body's discovery. This was the first of what author and investigative journalist John Cornwell would call "economies with the truth" perpetrated by the Vatican hierachy, leading to the suspicions that the pope had met an untimely, dastardly end.

No fewer than six books claim that the pope was murdered, poisoned to give the appearance of having succumbed to a heart attack

130

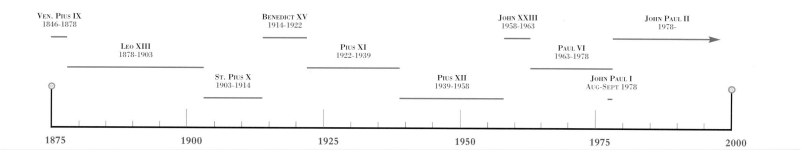
or a blood clot in the lungs. Many of the conspiracy theorists believe that he died because he was intent on clearing up the Vatican Bank, mired in corruption and scandal, and linked with the Mafia.

It wasn't until Cornwell, a lapsed Catholic, was given access inside the Vatican, that he changed his mind about the pope's death. Now he no longer believes he was murdered, but that the Vatican hierachy was responsible for his demise. In his book *A Thief in the Night* Cornwell puts forward the theory that Paul was tormented by the fact that his Vatican colleagues did not regard him as a worthy successor to lead the church. "The truth is much more shameful than if he had been murdered," he said. "That would have been the work of several criminals or madmen, where in fact the whole of the Vatican is responsible for the death of John Paul I. He was allowed to go to the solitary death he prayed for, untended and uncared for by those closest to him."

Cornwell contends that the Vatican, which declared his death as sudden and a shock, knew all along of his own feelings of inadequacy and that he was taking strong medication for a serious blood-clotting condition. Cornwell says he was despised by many of the papal fat-cats who mocked him for his modest ways and laughed at his anxiety at dealing with leading the largest Christian community in the world. Cornwell concludes that there was a coverup—but not of murder, rather of culpable neglect and "lack of love."

That, of course, is one theory—many other people, including David Yallop, still propound the notion that he was murdered. In his worldwide bestseller, *In God's Name,* he identifies six suspects with powerful motives for snuffing out the life of the supreme pontiff, but stops short of showing whose hand held the smoking gun. One of those suspects is Archbishop Marcinkus, whose financial morality is certainly questionable; as he was head of the Vatican Bank, and many feel that the corruption of that venerable institution may have lain behind the pope's death, there is a connection. The film *Godfather III* touched on this scandal with a scene in which the Mafia became deeply embroiled in the financial dealings of the Vatican bank. In truth, reality was not so very far behind. But it wasn't until a man named Roberto Calvi was found swinging from his neck beneath Blackfriars Bridge in London in 1982 that the tangled web of intrigue began to unfold.

If there is a key to the character of Roberto Calvi, it came during World War II when, as a 22-year-old lieutenant with a cavalry unit of the Italian army, he found himself facing starvation on the brutal Eastern Front. His soldiers in full retreat, he managed to smooth-talk a suspicious peasant farmer into accepting a promisory note for the value of a stable of horses to replace those lost in battle. Once out of sight of the farmer, the men butchered the animals, gorged themselves, and made it back to Italy. The debt was never paid, and Calvi went through later life with the same attitude—that he could get what he wanted without

Above: A Soviet ship steams toward Cuba bearing lethal nuclear missiles. The crisis brought the world to the brink of war, and the pope played a prominent role in bringing about a peaceful resolution to the standoff.

". . . the Vatican is responsible for the death of John Paul I. He was allowed to go to the solitary death he prayed for, untended and uncared for by those closest to him."

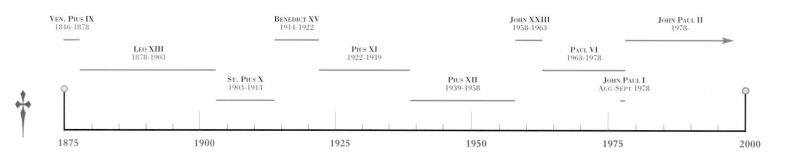

The third member of the trinity was Archbishop Paul Marcinkus himself, a burly, worldly, cigar-smoking cleric who acted as the pope's bodyguard and was a feared and loathed presence in the hallowed halls of the Vatican. Answerable only to the pope himself, Marcinkus main job was heading-up the Vatican Bank, particularly ensuring that its vast investments of $1.8 billion brought a suitable return for the papacy.

Right: Pope John XXIII, Supreme Pontiff from 1958 to 1963 and one of the popular and beloved popes of all time. He is responsible for healing the age-old breach between Catholicism and the Jewish faith.

there ever being a final reckoning. In this he was to be proved monumentally wrong.

After the war he resumed his career in the world of banking, becoming chairman of the prestigious Banco Ambrosiano, a Milan finance house that had been founded a century earlier. It had been nicknamed "The Priests' Bank" by Milanese merchants because of its ties to the Catholic Church and the founders' refusal to compete against profiteering commercial rivals. Calvi, however, was a man who didn't know the meaning of scruples and, in the world of currency restrictions which characterized the Italy of the late 1970s, he was a man who knew every loophole.

The currency regulations were brought in by successive left-wing governments in a bid to halt damaging speculation against the lira. It essentially meant it was illegal to salt money out of the country, but Calvi circumvented the regulations by setting up his own banking branches in the tax havens of Switzerland, Panama, and the Bahamas as secured loans to profitable foreign companies which would repay them later. Of course, these companies existed only on paper, were owned exclusively by Calvi, and the loans were used to buy more and more shares of the Banco Ambrosiano, which gave him more and more control over the bank.

Calvi made use of both witting and unwitting accomplices to his plan. One was Michael Sindona, a Sicilian wheeler-dealer who needed the benefit of an international network of contacts to launder the cash from his many shady business deals. The other was Licio Gelli, a wealthy Italian tycoon who was grandmaster of Rome's notorious P.2 Freemason's Lodge, a secret order with many Vatican members. All members of the lodge swore a sinister masonic oath, not dissimilar to the "omerta" taken by the killers of the mafia, acknowledging that betrayal of the secrets would entail "having my tongue torn out and being buried in the sand at the low water mark, or a cable length from the shore where the tide ebbs and flow . . ."

The third member of the trinity was Archbishop Paul Marcinkus himself, a burly, worldly, cigar-smoking cleric who acted as the pope's bodyguard and was a feared and loathed presence in the hallowed halls of the Vatican. Answerable only to the pope himself, Marcinkus main job was heading-up the Vatican Bank, particularly ensuring that its vast investments of $1.8 billion brought a suitable return for the papacy. It was a unique arrangement that suited all men—the power-hungry Calvi, the greedy Sindona and Gelli, and the ambitious Marcinkus, who openly boasted to more reverential members of the Vatican "that you can't run a church on Hail Marys alone."

It became clear that the Vatican Bank was inexorably linked to the dealings of Calvi and his Banco Ambrosiano. Calvi also used his bank as the chief money launderer of the Mafia, siphoning off billions of dollars

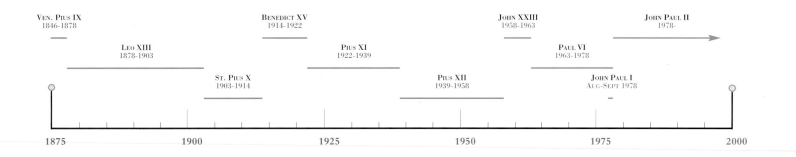

VEN. PIUS IX 1846-1878		BENEDICT XV 1914-1922		JOHN XXIII 1958-1963	JOHN PAUL II 1978-
LEO XIII 1878-1903		PIUS XI 1922-1939		PAUL VI 1963-1978	
	ST. PIUS X 1903-1914		PIUS XII 1939-1958	JOHN PAUL I AUG-SEPT 1978	

1875   1900   1925   1950   1975   2000

from the heroin trade into a network of front companies. So there was also the implication that the bank of the world's greatest Christian Church was benefiting from the misery of the drug trade which destroyed whole communities and countless lives.

It was a mafia informer who turned to the police, and they, in turn to the Bank of Italy, setting inspectors on to Calvi. They demanded to see his books in 1978, but the investigation was thwarted by P.2 Lodge contacts. It wasn't until March 1981, when Milan magistrates were probing an Italian-American businessman suspected of helping Sindona that the suspect revealed he had visited the home of Masonic grand-master Gelli for his help. When police raided Gelli's textile factory they found that he had already fled to South America, but a list of P.2 members was found—and Calvi's name was on it.

Arrested, Calvi confessed to many secret dealings with the Vatican over the years. He was handed down a four-year sentence on currency swindling, but amazingly was freed on appeal and even welcomed back to his job at the bank! For the next year he worked energetically to try to cover his tracks, dreaming up wild schemes to replace the $1.5 billion in foreign loans he knew could never be covered. He turned to Marcinkus at the Vatican to extend the guarantees on some of the loans, but he was flatly refused.

In May 1982, with the walls closing in on him, Calvi fled, using a forged passport to go to London where he rented out a small apartment in Chelsea. He was confident that his old friends and contacts would help him. The following month, on the 17th, he was found hanged beneath Blackfriars Bridge in London. His body was weighted with stones that dragged his corpse almost into the murky waters of the Thames below. His death was recorded as a suicide but later it was changed to an open verdict. The man who conned horses out of a poor peasant farmer on the Russian steppe all those years ago finally found out that debts have to be settled in full. But who killed him? It wasn' t until 15 years later that informants within the ranks of the Mafia itself came forward to reveal what they knew of his illegal and treacherous dealings. "Calvi was killed out of revenge," said the Mafia "super-grass" Tommaso Buscetta. "He was given Mafia money to recycle and he made poor use of it." It transpired that the Vatican, in the frantic weeks before his death, was trying to claw back from him $250 million he did not have.

Pope John Paul I may have touched on this financial morass and may have died for it. Whatever happened to him is certainly shrouded in mystery, and the treatment of his life and death within the Vatican is not one of the more glorious episodes in the papacy. It would be left to his charismatic and influential successor to initiate the reforms of the Vatican Bank to try to expunge the memory of, and the losses caused by, Roberto Calvi.

In John Paul II the Catholic Church has very much a man made

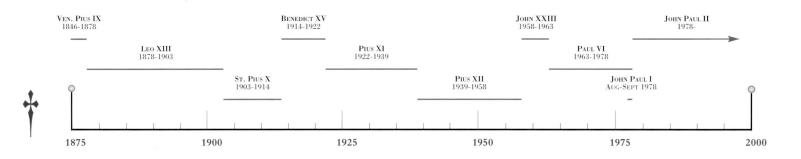

VEN. PIUS IX
1846-1878

LEO XIII
1878-1903

ST. PIUS X
1903-1914

BENEDICT XV
1914-1922

PIUS XI
1922-1939

PIUS XII
1939-1958

JOHN XXIII
1958-1963

PAUL VI
1963-1978

JOHN PAUL I
AUG-SEPT 1978

JOHN PAUL II
1978-

1875   1900   1925   1950   1975   2000

It wasn't until 15 years later that informants within the ranks of the Mafia itself came forward to reveal what they knew of his illegal and treacherous dealings. "Calvi was killed out of revenge," said the Mafia "super-grass" Tommaso Buscetta. "He was given Mafia money to recycle and he made poor use of it." It transpired that the Vatican, in the frantic weeks before his death, was trying to claw back from him £154 million in sterling he did not have.

for the moment, a charismatic, pious, and energetic individual, who has traveled more than any pope before in his mission to spread the word of God and strengthen the church for the coming millennium. A charmer, a player to the gallery, he nonetheless has proved implacable in the face of the Catholic faith's enemies. He will never countenance abortion, birth control, female priests, or any other move that he believes would diminish the church or the papacy. The first non-Italian pope since Adrian VI in 1522, and the only Pole ever chosen, he commands a unique respect around the world among believers and non-believers alike.

He was born Karol Wojtyla on May 18, 1920, in Wadowice, near Krakow, in a Polish state that was to enjoy just a few more years of liberty before it was carved up by the Nazis and the Russians at the onset of World War II. His mother, Emilia, was a frail woman, his father Karol a 40-year-old lieutenant in the army who looked after his other son Edmund, 13, while his wife went into labor.

From the beginning, Karol's mother took an inordinate interest in her new son, telling all who would listen that he was a boy destined to grow into a great man. As a young man he suffered two grievous blows—first the death of his mother, then the death of Edmund, struck down by scarlet fever, contracted from a patient he was trying to save in a hospital where he worked as a doctor. They were profound events that were to draw Karol closer to God and then the priesthood.

He was a popular boy at school, good at soccer and other sports. He had a natural charm that endeared him to young women. Halina Krolikiewicz was, it seems, the young woman who, under different circumstances, might have gone on to become the sweetheart, and perhaps wife, of Karol had he not chosen the path he did. A Jewish girl who studied at the girl's Gymnasium school when he was a teenager, Halina went on to become a famous Polish actress. She remembered the man who would become the most famous and populist pope in history as "different from the others; a tall boy, a handsome boy, with a very beautiful voice with excellent articulation." Their bond of friendship became so close—forged as young Karol excelled in his drama group at school—that many in small-town Wadowice thought they would eventually marry. To this day he is said to hold a special place in his heart for the schoolgirl friend.

After school he became a student in Polish literature at the Jagiellonian University of Krakow, where he displayed a keen ability in foreign languages and continued to pursue his love of outdoor sports. When the Germans invaded they targeted intellectuals, and the university professors were arrested, forcing the college to close. He became a chemical worker and a laborer in a limestone quarry, continuing his studies in secret with a friend and a teacher who had evaded arrest.

In 1942 he vanished. His father, now the retired army lieutenant, died that year. Scattered family relatives surmised that he had been

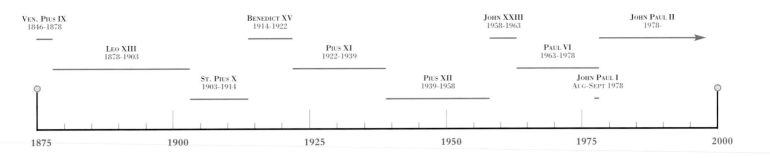

VEN. PIUS IX 1846-1878		BENEDICT XV 1914-1922		JOHN XXIII 1958-1963	JOHN PAUL II 1978-
LEO XIII 1878-1903		PIUS XI 1922-1939		PAUL VI 1963-1978	
	ST. PIUS X 1903-1914		PIUS XII 1939-1958	JOHN PAUL I AUG-SEPT 1978	

1875   1900   1925   1950   1975   2000

rounded up by the Germans for shipment to a slave labor camp, but in actuality he had been taken into the house of the archbishop of Krakow with four other clandestine students to continue his studies in safety. It was while he was under the cleric's tutelage that he decided once and for all on a career in the priesthood.

The students hardly ever left the palace. This gave rise to rumors later in life of a secret romance—even a marriage—conducted within the walls, but it was a fallacy; from the age of 21 the future pope had set his heart on the priesthood. Through his young eyes the clergy seemed to be the only body of men who cared about what was happening to Poland and the Polish people during the terrible Nazi occupation.

There were times during the dark days of the Third Reich's subjugation of Poland when it seemed that he might not live long enough to realize his ambition. On February 29, 1944, when he had emerged from hiding to take a job at the chemical works again, he was run over by a German truck that didn't even slow down, much less stop when he had been struck. Luckily a passing German official, far more humanitarian than the one who had been driving the truck, stopped and ordered his driver to take the young man to the hospital immediately. He was diagnosed with serious head wounds and spent 13 days in the hospital before he was released.

He was nearly liquidated by the Nazis in August that year when the Germans made a sweep of Krakow to prevent young men and intellectuals from rising up as the Red Army was banging on the gates of the city. Squads of SS men moved with efficiency through the city, bundling thousands of people off to concentration and extermination camps.

Karol survived by hiding in the basement of an apartment that the Germans, in their haste, didn't search. He finally made it back to the palace under cover of darkness. He was still there when the Red Army rolled into Krakow early in 1945 to drive the remaining Nazis out of the city. Karol was grateful that this gracious and historic Polish city was the only one in the country to escape destruction during World War II.

With the war over and the university reopened, he continued his studies. He actively studied for the priesthood, too, receiving ordination on November 1, 1946, the feast of All Saints. On the next day, All Souls Day, in the Wawel Cathedral, he celebrated his first mass.

Like St. Peter centuries before, the lure of the Eternal City was a powerful one for the young priest. He decided to resume his studies at the Angelicum University in Rome where he received a doctorate in ethics. Further degrees in philosophy followed at Lublin University and at Krakow where, in 1964, he was appointed archbishop. In 1967 he achieved election to the College of Cardinals thanks to the patronage of Paul VI. He was then 47 and the second-youngest living cardinal. Before he even achieved this dignified post he had made himself an authority in the church on matters ranging from birth control (to which

Above: Aldo Mori, the Italian premier murdered by Red Brigade terrorists. His death appalled the Vatican which placed itself firmly against terrorism.

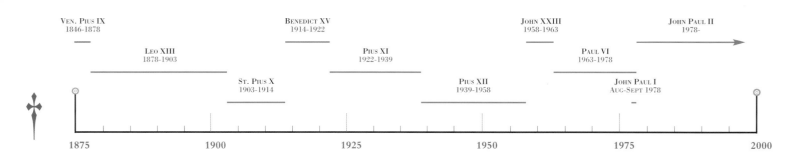

VEN. PIUS IX 1846-1878		BENEDICT XV 1914-1922		JOHN XXIII 1958-1963		JOHN PAUL II 1978-
LEO XIII 1878-1903		PIUS XI 1922-1939		PAUL VI 1963-1978		
	ST. PIUS X 1903-1914		PIUS XII 1939-1958		JOHN PAUL I AUG-SEPT 1978	

1875   1900   1925   1950   1975   2000

Above: Pope Paul VI, Supreme Pontiff from 1963 to 1978. He made it his mission to strengthen the position of the church in the post-war years and was instrumental in reorganizing the curia to run more efficiently.

he was, and remains, steadfastly opposed) to the education of Africans in missionary schools in Togo. The brilliance and clarity of mind which he had displayed at school and university grew during his rise through the ranks of the church, marking him out for great things. He had become so influential by the mid-1960s that it was his treatise on contraception that persuaded the pope in 1968 to issue his *Humane Vitae* encyclical, in which he reinforced the papacy's ban on all methods of artificial birth control. "We helped the pope," he said with satisfaction afterwards.

The conclave that was to elect him came with the death of John Paul I. By this time the Polish cardinal had been regularly appearing in papers as distinguished as the *New York Times* and the *Washington Post* as a hot favorite to succeed him, whenever that might be. But no-one, least of all Father Karol, was prepared for the suddenness with which the pope died. When the two-day conclave was over 99 out of 108 cardinals gave their vote to Wojtyla. "They had done the unimaginable," said his biographers Carl Bernstein and Marco Politi in their much-praised work *His Holiness*: "They had chosen a pope from a country subject to the Soviet Union, a country with a Marxist and atheist government." He was the first non-Italian pope in 450 years, a young pope, at the age of 58. Outside of Poland, few knew much about this Slav who had become shepherd to a flock of 800 million Catholics. Amid the silence the voice of the Cardinal President could be heard.

"Do you accept? What name will you take?"

Wojtyla accepted. The tension vanished from his face, which took on a solemn expression. Not only did he say "yes" as tradition demanded, with a clear voice, but added: "With obedience in faith to Christ, my Lord, and with trust in the Mother of Christ and of the church, in spite of the great difficulties, I accept." It was an appointment that was to change the world—and strike fear into the hearts of the communist despots that ruled his native land.

From the start he outlined a bold vision for the church as he saw its role in the latter quarter of the twentieth century:

"We will be at the service of the universal mission of the church, that is to say the service of the world. We will be at the service of truth, of justice, of peace, of harmony. Open up, no! Swing wide the gates to Christ. Open up to his saving power the confines of the state, open up economic and political systems, the vast empires of culture, civilization and development."

To the people who heard these words, it seemed as if the world had been delivered a pope who would stamp the authority of the Vatican upon modern secular societies like the papal rulers of old.

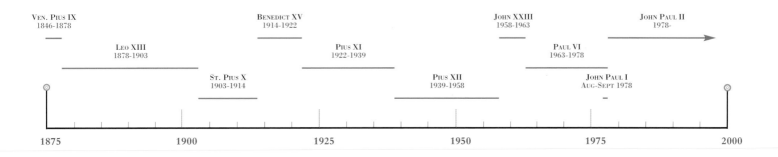

VEN. PIUS IX
1846-1878

LEO XIII
1878-1903

ST. PIUS X
1903-1914

BENEDICT XV
1914-1922

PIUS XI
1922-1939

PIUS XII
1939-1958

JOHN XXIII
1958-1963

PAUL VI
1963-1978

JOHN PAUL I
AUG-SEPT 1978

JOHN PAUL II
1978-

1875   1900   1925   1950   1975   2000

It was obvious, too, that the pope intended to target the godless regimes of Eastern Europe with the same fanaticism that predecessors had gone after the Moslems during the Crusades. Although he commanded no armies, had no men under arms save those of his Swiss Guard, he was the greatest threat to the Kremlin since Hitler's panzers rolled eastwards in 1941.

The communists knew their hold on Moscow's satellites—Poland, Hungary, East Germany, etc.—was tenuous at best. Twice Moscow had had to send in the tanks, to Hungary and Czechoslovakia. Now, with the promotion of a Polish pope, all eyes turned worryingly to Warsaw, and with good reason.

The Poles were among the most truculent citizens of an unwilling empire carved out of the ruins of Europe at the end of World War II. Not only was their nationalism profound, so was their religious feeling, with a full 95 percent of the population committed, practicing Catholics. KGB analysts predicted with accuracy that the election of Pope John Paul II could make him a magnet for disaffected Poles and the catalyst for a counter-revolution. At the time their analysis was made, the whole Eastern Bloc had less than 12 years of socialist life left in it. The initial report on the new supreme pontiff, compiled for polit-buro eyes by Oleg Bogomolov, read:

"According to high-ranking Catholic officials, the election of this Polish cardinal will mean he will promote the universalization of the church, that is its activity in all social-political systems, above all in the socialist system. It is likely that this dialogue with the socialist countries will have, on the part of the Vatican, a more aggressive and systematic character than under other popes. Wojtyla will apparently be less willing to compromise with the leadership of the socialist states, especially as regards the appointing of bishops to local churches. He will try to expand the church's influence not only in the socialist countries, but also among the working class in the capitalist world."

Sneeringly, during World War II, Stalin, when told of the power of the papacy, had said: "How many divisions does the pope have?" Stalin's heirs would soon find out. Not only has this present pope become the most high-profile in history, he must take a large percentage of the credit for speeding the collapse of communism.

Poland—and openness—were rapidly to become the hallmarks of this new, innovative pontiff. He took to straying from the Vatican for drives around Rome, hugging politicians and priests alike when his predecessors only proffered an outstretched hand. And he showed a ready wit which endeared him even to the staunchest right-wingers inside the curia. When he received the notoriously left-wing Bishop Mendez Arceo of Mexico at the Vatican, early on in his reign, an aide

KGB analysts predicted with accuracy that the election of Pope John Paul II could make him a magnet for disaffected Poles and the catalyst for a counter-revolution.

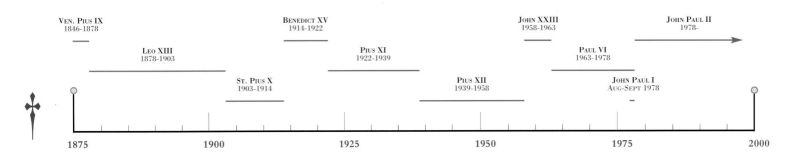

VEN. PIUS IX
1846-1878

LEO XIII
1878-1903

ST. PIUS X
1903-1914

BENEDICT XV
1914-1922

PIUS XI
1922-1939

PIUS XII
1939-1958

JOHN XXIII
1958-1963

PAUL VI
1963-1978

JOHN PAUL I
AUG-SEPT 1978

JOHN PAUL II
1978-

1875   1900   1925   1950   1975   2000

Above: Pope John Paul II, elected in 1978, has great energy and has visited many countries—particularly in South America. However, his conservatism has worried many catholics.

said to him: "Most Holy Father, he is a member of Christians for Socialism." The pope winked and said: "That's all right—socialism is something I am quite familiar with!"

It was the Holy Father's return to his homeland that set in motion the tumultuous events that would lead to the collapse of the Iron Curtain countries. When he landed there in June 1979 the country went wild. Breznhev, the Soviet leader, tried to get the Polish communists to cancel his visit, but even they knew they could not contain order without massive bloodshed if they tried to do so. Consequently, he landed in Warsaw to deliver an address that swept away decades of church policy.

Since the end of the war the papacy had sought accommodation with the Moscow satellites, recognizing their legitimate rule in order to keep priests in pulpits and churches, and out of prison. In Krakow John Paul threw down the gauntlet, saying: "Christ cannot be excluded from human history in any part of the globe, from any latitude or longitude of the earth. Excluding Christ from human history is a sin against humanity." Bernstein and Politi remarked:

"Everything he said marked a grand turnabout for the church—in Poland, in eastern Europe, in the Soviet Union, in world affairs. Through him the church was laying claim to a new role, no longer simply asking for space for itself. These demands represented a direct assault on the universal pretensions of Marxist ideology, which by now had become an empty shell in the countries under Soviet influence."

A few years later, during Ronald Reagan's presidenecy, William Casey, director of the Central Intelligence Agency, visited the Holy Father in Rome. He handed him spy satellite pictures of himself taken in Poland on his triumphant return. President Reagan, he told the pope, was aware of the immense power the pope wielded and he was willing to channel CIA information on the Eastern Bloc to him. Although the Vatican seeks to dispel the notion that there was some kind of alliance between Reagan and the pope, there was in fact just such a bond. Reagan saw him as the key to toppling what he termed "the evil empire"—and he intended to capitalize on the pope. Every important scrap of CIA data on Poland passed from America to the Holy See, and the pope and President Reagan were to meet six times during the latter's days in power. Reagan knew Poland was the weakest link in the chain of Soviet satellites and breaking it was his goal. When Solidarity, the worker's movement, came to power, they, too, looked to the Holy Father for support—and, it is argued, would never have formed in the first place had they not had a Polish pope who instilled them with such courage.

In the first 100 days of his pontificate, John Paul II honed his vision for the church. He exhorted priests not to water down the mission of

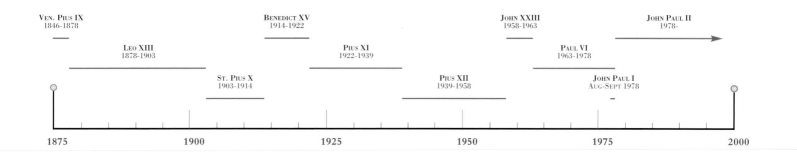

the church; he championed celibacy before marriage and fidelity in it; he lambasted abortion and praised mothers who refused to have them even when their own lives were at risk; he instructed American bishops to keep a close eye on church discipline and stood firmly against women priests, despite hopes that he would be susceptible to the idea.

It is one of the strange dichotomies of Pope John Paul II that he is so popular when he is also so entrenched in his views. Nothing has fundamentally changed in the church since he assumed power, despite all the pope-mobiles, the mass rallies, the photo opportunities, the traveling, the kissing of babies, and the mass rallies that have bordered at times on hysteria.

Popularity and openess have not added up to any willingness to change what he sees as the essential foundations of the church. South American bishops who pleaded for some form of birth control to save the lives of mothers giving birth to seven and more children in conditions of appalling poverty, led only to their excommunication. Nuns who pleaded for the right to ordination found themselves forever shut off from any papal audience in the future. The pope intended to change the role of the church in society—but not the church.

He moved with the speed of an international executive rather than an elderly religious cleric. Curia officials, unused to such frenzied activity, were hard put to keep up with him as he organized trips around the globe, worked on encyclicals with astonishing energy, and began giving regular lectures in the Vatican on human sin, destiny, sexuality, and theology. He took a keen interest in the Vatican's financial affairs, vowing there would never be another Calvi to deplete the coffers of the church, and promised in his first published encyclical, *The Redeemer of Man*, to put Christ and his message firmly back at the center of world history and affairs.

It was the Eastern Bloc that continued to be most worried about the pope and his mass appeal. Records from the now-defunct Soviet Union show that Breznhev held meeting after meeting of the politburo, seeking to find a way to negate his appeal. When Solidarity burst onto the scene, with its strikes, its confrontation with state authority, and its universal appeal, his worst fears were realized.

Lech Walensa, its leader, and the Holy Father seemed men made for each other, men of destiny to change the order of things. Such men were dangerous and Breznhev and his advisers plotted frantically to deal with them. Help came their way in the shape of a fanatic nsmed Mehmet Ali Agca who, clutching a Browning 9mm automatic pistol, fired several shots, two of which hit the pope, as he drove around St. Peter's Square on May 13, 1981.

The pope was wounded in his right elbow, the stomach, and the index finger of his left hand. Fortune was shining on the Holy Father that day, as doctors discovered one bullet had missed his central aorta by

It is one of the strange dichotomies of Pope John Paul II that he is so popular when he is also so entrenched in his views.

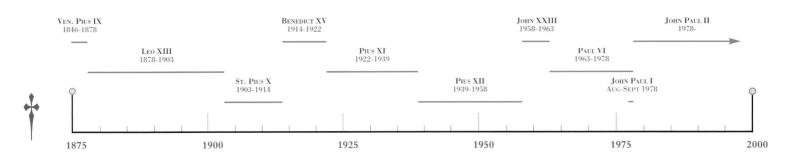

"Pope John Paul II always sees women in their biological dimension—either as mothers or as virgins . . . Wojtyla never sees women as persons in the same way as he sees a male as a person."

a fraction of a inch. It was bad news for the Soviets, but good news for humanity that his life was spared. Just who was behind the shooting remains, in the words of Robert Gates—Casey's successor as CIA chief—as "the last great secret of our time." Many theories abounded about who had put the young Turk up to the plot, and for a while the favorite contender was the Bulgarian secret service. The pope never bought into the conspiracy theory, preferring to say that the attempt on his life "was the work of the devil, nothing more." He even visited his would-be killer in a Roman prison, comforting him as he dropped to his knees and begged forgiveness. More recently it has been suggested that Islamic fanatics may have been behind the assassination attempt, but no new light has been shed on the incident.

Throughout the dark days of martial law in Poland, a futile attempt to break the national will forged between Walensa and the Vatican, Pope John Paul continued to be a beacon of light to the oppressed masses in his homeland. By the mid-1980s the old guard of Soviet leaders, the heirs of Stalin who ruled by fear and terror, were dead, and a new man named Mikhail Gorbachev was in power. Soon Pope John Paul's crusade would bear fruit and the evil empire would fall completely.

While politicians courted him and the faithful followed him, feminist attacks on his papacy mounted. Ida Magli, an eminent Italian anthropologist, said:

"Pope John Paul II always sees women in their biological dimension—either as mothers or as virgins who must follow the model of the Virgin. It is always the way they relate to their body—either they make children or they abstain from sexual intercourse. Wojtyla never sees women as persons in the same way as he sees a male as a person. I think that deep in his heart he fears the rebellion of women. His harsh prohibitions, especially regarding abortion in whatever situation, betray a sort of unconscious hatred of the freedom of women."

No matter how vitriolic the attack, the pontiff never wavers from his teachings and beliefs—a course that has set him against President Bill Clinton, whose support of abortion and birth control rights in America has led him to condemn America's "culture of death."

The pope has also moved swiftly and ruthlessly to crush dissent in the church. He made it his mission from the start to silence people who he thought preached a doctrine alien to his teachings. French theologian Jacques was banned from preaching, writing, and lecturing without specific authorization from the Vatican. Swiss theologian Hans Kung received the same treatment for calling into question the dogma of papal infallibility. In America, Father Charles Curran was sacked from his job at the Catholic University of America in Washington when he argued that sterilization and birth control is not necessarily wrong in all

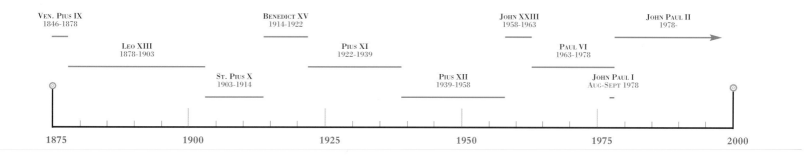
circumstances. The pope's willingness to confront unpleasant tasks head-on proves there is far more to him than the smiling, hand-shaking, avuncular old man of popular myth.

The pope's full qualities as a politician were seen in December 1989 when he became the first pontiff ever to meet with the general secretary of the Communist Party of the Soviet Union. Mikhail Gorbachev, the new leader in Moscow, realized what his predecessors had failed to see—that communism as it was practiced in his massive country and its satellite states was a bankrupt system. Consequently, he traveled to Rome to visit the man who nourished the spiritual void that Marxist-Leninism had failed to fill, and the streets of the Eternal City were thronged with thousands of people eagerly awaiting the historic summit.

The men met in private in the papal apartments. Here, general secretary Gorbachev spoke of the need for freedom and responsibility in the Soviet Union and her allied countries. He hoped the pope would provide the spiritual guidance and responsibility for that freedom to function without violence and confrontation. The pope was asked to avoid politics when he spoke to the masses in his homeland—something the Holy Father was only too happy to agree to. Yet if Gorbachev hoped that his policy of openness and democracy would still ensure a Soviet-style system of government, he was very much mistaken. Within two years everything that had been hammered out at Yalta, in the last conference of the war hosted by Stalin with Roosevelt and Churchill, was dead. The Iron Curtain was lifted from Europe and the Soviet Union splintered apart as communism self-destructed.

The victory was due in no small measure to John Paul II. No longer would the "how many divisions does the pope have?" insult be leveled at the Vatican.

Now, an old man who has undergone an operation for a cancerous tumor, a man who looks tired at his public meetings, Pope John Paul II—*Time*'s Man of the Year in 1995 and an international bestselling author with his book *Crossing the Threshold of Hope*—has no intention of giving up. He wants to lift the "Bamboo Curtain" on Chinese Catholics and draw them closer to Rome, as he drew the believers in the old Soviet Union. His message is as loud and clear as it ever was as he leads a church more united, stronger, and better equipped than it has ever been in the history of the papacy.

"Never has there been a more effective pope," said William Burrell, an American Catholic scholar. "He is truly the leader of the world, regardless of individual faith."

Above: Stalin's famous sneer at the pope— "How many divisions does he have then?"—would be shown as vainglorious when later in the century the unarmed "divisions" of the Catholic Church in Poland helped bring about the first cracks in the Eastern Bloc that would eventually help destroy Soviet communism.

"Never has there been a more effective pope."

THE POPES

1	St. Peter	died c66
2	St. Linus	c66-c76
3	St. Anacletus	c76-c88
4	St. Clement I	c88-c97
5	St. Evaristus	c97-c105
6	St. Alexander I	c105-c115
7	St. Sixtus I	c116-c125
8	St. Telesphorus	c125-c136
9	St. Hyginus	c137-c142
10	St. Pius I	c142-155
11	St. Anicetus	c155-c166
12	St. Soter	c166-c174
13	St. Eleutherius	c175-189
14	St. Victor I	189-198
15	St. Zephyrinus	199-217
16	St. Callistus I	217-222
17	St. Urban I	222-230
18	St. Pontain	230-235
19	St. Anterus	235-236
20	St. Fabian	236-250
21	St. Cornelius	251-253
22	St. Lucius I	253-254
23	St. Stephen I	254-257
24	St. Sixtus II	257-258
25	St. Dionysius	260-268
26	St. Felix I	269-274
27	St. Eutychian	275-283
28	St. Gaius	283-296
29	St. Marcellinus	296-304
30	St. Marcellus I	306-308
31	St. Eusebius	Apr-Oct 310
32	St. Miltiades	311-314
33	St. Silvester I	314-335
34	St. Mark	Jan-Oct 336
35	St. Julius I	337-352
36	Liberius	352-366
37	St. Damasus I	366-384
38	St. Siricius	384-399
39	St. Anastasius I	399-401
40	St. Innocent I	401-417
41	St. Zosimus	417-418
42	St. Boniface I	418-422
43	St. Celestine I	422-432
44	St. Sixtus III	432-440
45	St. Leo I	440-461
46	St. Hilarus	461-468
47	St. Simplicius	468-483
48	St. Felix III (II)	483-492
49	St. Gelasius I	492-496
50	Anastasius II	496-498
51	St. Symmachus	498-514
52	St. Hormisdas	514-523
53	St. John I	523-526
54	St. Felix IV (III)	526-530
55	Boniface II	530-532
56	John II	533-535
57	St. Agapitus I	535-536
58	St. Silverius	536-537
59	Vigilius	537-555
60	Pelagius I	556-561
61	John III	561-574
62	Benedict I	575-579
63	Pelagius II	579-590

64	St. Gregory I	590-604
65	Sabinian	604-606
66	Boniface III	Feb-Nov 607
67	St. Boniface IV	608-615
68	St. Adeodatus I	615-618
69	Boniface V	619-625
70	Honorius I	625-638
71	Severinus	May-Aug 640
72	John IV	640-642
73	Theodore I	642-649
74	St. Martin I	649-653
75	St. Eugene I	654-657
76	St. Vitalian	657-672
77	Adeodatus II	672-676
78	Donus	676-678
79	St. Agatho	678-681
80	St. Leo II	682-683
81	St. Benedict II	684-685
82	John V	685-686
83	Conon	686-687
84	St. Sergius I	687-701
85	John VI	701-705
86	John VII	705-707
87	Sisinnius	Jan-Feb 708
88	Constantine	708-713
89	St. Gregory II	713-731
90	St. Gregory III	731-741
91	St. Zacharias	741-752
	Stephen I (II)	March 752 (unconsecrated)
92	Stephen II (III)	752-757
93	St. Paul I	757-767
94	Stephen III (IV)	768-772
95	Adrian I	772-795
96	St. Leo III	795-816
97	Stephen IV (V)	816-817
98	St. Paschal I	817-824
99	Eugene II	824-c827
100	Valentine	Aug-Sept 827
101	Gregory IV	827-844
102	Sergius II	844-847
103	St. Leo IV	847-855
104	Benedict III	855-858
105	St. Nicholas I	858-867
106	Adrian II	867-872
107	John VIII	872-882
108	Marinus I	882-884
109	St. Adrian III	884-885
110	Stephen V (VI)	885-891
111	Formosus	891-896
112	Boniface VI	April 896
113	Stephen VI (VII)	896-897
114	Romanus	Aug-Nov 897
115	Theodore II	Nov-Dec 897
116	John IX	898-900
117	Benedict IV	900-903
118	Leo V	Aug-Sept 903
119	Sergius III	904-911
120	Anastasius III	911-913
121	Lando	913-914
122	John X	914-928
123	Leo VI	May-Dec 928
124	Stephen VII (VIII)	929-931
125	John XI	931-c935

126	Leo VII	936-939	
127	Stephen VIII (IX)	939-942	
128	Marinus II	942-946	
129	Agapitus II	946-955	
130	John XII	955-964	
131	Leo VIII	963-965	
132	Benedict V	May-June 964	
133	John XIII	965-972	
134	Benedict VI	973-974	
135	Benedict VII	974-983	
136	John XIV	983-984	
137	John XV	985-996	
138	Gregory V	996-999	
139	Silvester II	999-1003	
140	John XVII	May-Nov 1003	
141	John XVIII	1003-1009	
142	Sergius IV	1009-1012	
143	Benedict VIII	1012-1024	
144	John XIX	1024-1032	
145	Benedict IX	1032-1044	
146	Silvester III	Jan-Mar 1045	
	Benedict IX	Mar-May 1045	
147	Gregory VI	1045-1046	
148	Clement II	1046-1047	
	Benedict IX	1047-48	
149	Damasus II	July-Aug 1048	
150	St. Leo IX	1049-1054	
151	Victor II	1055-1057	
152	Stephen IX (X)	1057-1058	
153	Nicholas II	1058-1061	
154	Alexander II	1061-1073	
155	St. Gregory VII	1073-1085	
156	Blessed Victor III	1086-1087	
157	Blessed Urban II	1088-1099	
158	Paschal II	1099-1118	
159	Gelasius II	1118-1119	
160	Callistus II	1119-1124	
161	Celestine (II)	1124-c1125	
162	Innocent II	1130-1143	
163	Celestine II	1143-1144	
164	Lucius II	1144-1145	
165	Blessed Eugene III	1145-1153	
166	Anastasius IV	1153-1154	
167	Adrian IV	1154-1159	
168	Alexander III	1159-1181	
169	Lucius III	1181-1185	
170	Urban III	1185-1187	
171	Gregory VIII	Oct-Dec 1187	
172	Clement III	1187-1191	
173	Celestine III	1191-1198	
174	Innocent III	1198-1216	
175	Honorius III	1216-1227	
176	Gregory IX	1227-1241	
177	Celestine IV	Oct-Nov 1241	
178	Innocent IV	1243-1254	
179	Alexander IV	1254-1261	
180	Urban IV	1261-1264	
181	Clement IV	1265-1268	
182	Blessed Gregory X	1271-1276	
183	Blessed Innocent V	Jan-June 1276	
184	Adrian V	July-Aug 1276	
185	John XXI	1276-1277	
186	Nicholas III	1277-1280	
187	Martin IV	1281-1285	
188	Honorius IV	1285-1287	
189	Nicholas IV	1288-1292	
190	St. Celestine V	July-Dec 1294	
191	Boniface VIII	1294-1303	
192	Blessed Benedict XI	1303-1304	
193	Clement V	1305-1314	
194	John XXII	1316-1334	
195	Benedict XII	1334-1342	
196	Clement VI	1342-1352	
197	Innocent VI	1352-1362	
198	Blessed Urban V	1362-1370	
199	Gregory XI	1370-1378	
200	Urban VI	1378-1389	
201	Boniface IX	1389-1404	
202	Innocent VII	1404-1406	
203	Gregory XII	1406-1415	
204	Martin V	1417-1431	
205	Eugene IV	1431-1447	
206	Nicholas V	1447-1455	
207	Callistus III	1455-1458	
208	Pius II	1458-1464	
209	Paul II	1464-1471	
210	Sixtus IV	1471-1484	
211	Innocent VIII	1484-1492	
212	Alexander VI	1492-1503	
213	Pius III	Sept-Oct 1503	
214	Julius II	1503-1513	
215	Leo X	1513-1521	
216	Adrian VI	1522-1523	
217	Clement VII	1523-1534	
218	Paul III	1534-1549	
219	Julius III	1550-1555	
220	Marcellus II	April 1555	
221	Paul IV	1555-1559	
222	Pius IV	1559-1565	
223	St. Pius V	1566-1572	
224	Gregory XIII	1572-1585	
225	Sixtus V	1585-1590	
226	Urban VII	Sept 1590	
227	Gregory XIV	1590-1591	
228	Innocent IX	Oct-Nov 1591	
229	Clement VIII	1592-1605	
230	Leo XI	April 1605	
231	Paul V	1605-1621	
232	Gregory XV	1621-1623	
233	Urban VIII	1623-1644	
234	Innocent X	1644-1655	
235	Alexander VII	1655-1667	
236	Clement IX	1667-1669	
237	Clement X	1670-1676	
238	Blessed Innocent XI	1676-1689	
239	Alexander VIII	1689-1691	
240	Innocent XII	1691-1700	
241	Clement XI	1700-1721	
242	Innocent XIII	1721-1724	
243	Benedict XIII	1724-1730	
244	Clement XII	1730-1740	
245	Benedict XIV	1740-1758	
246	Clement XIII	1758-1769	
247	Clement XIV	1769-1774	
248	Pius VI	1775-1799	
249	Pius VII	1800-1823	
250	Leo XII	1823-1829	
251	Pius VIII	1829-1830	
252	Gregory XVI	1831-1846	
253	Ven. Pius IX	1846-1878	
254	Leo XIII	1878-1903	
255	St. Pius X	1903-1914	
256	Benedict XV	1914-1922	
257	Pius XI	1922-1939	
258	Pius XII	1939-1958	
259	John XXIII	1958-1963	
260	Paul VI	1963-1978	
261	John Paul I	Aug-Sept 1978	
262	John Paul II	1978-	

INDEX